British Studies Series

General Editor JEREMY BLACK

(*List continued overleaf*)

W. Rubinstein **History of Britain in the Twentieth Century**
Howard Temperley **Britain and America**

British Studies Series
Series Standing Order ISBN 0–333–69332–9

You can receive future titles in this series as they are published by placing
a standing order. Please contact your bookseller or, in case of difficulty,
write to us at the address below with your name and address, the title of the
series and the ISBN quoted above.

Customer Services Department, Macmillan Distribution Ltd
Houndmills, Basingstoke, Hampshire RG21 6XS, England

Government and Community in the English Provinces, 1700–1870

David Eastwood

First published 1997 by
MACMILLAN PRESS LTD
Houndmills, Basingstoke, Hampshire RG21 6XS
and London
Companies and representatives
throughout the world

ISBN 0–333–55285–7 hardcover
ISBN 0–333–55286–5 paperback

A catalogue record for this book is available
from the British Library.

This book is printed on paper suitable
for recycling and made from fully
managed and sustained forest sources.

10   9   8   7   6   5   4   3   2   1
06 05 04 03 02 01 00 99 98 97

Typeset by Expo Holdings, Malaysia

Printed in Hong Kong

 Published in the United States of America 1997 by
ST. MARTIN'S PRESS, INC.,
Scholarly and Reference Division
175 Fifth Avenue, New York, N.Y. 10010

ISBN 0–312–16577–3

To Mum and Dad

Contents

Contents

Preface

This is a study of neglected but important aspects of state and social formation in England. I have here sought to develop an argument about the changes in the structural and cultural relationships between state and society in England. Much of what I say would apply to that other state, the British state, and on another occasion I will venture into the broader question of relationships within the British state. Nevertheless, English provincialism has been at least as neglected a theme as the relationships between England, Wales, Scotland, and Ireland, and even in restricting myself to the more modest ambition of writing about the English experience much has had to be left unsaid. In what follows, therefore, I explore relationships between centre and locality in England, the decline of English provincialism, and the profound cultural, ideological, economic, and social changes that determined structural developments within the English polity. To colleagues working in Welsh, Irish, and Scottish history, aspects of the story that I tell will, I hope, seem familiar.

Many friends have contributed intentionally or inadvertently to the making of this short book. Jeremy Black asked me to write it, and was typically good-humoured as its shape changed and its completion was delayed. Richard English invited me to contribute to a series of lectures on the state at Queen's University, Belfast, which made me begin to think systematically about English exceptionalism, and present my ideas in a context in which understanding English state power and political culture still matters enormously. James Campbell kindly gave me an offprint of his richly suggestive Stenton Lecture and taught me much about medieval England through agreeable conversation. For a number of years John Prest and I shared both teaching duties and research interests with pleasure and profit. Paul Langford has been a consistent source of ideas, advice, and kind encouragement. Joanna Innes has made me rethink some of my more fanciful readings of eighteenth-century developments, and Peter Ghosh has done the same for the nineteenth century. My friend and former colleague, Miri Rubin, reminded me that I was still a historian when mushrooming administrative duties seemed to suggest otherwise. The Annual Conference on the English state at St Peter's College, Oxford, has done much to refine my understanding of its long-run development. The bulk of this book was written after I joined the Department of History at the University of Wales Swansea and, although this is a book which is resolutely about England, it has gained much by way of perspective from being written in so agreeable a Welsh setting. My father has again been unstinting of his time in reading and commenting on the text, while the dedication is a small token of a vastly deeper gratitude. Finally, my family have tolerated my spending too long in my study and too little time with them. I shouldn't promise them that things will be different in the future, but no doubt I will try.

David Eastwood
University of Wales Swansea

1 English Exceptionalism

Convergence and Divergence: English State Formation in Context

English history, and indeed much English historical writing, is strikingly self-referential. References to 'English exceptionalism' are legion, and reflect a widely accepted orthodoxy that state and society developed differently in England.[1] At one level, of course, this emphasis on English exceptionalism is neither surprising nor objectionable: there is no one master-narrative of state formation but, rather, many historically specific experiences of it. Indeed, the more closely one probes the processes through which public institutions and political cultures are shaped, the more contingent such processes appear. When we begin to anatomize the political cultures of different societies, it rapidly becomes apparent that cultural formation is a dialectic of the generic and the unique. At one level, modern Europe – or at least modern Western Europe – might be said to have developed a common, or converging, political culture. Representative institutions, through which state power is legitimized in terms of popular sovereignty, are the norm. Pervasive bureaucratic systems regulate, provide, coerce, and arbitrate. Governments seek delicately to balance a commitment to market ideologies on the one hand, with their own desire to control and a rhetoric of popular accountability on the other. Institutional practice and public policy in Western Europe is sufficiently similar for relatively weak European institutions to orchestrate further 'harmonization'; if not yet of institutions, then at least of policy and public entitlements.

Even so, Western European states have developed convergent political institutions and political cultures through quite divergent historical processes.[2] The politics of medieval France, like those of medieval England, might have been dominated by recurrent tension between the claims of the crown and the power of

1

nobles, but the path from this to representative democracy was quite different. Whereas England developed a functioning parliament from the later medieval period, and an embryonic parliamentary *system* from the sixteenth century, France recovered from the violent destabilization of the counter-reformation and *Frondes* by creating a Catholic absolutism, with a fiscal and military capacity that English monarchs could only envy and fear. Yet French royal absolutism, with pretensions to 'universal monarchy', overreached itself.[3] A chronically sclerotic French *Ancien Régime* was out-gunned by an eighteenth-century British state which built a formidable navy and its first Empire on the basis of parliamentary sovereignty and a sophisticated system of public credit.[4] The French state's collapse into revolution between 1787 and 1789 inaugurated the crucial, defining moment in the creation of modern Europe. The French Revolution not only unleashed the politics of democratic participation and popular citizenship which would eventually reshape all European states but also improvised a new political idiom: that of a self-consciously revolutionary politics.[5] In the name of revolution all that makes up the fabric of the state – public institutions, law, property, religion, and public administration – could be remade and even forcibly transformed. As Tocqueville was to argue in the nineteenth century, it was as if the normal processes of political and cultural evolution had been short-circuited.[6] As English Whigs, who greeted the French Revolution with some enthusiasm, pointed out in the early 1790s, France was now trying to accomplish swiftly what England had accomplished with greater leisure, if not without incident, through its civil wars, 'Glorious Revolution', and long struggle for parliamentary ascendancy.[7] In a momentous address to the 'Society for Commemorating the Revolution in Great Britain' on 4 November 1789, Richard Price looked back to the rekindling of English liberty in the Revolution of 1688 and forward to the universalization of a still more extensive liberty through the American and French Revolutions: 'After sharing in the benefits of one Revolution [that of 1688], I have been spared to be a witness to two other Revolutions, both glorious. And now, methinks, I see the ardor for liberty catching and spreading, a general amendment beginning in human affairs ... The times are auspicious. Your labours have not been in vain ... Behold, the light you have struck out, after setting America free, reflected to France and there kindled into a blaze that lays despotism in ashes and warms and illuminates Europe!'.[8] The moderate English supporters of the French Revolution could not have been more wrong. What James Mackintosh, Mary Wollstonecraft, Richard Watson, and others misunderstood was less the objectives of the French Revolution than its methods.[9] From 1789 a new politics, a politics of transformation, had not only been born but was also available, carried abroad by its universal imperatives. In resisting not only the French Revolution's ideological imperialism but also its transforming power, the English state confirmed its distinctiveness.[10] It came to celebrate the non-revolutionary character of its development, and it achieved representative democracy not by overthrowing parliament and monarchy but by transforming them. In the process the deep continuities of English history were underscored. The English monarchy transformed itself, through a rather opportunistic commitment to importing superior foreign products in 1688 and 1714, while France oscillated uneasily between republican, imperial, and monarchical forms. France swept away its traditional *pays* and replaced them with the Euclidean system of *départments, arrondissements, cantons,* and *communes;* while the most the English poor law commissioners could muster after 1834 was the superposition of poor laws unions on the ancient matrix of counties and parishes. The common law persisted while continental Europe codified its legal systems. As revolutionary politics convulsed Europe in 1848, the British state mustered the Iron Duke and an army of small property owners as special constables, and Chartism dissolved in the London drizzle. Hector Berlioz, who supported the Chartists and wrote truly great symphonies, commented that the Chartists knew 'as much about starting a riot as the Italians about writing a symphony'.[11]

The failure of revolution in Britain in 1848 was more than simply a failure of Chartist organization. As with Italian composers, so with English political culture: radicals and conservatives alike hallowed different idioms and imbued politics with what they took to be the evolutionary sonorities of English history rather than the dissonance of revolutionary violence.[12] While it would be wrong to suggest that revolutionary politics liberate the present from the past, in a quite self-conscious way revolutions seek to renegotiate the relationship between the past and the present. They turn Edmund Burke's reverence for the past into active contempt, seeking to empower the present generation by casting off the shackles of accumulated tradition, turning minds away from what is to what might be. In one sense, befitting its preciosity, England had its revolution first, between 1640 and 1689, and it would be quite misleading to minimize the importance of the seventeenth century in the long-run development of England's political apparatus.[13] Similarly, historians – or at least those working in Cambridge in the 1950s and 1960s – perceived two decisive 'revolutions in government', one associated with Thomas Cromwell's enforcement of the English Reformation in the 1530s, and the other with the extension of government activity in the middle decades of the nineteenth century.[14] We will return to these 'revolutions in government' in due course, and I will argue that these were indeed transforming moments in English state formation. What they did not do, however, was infuse English or British political culture with a genuinely revolutionary tradition. Indeed, the alleged agents of change were generally politicians and bureaucrats rather than the people. Moreover, the very fact that such 'revolutions' were only discovered in the 1950s says something about their status and salience. Indeed, it problematizes English socio-political history in a quite distinctive way, suggesting that important moments of transformation were veiled by a pervasive, but misplaced sense of evolutionary calm.

The principal difficulty with emphasizing English exceptionalism is not that it exaggerates English distinctiveness but, rather, that it exaggerates the continuities in English history. More than that, in so far as there is a meta-narrative of English state formation, it tends to conceive of the state narrowly: it is a narrative the foci of which are crown, parliament, and executive, thus doing scant justice to the local institutions of the English state. Historians of late-medieval and early-modern England have traced the contours of county communities and developed a clear sense of the dialectic between centre and localities.[15] But in the modern period the absence of such a body of work is interpretatively impoverishing. There are a few suggestive local studies, but relatively few of these attempt to chart changes in political culture and still fewer chart changes in the distribution of power between the centre and locality.[16] In what follows I want to rethink the nature of state formation in England, and to do so by adopting a different perspective. My vantage point for observing state formation will be the localities more than the centre. In seeking to evaluate the capacity of the state I will look at local rather than national institutions. In so doing I hope to explain the complexity of relationships between the governed and government on the one hand and between locality and centre on the other. At the same time, I will offer a reading of the ways in which the local framework of the English state adapted to profound changes in public culture, political ideology, and the national economy. The story which emerges is a story of quasi-revolutionary change accomplished by non-revolutionary means.

From Medieval to Modern: The Long-run Development of the English Polity

In England, language, geography, religion, and political institutions conspired to fashion a coherent system of state power which appeared precocious by comparison with continental political systems. At present historians of Anglo-Saxon England are engaged in fierce controversies over the scale and capacity of Anglo-Saxon government.[17] Whatever its military weaknesses, the Anglo-Saxon state from Alfred onwards was strikingly successful in promoting linguistic unity, legal uniformity, and fiscal efficacy. Moreover, it was beginning to develop a network of law and of local agencies which came to constitute the basis of a united English realm.[18] The sense of the deep-rootedness of English state formation is not confined to historians, still less to those who happen to specialize in the early-medieval period. Eighteenth-century reformers were fond of describing their attempts to reform parliament and extend legal rights as a quest to restore 'Anglo-Saxon liberties'.[19] These political rights, the rights of free-born Englishmen, had been expropriated by the conquering Normans. For self-consciously English Radicals such as Major John Cartwright, William Cobbett, and – in a distinctive way – even the Radical cosmopolitan Tom Paine, the 'Norman Yoke' had hung like a pall over English history, distorting institutions such as the crown, parliament, and even the church.[20] Ancient liberties had been lost as an alien aristocracy, a tithe-devouring church, and an exclusive educational system had been intruded into the liberal, participatory, and aggressively *English* state which had flourished before 1066. In similar vein Joseph Arch – who founded the Agricultural Labourers' Union in 1872 and took his seat in 1885 as the first rural labourer to be elected to parliament – styled himself 'a peaceable Wat Tyler of the fields'. In equally sonorous tones, he heralded three founder members of the Union as being 'like the old Barons of Runnymede, for they put their sign and seal as best they could to the Magna Charta of the English Agricultural Labourer'.[21]

Thus the radicals of Hanoverian England mourned what they took to be a long deviation in the development of the English state, which privileged the few at the expense of the many and led to an alien aristocratic politics displacing a vernacular political culture. Conservatives, by contrast, celebrated the forging of distinctive English institutions which underpinned equally distinctive, and enduring, English liberties. This sense of the antique, local, and essentially Saxon character of England's law and liberties was captured almost incidentally in James Montagu's *Charge* to the Grand Jury of Wiltshire in April 1720: 'I think I may venture to affirm, that the Tryal of Causes, whether Civil or Criminal, by Jurys ... is the darling Privilege of the Subject, and a Peculiar Franchise, which no People, as I know of, enjoy, besides ourselves. It is a Liberty immemorially delivr'd down to us, and of so inestimable a Value, that King *Alfred* ... put [one] of his Judges to death, for Passing Sentence of Death upon an *Ignoramus* returned by the Grand Jury'.[22] If Montagu used his Charge to celebrate the Saxon origins of England's local legal liberties, other magistrates used their Charges to remind fellow justices of the majestic maturation of English law and legal culture. Thus Richard Witton began his *Charge to the Grand Jury* at Barnsley in October 1741 by invoking Bracton, while eight years later Henry Fielding took his fellow Westminster justices through Fortescue, Spelman's *Life of Alfred*, Bracton, and Lambarde, and then on to Hale, Coke, and Locke.[23] Thus magistrates and jurors – in short, the governing elites of provincial England – were left in no doubt that they stood in a privileged relationship to a specific process of state formation. To this extent at least, the mystification of English state formation was crucial to its self-image and self-understanding. Later, in repudiating both the French Revolution and abstract notions of political rights, Edmund Burke captured, in still more baroque language, the essence of conservatives' essentially celebratory reading of English history: 'The very idea of the fabrication of a new government, is enough to fill us with disgust and horror. We wished at the period of the Revolution, and do now wish, to derive all we possess as *an inheritance from our forefathers* ... All the reformations we have hitherto made, have proceeded upon the principle of reference to antiquity'.[24] In political terms Burke's account, which was echoed and embroidered by conservatives throughout the nineteenth century, was diametrically opposed to historical accounts of radicals and reformers. Yet what was shared was a common perception that English historical development was distinctive, and that the debate on the present nature and future shape of the English polity had to recognize this distinctiveness.

If the history of the English state was distinctive, it was also ambiguous, and attempts to impute normative political meanings to the evolution of public institutions and social customs served to heighten this ambiguity. This was well captured by Matthew Arnold in *Culture and Anarchy* (1869):

Our familiar praise of the British Constitution under which we live, is that it is a system of checks, – a system which stops and paralyses any power in interfering with the free action of individuals. To this effect Mr Bright, who loves to walk in the old ways of the Constitution, said forcibly in one of his great speeches, what many of the people are every day saying less forcibly, that the central idea of English life and politics is *the assertion of personal liberty*. Evidently this is so; but evidently, also, feudalism, which with its ideas and habits of subordination was for many centuries silently behind the British Constitution, dies out, and we are left with nothing but a system of checks, and our notion of its being the great right and happiness of an Englishman to do as far a possible what he likes, we are in danger of drifting towards anarchy. We have not the notion, so familiar on the Continent and in antiquity, of *the State*, – the nation in its collective and corporate character, entrusted with stringent powers for the general advantage, and controlling individual wills in the name of an interest wider than that of individuals.[25]

What Arnold here focuses is the extent to which the English state was fashioned not by one dominant political culture but through a clash of two cultures, one aristocratic (or feudal) the other popular. Thus parliament, measured in terms of its social composition, remained an elite institution until at least the Reform Act of 1884. Yet many English elections were popular events, upon which non-electors had a powerful impact, as early as the eighteenth century.[26] Similarly, parliamentary reformers, from the 1790s through to the Chartists, were prone to defend their programmes as an attempt to *restore* parliament to the people. The same kind of cultural fission occurred within the local institutions. The parish vestry enfranchised all ratepayers and, in terms of its formal composition, was the most representative single institution in the pre-twentieth-century English state; but in practice parishes created their own elites – a local aristocracy every bit as sharply delineated as the peerage itself – and through this the politics of local oligarchy colonized government. Moreover, as Arnold suggests, this process of reshaping state institutions was facilitated by the absence of a formal discourse on the English state. An English political language which centred on 'the constitution', 'parliament', and custom was a language which venerated practice over theory. In his highly influential essay, *The English Constitution* (1867), Walter Bagehot dismissed theoretical debates about the nature and ideological character of the English constitution as 'an undergrowth of irrelevant ideas', and his work was concerned unflinchingly with 'sketch[ing] a living Constitution'.[27]

One of the more striking moments in Bagehot's austerely technical reading of the English Constitution is his indifference to the way in which power was distributed within the English polity. At almost the same time as the great French historical sociologist, Alexis de Tocqueville, was inveighing against the over-centralization of the French state, and the German jurist Rudolph Gneist was exploring the mechanisms through which the English state had decentralized power, Bagehot tossed such problems aside.[28] 'We', Bagehot declared, 'need not care how much power is delegated to outlying bodies, and how much is kept for the central body'.[29] One effect of such theoretical insouciance was to pave the way for parliamentary centralization, but equally striking was its commitment to a very thin reading of the nature and historical evolution of English constitutional practice. Viewed in terms of the long-run development of the English state, the struggle to determine the proper spheres of central and local government was profoundly significant. Moreover, the manner in which the localities were governed did much to determine the character of English governance more generally. The corollary of England's having, relative to continental absolutisms, a weak central state in the sixteenth and seventeenth centuries was its ability to develop a flexible and capacious system of local government. In the midst of an indictment of central government taxation, Tom Paine paused to celebrate not only the distribution of power as between centre and locality but also the essentially voluntaristic culture of power in the localities: 'In a country like England, where the whole of the civil government is executed by the people of every town and county, by means of parish officers, magistrates, quarter sessions, juries and assize; without any trouble to *what is called the government,* or any expense to the revenue than the salary of judges, it is astonishing how such a mass of taxes can be employed'.[30] Paine himself had served as an elected member of Lewes Town Council, the so-called committee of twelve, in the early 1770s. Predictably, but not wholly inaccurately, Paine described this system, under which 'the nation is left to govern itself', as republican.[31]

Paine reminds us, as Montesquieu had argued a generation earlier, that simple typologies of constitutions, still less of functioning political systems, are at best inadequate and sometimes flatly misleading. Nowhere is this more true than of the British constitution, which was improvised over centuries. The form of the English constitution by the eighteenth century might have been monarchical, parliamentary, and moderately oligarchic, but the Hanoverian political system embodied institutions the character of which might best be described as republican, participatory, and communitarian. It is here that organic metaphors are most illuminating. Local communities had moulded local institutions and developed their own political cultures. Parish officers and county magistrates, such as jurors, coroners, sheriffs, and local constables, were creatures of the communities, classes, and social experiences which had shaped them. Public office did not transform them, in some desiccated way, into mere public officials, imbued with the programmed reflexes of the official mind. In the 1860s another Frenchman, Hippolyte Taine, illuminated precisely this interplay between official forms and public offices on the one hand, and local traditions, social alignments, and political cultures on the other: 'The Constitution of a nation is an organic phenomenon, like that of a living body. Consequently that Constitution is peculiar to the state in question, no other state can assimilate it ... For beneath these ... institutions and charters, the bills of rights and the official almanacs, there are the ideas, the habits and customs and character of the people and classes; there are the respective positions of classes, their reciprocal feelings'.[32]

From its medieval origins, the capacity of the English state was crucially dependent upon its ability to mobilize local elites as governing elites.[33] Initially sheriffs, appointed from the eleventh century, and then justices of the peace, first so named in 1361, were the key agents of governance in the localities. Both offices were nominated by the crown but office-holders had local affinities and local roots. To a significant extent, their authority rested upon and was bounded by local opinion.[34] Not for nothing was 'sheriff' a corruption of 'shire-reeve'. Similarly jurors, coroners, and the lesser officials of the sheriff were local men committed or conscripted to public service. The system which emerged has been well described as 'local government at the king's command', with official authority being exercised in the name of the king but in the interest of the locality. This is not to suggest that central–local relations in medieval England were harmonious – far from it. What the king gave, the king could take back; and those whom the king appointed, the king could dismiss. The inquest of 1170 led to 20 of 26 sheriffs being dismissed.[35] Commissions of the Peace, which named all magistrates, could be remodelled and individuals stripped of their authority. Moreover, the struggle between local rights and local elites on the one hand and the crown on the other was passionately – even violently – contested. The struggle which culminated in the issuing of Magna Charta in 1215 and its reissuing in 1216, 1217, 1225, and 1237, represented the apotheosis of one episode in this struggle: the Baronial Rebellion of 1258–65, Bastard Feudalism and the Wars of the Roses were others.[36] Nevertheless, between and even during these struggles the governance of the localities was principally in the hands of representatives of local elites. A social distribution of power had been forged which would persist, albeit in different social forms, into the modern period.

This system of local government was not founded in any one period or established by any one cluster of statutes: it emerged and mutated over time. Its basic units, for example, were the county and the hundred. These were Anglo-Saxon territorial terms which the Normans took over and modified.[37] The parish, too, which emerged as the basic unit of secular administration in the sixteenth century, had its roots in patterns of church organization and lordship in Anglo-Saxon England. Thus what William Stubbs dubbed England's 'ancient local organization' largely survived the Norman attempts to remodel the English state. Indeed, what struck Stubbs was 'the tenacity of primitive institutions in the lower ranges of the [state] fabric'.[38] Here, of course, 'primitive' carries none of its now conventional pejorative connotations. Rather, from this very early stage, the English state had equipped itself with state forms which were inherently flexible and could be remoulded to suit new circumstances, and which proved highly receptive to the grafting-on of new institutions. Thus Henry II's legal reforms, developing networks of Assizes and justices, could be embodied within the existing framework.[39] Similarly, the state's attempt to regulate labourers' wages in the wake of the Black Death involved the extension of quasi-governmental powers to justices of the peace through the Statute of Labourers in 1351.[40] As the formal authority of local officials was enhanced by statute or ordinance, so it was also developed by the ambitions and through the discretionary authority of local elites themselves. 'Local government at the King's command' thus legitimized an ideological context and developed political frameworks within which the nature and extent of decentralization could be negotiated. This process of negotiation was bounded at one extreme by the centre's capacity and disposition to control local government. At times, perhaps notably under Henry II and Edward I, this disposition was relatively strong; at other times, under John, Henry III, and Henry VI, this capacity to control the localities was weak. At the other extreme the decentralization of power was limited by local elites' perception that local autonomy implied a clear recognition of complex – even intense – relationships between centre and locality. Moreover, in so far as those local elites grounded their status in claims to the authority of property and rights of law, they recognized that the nature of property rights and the authority of law were crucially dependent upon the crown.

It is at least arguable that the grumbling civil war which convulsed fifteenth-century England retarded the pace of institutional development. Certainly the civil peace of the sixteenth
century was accompanied by a massive extension in the scope of
local government and modifications in the machinery of governance which were to have profound long-term consequences. The
debate over the reality, or otherwise, of Professor Elton's 'Tudor
Revolution in Government' has obscured broader and more
unequivocal developments.[41] The Henrician Reformation, the
forcible secularization of monastic property, and repeated
attempts to enforce new patterns of religious observance
demanded modified patterns of partnership between centre and
locality and imposed quite new conditions upon public service
and office-holding. Without local officials to police them, the
statutory frameworks through which the Protestant Reformation,
and brief Marian Counter-Reformation, were articulated were
largely nugatory. Corporations, justices of the peace, church
courts, and churchwardens constituted crucially important agencies through which religious policy was policed.[42] As Gerald
Aylmer put it, without the active support, and thus implied
consent, of local officials, 'central government was helpless'.[43]
The Privy Council developed an ever more important role in
managing and monitoring contact between the centre and the
localities. Similarly important, in real and symbolic terms, were
the Assizes, developed in the fourteenth century and now playing
a pivotal role in meshing central courts and the localities. Six
assize circuits were travelled biannually by royal judges, and their
sittings constituted perhaps the most elaborate ritual of authority
in early-modern English counties.[44] But behind ritualized power
lay real politics. The Assizes brought the king's justices into the
counties, powerfully articulating the extent to which legal authority and royal majesty were interdependent. Judges could constitute conduits through which policy could be communicated
and, through their contacts with leading members of the county
elite on the grand jury, Assize judges could direct the political
energies of the localities towards priorities identified by the
crown. Similarly, through the political set-pieces of the Assizes
and the socio-political status of their Lords Lieutenant, counties
could communicate with the centre and reinforce their own sense
of distinct local identities.[45]

At the same time, the English parish emerged as the fundamental unit of local government. As we have seen, the ecclesiastical origins of the parish lie deep in the Anglo-Saxon period, and the territorial configuration of the parochial system was refined throughout the later medieval period.[46] Only in the sixteenth century, however, did the parish come to be invested with substantial secular administrative functions. Prior to that, the smaller communities of England had been governed through manorial or monastic jurisdictions and through the increasingly pervasive authority of justices of the peace. The changed circumstances of sixteenth-century England had profound consequences for the nature and structures of authority at the lower levels of the English state. The end of the Wars of the Roses did not so much institute a 'new monarchy' as reorient the energies and priorities of royal administration. New patterns of landownership and new religious and ecclesiastical forms served, if not to secularize, then to broaden responsibility for enforcing patterns of public worship and piety. At the same time, the fearsome demographic pressures of the sixteenth century (with the English population rising from around 2.77 million in 1541 to 4.25 million by 1606) gave a new intensity to the pervasive problems of poverty, vagrancy, and disorder.[47] Confronting these burgeoning social problems demanded that the state mobilize local people and local resources through newly empowered local agencies. In a series of statutes – notably Acts of 1536, 1572, 1598, and 1601 – the Tudor state augmented the responsibilities of parishes for the provision of relief and employment for their poor. By 1601 the Tudor state had, in effect, reconstituted the parish as the primary component of the polity, with substantial powers of taxation in the form of local rates, an elected executive dominated by churchwardens and overseers, and substantial autonomous authority over the local poor, roads, and policing. Significantly, though, the Elizabethan statutes of 1572, 1598, and 1601, which codified the poor law and with it parochial jurisdiction, themselves owed much to experiments in the management of poor relief in towns such as Norwich, Colchester, Ipswich, and Cambridge. Thus the politics of poverty were, from the mid-sixteenth century onwards, central to the debate on the distribution of power within the English polity.[48]

The re-invention of the English parish as a unit of local government was driven by religious and secular imperatives: hence the deep interfusion of secular and religious forms. Not only were secular governmental responsibilities superimposed on traditional ecclesiastical jurisdictions: the central political institution of the parish, the vestry, proclaimed the fusion of the secular and the religious. Parish officers and principal ratepayers met in the only appropriate public place, the vestry of the local church. The churchwardens and the incumbent played leading roles in the affairs both of the parish and the vestry, overseers of the poor trumpeted the association of piety and entitlement to poor relief, and constables were frequently charged with policing public behaviour on the Sabbath. Indeed so intimate was this fusion of the religious and the secular, of what we would now call religious and social policy, that this very mode of analysis is misleading. Rather, we should see the Reformation as extending the size and social composition of the English ruling elite and thereby creating the conditions in which a new governing elite was forged. In quite novel ways, local people were invited to take power in local communities. The language of Protestantism empowered them not only as saints but as Godly governors of the public weal.[49]

Tudor legislation and – we might add – the governing imperatives of the Tudor regime, made England a more intensely *governed* country by the early seventeenth century.[50] A system of local government through parish officers, parish institutions, and parish elites was elaborated which would survive, albeit with important modifications and augmentations, into the nineteenth century. But this construction of the parish as an organ of government should not be understood in narrowly administrative terms. The processes through which the parish was reforged as an agency of government were social as much as they were administrative, and the public life of the parish generated its own distinctive politics. Parish offices offered a means by which a new parish elite could articulate its status, while the vestry constituted the stage on which the political contests within that new parish elite could be fought out. Farmers, tradesmen, and men of modest but independent means in the localities could, by the end of the sixteenth century, aspire to a public life previously denied to them. As parish officers, through the poor law, by instructing their constables, and through management of local rates, those who ran the parish also governed their fellow parishioners.[51]

It would be pleasingly symmetrical to see social, political, and cultural processes in early-modern England as synchronous and mutually reinforcing: a parish elite emerging to run the newly created parishes and the increasing scope of justices of the peace shaping a county community and a county culture which further empowered the gentry. The public culture of England could then be read within a tripartite typology of court, county, and parish. Such a typology is not without its uses. It explains some individuals' sense of social location and others' strategies for social advancement. Both were well illustrated in Norfolk in 1585 when the Gawdy family fought a fierce, but unavailing, battle to prevent Thomas Lovell from being named on the Commission of the Peace.[52] Moreover, there were recurrent conflicts between the royal administration and local authorities at county and parish levels. However, many individuals were members of more than one community and defined their public identity in these more complex ways. Professor Hassell Smith has identified a 'court' and a 'country' gentry in Norfolk. Some justices in Elizabethan Norfolk, according to Hassell Smith, 'consistently took a "Court" view ... they worked efficiently, if not ruthlessly, as deputy lieutenants and commissioners for purveyance, no matter what additional burdens they imposed on the county'. Simultaneously, other justices 'were equally consistent in their opposition to the authority of these "Court" justices', and regarded themselves as having 'an overriding duty to reconcile County interests ... with national requirements as seen by Court and Council'.[53] The growing attraction of London and the increasing importance of parliament and the Inns of Court may have more sharply differentiated metropolitan and provincial life, but that did not stop individuals moving between these cultural *milieux*.[54] Similarly, some landowners found greater satisfaction in parish than in county politics; others were active in both, and others still in neither.

The upheavals of the seventeenth century might have subverted this process of intense evolution through which the local institutions of the English state were forged and reforged. In the short term the civil wars disturbed and the Puritan revolution challenged the emergent patterns of local government. The long-term effects, however, were to consolidate not only the existing institutional framework but also the long-negotiated patterns through which power was consolidated and dispersed within the English polity.[55] Under the Protectorate the powers of magistrates to influence appointments of overseers, surveyors, and constables were extended; parish officers became increasingly subject to fines for the non-performance or mal-performance of their duties; and repeated attempts were made to oblige parishes to greater vigilance in purging vagrancy and dissidence.[56] Individual officers might have been purged, new religious tests, formal or informal, might have operated, and the centre, through statute or the privy council, might have been intermittently more influential; but in the localities the English state retained its voluntaristic, participatory, and communitarian character. There were no Intendents and the most visible agents of central government in the provinces remained Assize judges. Attempts to intrude more powerful agents of central government into the localities met with widespread resistance and proved at best evanescent. In some ways at least, the failure of the rule of the Major Generals in the 1650s and of James II's attempts to remodel municipal corporations, Commissions of the Peace, and lords lieutenancies between 1685 and 1688 represented a victory of localities over the centre just as much as it did a triumph for country over court, or limited Anglican comprehension over religious enthusiasm of one form or another.[57]

Over the early-modern period the mode of articulating the influence of the centre over the localities was shifting from the personal to the institutional. The growth of court politics and the refinement and extension of court (and later metropolitan) culture led to the emergence of a 'court elite' that was, in function and disposition, clearly differentiated from the 'county elite'.[58] Central instruments of control, notably the Privy Council, thus became crucial determinants of the ability of the centre to influence the localities. As the institutions of central control weakened after 1688, and the disposition of the executive to shape the structure of county government weakened from the 1720s, so the effective autonomy of the localities grew.[59] Indeed, as the disposition of power between crown and parliament was renegotiated after 1688, so too was the distribution of power between centre and locality. In this context, the establishment of parliament's political pre-eminence in the eighteenth century was paralleled by the growth in local autonomy. This synchronous development of central and local government in the eighteenth century was not casually related but rather structurally interconnected.

It has recently become fashionable to characterize the Hanoverian state as a 'fiscal–military state'.[60] This captures something of its capacity and priorities. As John Brewer has argued, the early-modern English state, when viewed in terms of its capacity to wage war and intervene decisively in the European theatre, was relatively weak. Its ambitions were necessarily modest and its position easily eclipsed by the imperial ambitions and greater military capacity of continental states, notably Spain in the sixteenth and France in the seventeenth centuries. The Revolution of 1688 transformed England's international standing in intended and unintended ways. William III's avowed objective in invading was to draw England and English resources into the struggle against Louis XIV's Catholic absolutism. What was unclear, in 1689 at least, was how England could mobilize sufficient resources to be anything other than a bit-part player in international dramas.[61] The so-called 'financial revolution' that was central to the Revolution settlement transformed England's, and later Britain's, fiscal capacity. The establishment of the Bank of England in 1694 and with it a new system of public finance resting on public credit and parliamentary taxation gave Britain the ability to raise quite prodigious sums at modest rates of interest.[62] On the back of this system of public credit, Britain built a formidable navy and, by 1763, had displaced France in North America and India. Deficit financing, coupled with massive commercial and later industrial expansion, carried the British state victorious through two great world wars (1755–63 and 1793–1815).

What is as yet less clear is how this increasingly outward-looking 'fiscal–military state' harmonized with traditions of local self-government. Conrad Russell has suggested that 'a successful war could not readily be combined with local self-government which was the tradition of the English counties'.[63] Stuart governments were thus constrained by the distribution of power and the style of decision-making within the English polity. This kind of analysis is, of course, strengthened when we recall that the intensification of central control under the Cromwellian Protectorate was combined with a much enhanced commitment of state resources to war overseas. Nevertheless, Cromwellian innovations did not survive the Restoration, and the development of a 'military state' in eighteenth-century England took a quite different form. Here the English state developed a distinctive structure of limited, but highly effective central agencies to resource the state at war. Public credit was grounded in large and efficient departments of excise and customs, and the state developed complex networks of military supply. The result was a considerable, but functionally delimited, increase in the power of the centre to control policy and mobilize resources. Nevertheless, much of the responsibility for *domestic* government continued to be devolved to the localities. Indeed, as we shall see, local government independently augmented its scope and deployed new resources to ameliorate or contain burdening social problems, notably poverty, vagrancy, crime, and lunacy.[64] In so far as the development of the 'fiscal–military state' and a more capacious local government were dependent upon the growing power and sophistication of Hanoverian parliaments, developments at the centre and in the localities were not casually, but causally, interrelated. It would, however, be misleading to construe the development of local institutions and the expansion of provincial political culture in Hanoverian Britain as some of the many faces of the 'fiscal–military state'. Rather, they further developed the complex counterpoint between centre and locality and represented an increase in governance rather than a transfer of power between centre and locality.

By the eighteenth century, what had begun as 'local government at the King's command' was becoming 'local government at parliament's command'. Quite when this occurred is difficult to establish with any certainty, not least because the process was epiphenomenal to the long-run struggle between crown and parliament. What is clear, though, is that by decisively resolving this latter struggle in parliament's favour, the Revolution of 1688–9 established 'the crown in parliament' as the fulcrum of political authority within England and Wales, and, from 1707, within Britain. The powers of local government were defined, ultimately, in terms of parliamentary statute and, increasingly, the localities would seek to use parliament and legislation to broaden their jurisdiction and to underwrite locally inspired policy initiatives. Day-to-day contacts between centre and locality continued through a wide variety of channels including instructions from the Lord Chancellor to Lords Lieutenant, through the Privy

Council, through Royal Proclamations, and, from 1782, through the newly established Home Office. Nevertheless, within the complex of customary institutions that constituted the essential fabric of the British state, parliament had, by the beginning of the eighteenth century, established an unequivocal and – as it transpired – an unassailable primacy. The effect of this system of 'local government at parliament's command' was, in the Hanoverian period, to give local government very considerable autonomy. This functional separation of powers should not be mistaken for a constitutional axiom. What parliament gave, or at any rate underwrote, parliament could take back in order forcibly to reform the British state. That forcible remodelling of the relationship between centre and locality has been a *leitmotif* of the post-1830 period, culminating in the displacement of formal governmental institutions by nominated quasi-governmental agencies. An English parliament which, by the eighteenth century, had appropriated power substantially at the expense of the monarchy, could, by the late twentieth century, systematically centralize power with a striking intensity. If the century and a half after 1700 witnessed the apotheosis of English local government and provincial culture, it also heralded their slow demise.

NOTES

1.   G. E. Aylmer, 'The Peculiarities of the English State', *Journal of Historical Sociology*, iii (1990), 91–108; Philip Corrigan and Derek Sayer, *The Great Arch. English State Formation as Cultural Revolution*, new edn (Oxford, 1991); E. P. Thompson, 'The Peculiarities of the English', in Thompson, *The Poverty of Theory and Other Essays* (London, 1978), pp. 245–301; David Lindsey Keir, *The Constitutional History of Modern Britain 1485–1937*, 4th edn (London, 1950), pp. 1–4, and *passim*.
2.   For a suggestive, although different, reading of these processes, see Jeremy Black, *Convergence or Divergence? Britain and the Continent* (London, 1994).
3.   The idea of 'universal monarchy' and the British critique of its political and illiberal tendencies has been developed most suggestively by John Robertson in his 'Universal Monarchy and the Liberties of Europe: David Hume's critique of an English Whig Doctrine', in Quentin Skinner and Nicholas Phillipson (eds), *Political Discourse in Early Modern*

Britain (Cambridge, 1993), pp. 349–73, esp. pp. 356–68. For general accounts, see Pierre Goubert's massive and subtle *L'Ancien Régime*, 2 vols (Paris, 1962, 1973); and William Doyle's compressed but suggestive *The Ancien Régime* (London, 1986).

4.   John Brewer, *The Sinews of Power. War, Money and the English State, 1688–1783* (London, 1989); P. G. M. Dickson, *The Financial Revolution in England: a Study in the Development of Public Credit, 1688–1756* (London, 1967); Lawrence Stone (ed.), *An Imperial State at War: Britain from 1689–1815* (London and New York, 1994).

5.   This is not the place even to hint at, still less to rehearse, the vast French Revolutionary bibliography. Suffice it to say that modern readings of the Revolution have revisited traditional problems with a striking conceptual freshness. See, for example, Keith Michael Baker, *Inventing the French Revolution* (Cambridge, 1990); Colin Lucas (ed.), *The Political Culture of the French Revolution* (Oxford, 1988); Colin Lucas (ed.), *Rewriting the French Revolution* (Oxford, 1991); Lynn Hunt, *Politics, Culture and Class in the French Revolution* (London, 1986).

6.   Alexis de Tocqueville, *The Ancien Regime*, English trans., intro. Norman Hampson (London, 1988); Alexis de Tocqueville, *Recollections,* intro. J. P. Mayer (London, 1971), esp. pp. 3–74.

7.   See, for example, James Mackintosh, *A Defence of the French Revolution and its English Admirers ...*, in *The Miscellaneous Works of Rt. Hon. Sir James Mackintosh,* 2nd edn (London, 1851), pp. 543–623, esp. pp. 605–19.

8.   Richard Price, *A Discourse on the Love of our Country* [1789], printed in D. O. Thomas (ed.), *Richard Price: Political Writings* (Cambridge, 1991), pp. 195–6.

9.   For an introduction to what they said, see Marilyn Butler, *Burke, Paine, Godwin, and the Revolution Controversy* (Cambridge, 1984), and Alfred Cobban, *The Debate on the French Revolution 1789–1800,* 2nd edn (London, 1960). For analysis, see Albert Goodwin, *The Friends of Liberty. The English Democratic Movement in the Age of the French Revolution* (London, 1979).

10.   David Eastwood, 'Patriotism and the English State in the 1790s', in Mark Philp (ed.), *The French Revolution and British Popular Politics* (Cambridge, 1991), pp. 146–68; David Eastwood, 'E. P. Thompson, Britain, and the French Revolution', *History Workshop Journal,* 39 (1995), 79–88.

11.   David Cairns (ed.), *The Memoirs of Hector Berlioz* (London, 1969), p. 44: cf. also John Saville, *1848. The British State and the Chartist Movement* (Cambridge, 1987); Dorothy Thompson, *The Chartists. Popular Politics in the Industrial Revolution* (London, 1984), pp. 307–29.

12.   This case is brilliantly argued in Gareth Stedman Jones, 'Rethinking Chartism' in his *Languages of Class. Studies in English Working Class History 1832–1982* (Cambridge, 1983), pp. 90–178.

13.   Yet again the literature is voluminous, but for a judicious, concise survey, see G. E. Aylmer, *Rebellion or Revolution? England 1640–1660* (Oxford, 1986). A different perspective is offered in John Morrill, *The Nature of the English Revolution* (London, 1993).

14.   The key texts for the 1530s are as follows: G. R. Elton, *The Tudor Revolution in Government: Administrative Changes in the Reign of Henry VIII* (Cambridge, 1953); G. R. Elton, *Policy and Police: the Enforcement of the Reformation in the Age of Thomas Cromwell* (London, 1972); Penry Williams and G. H. Harriss, 'A Revolution in Tudor History?', *Past and Present*, 25 (1963), 3–58; G. R. Elton, 'The Tudor Revolution: a Reply', *Past and Present*, 29 (1964), 26–49. For the 'nineteenth-century revolution in government', key texts have been collected in Peter Stansky, *The Victorian Revolution. Government and Society in Victoria's Britain* (New York, 1973). See also Valerie Cromwell, 'Interpretations of Nineteenth-Century Administration: an Analysis', *Victorian Studies*, ix (1966), 245–55; Oliver MacDonagh, *Early Victorian Government 1830–1870* (London, 1977).

15.   See, for example, Christine Carpenter, *Locality and Polity: a Study of Warwickshire Landed Society, 1401–1499* (Cambridge, 1992); A. Hassell Smith, *County and Court. Government and Politics in Norfolk, 1558–1603* (Oxford, 1974); A. M. Everitt, *The Community of Kent and the Great Rebellion, 1640–1660* (Leicester, 1966); David Underdown, *Somerset in the Civil War and Interregnum* (Newton Abbot, 1973); David Underdown, *Revel, Riot, and Rebellion. Popular Politics and Culture in England 1603–1660* (Oxford, 1985); Ann Hughes, *Politics, Society and Civil War in Warwickshire, 1620–1660* (Cambridge, 1987); J. S. Morrill, *Cheshire 1630–1660: County Government and Society during the English Revolution* (London, 1974).

16.   Amongst general works which attempt to think structurally about the relationships between centre and locality are the following: Paul Langford, *Public Life and the Propertied Englishman 1689–1798* (Oxford, 1991); John Prest, *Liberty and Locality. Parliament, Permissive Legislation and Ratepayers' Democracies in the Mid-nineteenth Century* (Oxford, 1990); David Eastwood, *Governing Rural England. Tradition and Transformation in Local Government* (Oxford, 1994). See also Ruscombe Foster, *The Politics of County Power. Wellington and the Hampshire Gentlemen 1820–52* (London, 1990); J. Money, *Experience and Identity. Birmingham and the West Midlands, 1760–1800* (Manchester, 1977); and Philip Jenkins, *The Making of a Ruling Class. The Glamorgan Gentry 1640–1790* (Cambridge, 1983).

17.   James Campbell, *Essays in Anglo-Saxon History* (London, 1986); H. R. Loyn, *The Governance of Anglo-Saxon England 500–1087* (London, 1984).

18.   Sarah Foot, 'The Making of *Angelcynn*: English Identity Before the Norman Conquest', *Transactions of the Royal Historical Society*, 6th ser., vi (1996); Patrick Wormald, '*Engla lond*: the Making of an Allegiance', *Journal of Historical Sociology*, vii (1994), 1–24.

19.   R. J. Smith, *The Gothic Bequest. Medieval Institutions in British Thought, 1688–1863* (Cambridge, 1987), esp. pp. 97–170; Margot C. Finn, *After Chartism. Class and Nation in English Radical Politics, 1848–1874* (Cambridge, 1993), esp. pp. 36, 320–1.

20.   Christopher Hill, 'The Norman Yoke', in Hill, *Puritanism and Revolution. Studies in Interpretation of the English Revolution of the Seventeenth Century* (London, 1958), pp. 50–122; E. P. Thompson, *Making of the English Working Class,* Penguin edn (Harmondsworth, 1968), pp. 84–110.

21.   Joseph Arch, *From Ploughtail to Parliament. An Autobiography,* new edn, intro. Alun Howkins (The Cresset Library, 1986), pp. 74–5. Arch wrote his autobiography between 1897 and 1899.

22.   James Montagu, *Charge to the Grand Jury and other Jurors of the County of Wiltshire,* 26 April 1720, reprinted in Georges Lamonie (ed.), *Charges to the Grand Jury 1689–1803,* Camden Fourth Series, xliii (London, 1992), p. 142.

23.   Richard Witton, *A Charge to the Grand-Jury at the Quarter Sessions Held at Barnsley* [15 October 1741], printed in Lamonie, *Charges to the Grand Jury,* p. 319; Henry Fielding, *A Charge Delivered to the Grand Jury at the Sessions of the Peace Held for the City and Liberty of Westminster* [29 June 1749], printed ibid., pp. 325–43.

24.   Edmund Burke, *Reflections on the Revolution in France* [1790], ed. C. C. O'Brien (Harmondsworth, 1968), p. 117.

25.   Matthew Arnold, *Culture and Anarchy and Other Writings,* ed. Stefan Collini (Cambridge, 1993), p. 83.

26.   Frank O'Gorman, *Voters, Patrons and Parties. The Unreformed Electorate of Hanoverian England, 1734–1832* (Oxford, 1989); H. T. Dickinson, *The Politics of the People in Eighteenth-century Britain* (London, 1995), pp. 13–55; Nicholas Rogers, *Whigs and Cities. Popular Politics in the Age of Walpole and Pitt* (Oxford, 1989); John Phillips, *Electoral Behaviour in Unreformed England, 1761–1802* (Princeton, NJ, 1982).

27.   Walter Bagehot, *The English Constitution,* ed. R. H. S. Crossman (London, 1963), pp. 59, 267.

28.   Rudolph Gneist, *The History of the English Constitution,* Eng. edn (London, 1891). Gneist had published extensively on English 'self-government' in the 1850s and 1860s. For Tocqueville's position, see his *Recollections* and *Ancien Régime, passim*; and Larry Siedentop, *Tocqueville* (Oxford, 1994), pp. 41–68.

29.   Bagehot, *English Constitution,* p. 265.

30.   Thomas Paine, *Rights of Man* [1791–2], ed. Eric Foner (Harmondsworth, 1985), p. 194, my italics.

31.   Paine, *Rights of Man,* p. 126. On Paine's career in local government, see Ian Dyck, *Citizen of the World. Essays on Thomas Paine* (London, 1987), pp. 20–1.

32. Hippolyte Taine, *Notes on England*, trans. Edward Hyams (London, 1957), p. 162. Taine travelled to England on three separate occasions between 1859 and 1861.

33. The point is well made in Corrigan and Derek, *The Great Arch*, esp. p. 16.

34. W. A. Morris, *The English Medieval Sheriff to 1300* (Manchester, 1927); Irene Gladwin, *The Sheriff: the Man and his Office* (London, 1974); Esther Moir, *The Justice of the Peace* (Harmondsworth, 1969).

35. Julia Boorman, 'The Sheriffs of Henry II and the Significance of 1170', in George Garnett and John Hudson (eds), *Law and Government in Medieval England and Normandy* (Cambridge, 1994), pp. 255–75; W. L. Warren, *Henry II* (London, 1973), pp. 290–1.

36. The 1237 issue was a confirmation by Henry III of the Charta: see J. C. Holt, *Magna Carta*, 2nd edn (Cambridge, 1992), pp. 378–405. More generally, see J. R. Maddicott, 'Magna Carta and the Local Community 1215–1259', *Past and Present*, 102 (1984), 25–65; K. B. McFarlane, *The Nobility of Later Medieval England* (Oxford, 1978); R. A. Griffiths, *The Reign of King Henry the Sixth* (London, 1981); S. B. Chrimes, C. D. Ross, and R. A. Griffiths, *Fifteenth Century England 1399–1509*, 2nd edn (Stroud, 1995).

37. Helen M. Jewell, *English Local Administration in the Middle Ages* (Newton Abbot, 1972), pp. 42–68.

38. I owe this reference to James Campbell's richly suggestive Stenton Lecture, *Stubbs and the English State* (Reading, 1989), p. 10. See also William Stubbs, *Constitutional History of England*, 3rd edn, 3 vols (London, 1880), i, pp. 544–638; ii, pp. 165–316.

39. A. L. Brown, *The Governance of Late Medieval England 1272–1461* (London, 1989), pp. 100–55.

40. A. E. Bland, P. A. Brown, and R. H. Tawney (eds), *English Economic History. Select Documents* (London, 1914), pp. 164–68; Corrigan and Sayer, *The Great Arch*, p. 39.

41. For a balanced view, see Penry Williams, *The Tudor Regime* (Oxford, 1979).

42. Williams, *Tudor Regime*, pp. 253–92; J. Bettey, 'The Reformation and the Parish Church. Local Responses to National Directives', *The Historian*, xliv (1995), pp. 11–14; Christopher Haigh, *English Reformations. Religion, Politics, and Society under the Tudors* (Oxford, 1993); J. H. Gleason, *The Justices of the Peace in England 1558–1640* (Oxford, 1969).

43. G. E. Aylmer, *The King's Servants. The Civil Service of Charles I, 1625–1642* (London, 1961), p. 7.

44. Williams, *Tudor Regime*, pp. 218–35; J. S. Cockburn, *A History of English Assizes, 1558–1714* (Cambridge, 1972), esp. chs 1–3.

45. Gladys Scott Thomson, *Lords Lieutenant in the Sixteenth Century. A Study in Tudor Local Administration* (London, 1923).

46.   See Christopher Dyer's important 'The English Medieval Village Community and its Decline', *Journal of British Studies*, 33 (1994), 407–39. On the formal constitution of the parish, see Charles Arnold-Baker, *Parish Administration* (London, 1958), pp. 1–14.

47.   E. A. Wrigley and R. S. Schofield, *The Population History of England, 1541–1871. A Reconstruction*, new edn (Cambridge, 1989), pp. 208–9.

48.   Paul Slack, *Poverty and Policy in Tudor and Stuart England* (London, 1988), esp. pp. 114–31; Paul Slack, *The English Poor Law 1531–1782* (Basingstoke, 1990).

49.   David Underdown, *Fire From Heaven. Life in an English Town in the Seventeenth Century* (London, 1992); Keith Wrightson and David Levine, *Poverty and Piety in an English Village: Terling, 1525–1700*, new edn (Oxford, 1995); V. M. Larminie, *The Godly Magistrate: the Private Philosophy and Public Life of Sir John Newdigate*, Dugdale Society Occasional Papers, 28 (1982).

50.   Penry Williams, 'The Crown and the Counties', in C. Haigh (ed.), *The Reign of Elizabeth* (London, 1984), p. 128; Keith Wrightson, *English Society 1580–1680* (London, 1982), esp. pp. 152–5.

51.   Wrightson, *English Society 1580–1680*, pp. 164–73, 180–2; Keith Wrightson, 'Two Concepts of Law', in John Brewer and John Styles (eds), *An Ungovernable People: the English and their Law in the 17th and 18th Centuries* (London, 1980), pp. 21–46; Slack, *English Poor Law 1531–1782*, esp. pp. 56–8.

52.   Felicity Heal and Clive Holmes, *The Gentry in England and Wales 1500–1700* (London, 1994), p. 170.

53.   A. Hassell Smith, *County and Court. Government and Politics in Norfolk, 1559–1603* (Oxford, 1974), p. 333.

54.   This is carefully argued and well illustrated in Clive Holmes, *Seventeenth-century Lincolnshire* (Lincoln, 1980), esp. pp. 65–79, 96–101.

55.   This case is well made in Joan Kent, 'The Centre and the Localities: State Formation and Parish Government in England, c. 1640–1740', *Historical Journal*, xxxviii (1995), 363–404; Anthony Fletcher, *Reform in the Provinces: the Government of Stuart England* (New Haven, CT, 1986); and Christopher Hill, 'Parliament and People in Seventeenth-century England', *Past and Present*, no. 92 (1981), 100–24.

56.   Lane, 'State Formation and Parish Government', esp. pp. 376–91.

57.   David Underdown, 'Settlement in the Counties 1653–1658', and Austin Woolrych, 'Last Quests for a Settlement 1657–1660', both in G. E. Alymer (ed.), *The Interregnum. The Last Quest for Settlement 1646–1660* (London and Basingstoke, 1972), pp. 165–204; Andrew M. Coleby, *Central Government and the Localities: Hampshire 1649–1689* (Cambridge, 1987); J. H. Plumb, *The Growth of Political Stability in England 1675–1725*, Penguin edn (Harmondsworth, 1973), pp. 67–74; W. A. Speck, *Reluctant*

Revolutionaries. Englishmen and the Revolution of 1688 (Oxford, 1988), pp. 139–65, 213–40.

    58. Williams, 'Crown and Counties', p. 138.

    59. Norma Landau, *The Justices of the Peace, 1689–1760* (Berkeley, CA., 1984); Lionel K. J. Glassey, *Politics and the Appointment of Justice of the Peace, 1675–1725* (Oxford, 1979); E. G. Dowdell, *A Hundred Years of Quarter Sessions. The Government of Middlesex from 1660–1760* (Cambridge, 1932).

    60. The term is John Brewer's, coined in his *Sinews of Power.*

    61. J. R. Jones, *The Revolution of 1688 in England* (London, 1972), pp. 176–287, 311–31.

    62. Dickson, *The Financial Revolution*; Edward Hughes, *Studies in Administration and Finance 1558–1825* (Manchester, 1934), pp. 116–224; C. D. Chandaman, *The English Public Revenue, 1660–1688* (Oxford, 1975).

    63. Williams, 'Crown and Counties', citing Conrad Russell, *Parliaments and English Politics, 1621–1629* (Oxford, 1979), pp. 70–84, 324.

    64. This case is well argued in Joanna Innes, 'Parliament and the Shaping of Eighteenth-century English Social Policy', *Transactions of the Royal Historical Society*, 5th ser., xl (1990), 63–92.

2 Public Life in Rural England

Political Culture and Public Life in the English Parish

Our understanding of the relationship between state and society in England can all too easily be impoverished by adopting a very narrow conception of what constituted the public sphere. Few would doubt that there has always been an intimate connection between the holding of major offices of state and active participation in English public culture. The symbiosis between public office and public life at the centre of the English polity is too obvious to be laboured. The politics of the court, office-holding, and court life were of a piece. Similarly, the development of the London Season and the establishment of annual parliamentary sessions were not unconnected.[1] Also, historians of the early-modern period have demonstrated the ways in which the development of county government, notably the greater sophistication of the Quarter Sessions, rested on the emergence of a distinctive, self-referential, and vibrant 'county community'.[2] What has been less fully appreciated, and largely ignored by historians of the Hanoverian period, is the extent to which the development of the parish as a political unit was predicated on the parallel development of a distinctive parochial political culture.

News of national events reached parishes through a variety of routes. Bells tolled to proclaim news events to parishioners. Coronations, royal deaths, and military victories were broadcast by the sonorous intoning of bells. When puritans did not intervene, bells and bonfires solemnized and celebrated England's Protestant calendar. As late as the 1870s, as Francis Kilvert's Diary shows, bells still played a part in disseminating local and national news in rural England and Wales.[3] Before the advent of a provincial press, and to some extent even thereafter, the clergy were

26

important communicators of information. Sermons may have imparted news in varnished forms, but they imparted it nonetheless, and few clerics could resist expounding on war, peace, and the state of the nation. Victory in the Seven Years' War and defeat two decades later in the American War of Independence resulted in a cacophony of preachings and a minor epidemic of published patriotic sermons.[4] News of George III's not infrequent illnesses prompted Dissenting clerics such as James Hinton of Oxford to prayers for his recovery and protestations of Dissenters' loyalty; while news of the King's recovery in November 1788 so moved the normally liturgically minded Parson Woodforde of Weston Longeville that he resorted to extemporary prayer. Woodforde boasted to his diary of giving prayerful thanks in public, 'I did it out of my own head, no prayer yet [having] arrived'.[5] During the Crimean War, Drummond Rawnsley, vicar of the small parish of Shiplake in Oxfordshire, treated his parishioners to a disquisition that reaffirmed the rightness of the War while recognizing the Cobdenite case for peace. War, he told the people of Shiplake, 'retards civilization – it throws the world back – it adds to the burdens of the people – it increases the price of the means of life – it makes the poor man poorer, and the rich man richer, adding thereby to the inequality, already sufficiently wide, which parts man from his fellow'. But this, he assured his flock, was no self-interested military adventure: 'we have established more firmly the conviction, that England will not stand by, and overlook injustice – that she – the shopkeeper nation, as she has been tauntingly called – the great trafficker of the earth, will forgo her ease, and part with her wealth, and spend her best blood, for no direct benefit for herself, but to maintain the cause of the helpless, and to throw back the encroachment of the oppressor'.[6]

This propensity to comment on national events, and indeed national *mores*, was not confined to the clergy. Thomas Turner, a shopkeeper and parish officer in East Hoathly (Sussex), regularly punctuated his diary with comments of national and international events. When Admiral Byng was executed in 1757 for failing to relieve the garrison at Minorca, Turner was scandalized: 'I think him not that guilty person as many represent him, neither do I think it a prudent thing for him to be executed; but I suppose there was no calming a clamorous and enraged populace without taking away the life of this man, though if he is an innocent person, I think innocence should more than balance popular clamour'.[7] When news of the victory of Frederick II at Rossbach reached East Hoathly in November of 1757, Turner celebrated the Prussian victory and began melancholy speculations on English public culture: 'How can we expect to find such courage in the poor degenerated people of England ... For dissoluteness of manners, a spirit of effeminacy and self-interest, together with an intolerable share of pride and luxury, seem almost to overspread the whole face of the kingdom. And I presume when such are the vices of a nation, they must be ruined without a speedy reformation'.[8] For the next six years, Turner inveighed against tea drinking, the excessive imbibing of spirits, and 'that bane of private property LUXURY'.[9]

Turner's interweaving of patriotism, moralizing, and political speculation was hardly original, but is striking precisely because it was derivative. It hints at a language of public debate in rural parishes, and suggests the frame of mind in which some parishioners took on public office and with it parish governance. Culture, education, and economic standing defined a governing elite within parishes. While staying in Nettlebed in the summer of 1782, the German traveller Carl Philipp Moritz sought to characterize the parish elite: 'The farmers, whom I saw here, were dressed, not as ours, in course frocks, but with some taste, in fine cloth; and were to be distinguished from the people of the town, not so much by their dress, as by the greater simplicity and modesty of their behaviour'.[10] This class, from which parish officeholders were drawn, was both self-defining and increasingly self-confident. Its roots were firmly parochial and its horizons were limited, but its members defined their status within their parish and against a labouring class without means and public status. William Cobbett, writing in 1830, aptly described this parish elite as 'the small gentry'. The Reverend John Coker Egerton's description of precisely the same class in 1867 as 'our local parochial aristocracy' was equally apt, and exhaustive in its social reference.[11] The social standing of this parochial aristocracy was constantly reinforced. In Flora Thompson's Juniper Hill the congregation of the parish church was 'nicely graded, with the farmer's family in the front row, then the Squire's gardener and coachman, the schoolmistress, the maidservants, and the cottagers, with the Parish Clerk at the back to keep them in order'.[12] Joseph Arch recalled that in the Warwickshire village of Barford in the 1830s the rituals associated with taking holy communion articulated a social order that was both patriarchal and hierarchical. Before communion the women and children would leave and then the social distinctions were paraded before the throne of grace: 'First, up walked the squire to the communion rails; the farmers went up next; then up went the tradesmen, the shopkeepers, the wheel wright, and the blacksmith; and then, very last of all, went the poor agricultural labourers in their smock coats'.[13] Within most parishes, status was visible, official, and material.[14]

Social status is bewitching precisely because it represents a status which is artificial and constructed as something which is natural and necessary. Within parishes, social distances were carefully contrived and constantly policed. When Parson Woodforde arrived at Thurloxton in Somerset in 1763 the custom was for the poor to dine with the curate on Christmas day. Joseph Arch recalled that, in Barford, the rector's wife would sit in her pew in the chancel while 'the poor women used to walk up the church and make a courtesy to her before taking seats set apart for them'.[15] Such rituals dramatized status and obligation, articulating a social structure resting upon a complex, sometimes intuitively understood, ideology of deference. Fashion, manners, and social aspiration celebrated the social distances which held parochial society in dynamic tensions. From the late eighteenth century there was a litany of complaints that the more substantial farmers in rural England were repudiating a traditional, communal culture in a quest for gentility. In the seventeenth and earlier eighteenth centuries it was common for some agricultural labourers (farm servants) to reside in or by the farmhouse and eat with the farmer and his family.[16] In the 1820s Cobbett lamented that farm servants had been banished from the farmhouse, and with them the old symbols of 'plain manners' (oak chests and oak tables) had given way to new parlours with decanters, mahogany, and glass crockery, 'all just in the true stock-jobber style'.[17] Joseph Arch, who was inclined to attribute the embourgeoisement of tenant farmers to the social pretentions of their wives, observed that, 'Farmers' wives are ashamed nowadays to go to market and sell their eggs and butter as they used commonly to do. They want to play the piano, dress fine, make calls and ape the county [sic] gentry ... And the farmers want to hunt, and shoot, and play the gentleman at ease'.[18] Richard Jefferies, a suble conservative oberserver of rural trends in the 1870s, varied Arch's theme, hinting that an intrusion of urban *mores* enervated rustic virtue: 'The "civilization" of the town has, in fact, gone out and taken root afresh in the country. There is no reason why the farmer should not be educated; there is no reason why his wife should not wear a sealskin jacket, or his daughter interpret Beethoven. But the question arises, Has not some of the old stubborn spirit of earnest work and careful prudence gone with the advent of the piano and the oil painting?'.[19] Manners and material life were, as ever, of a piece. The parochial aristocracy aspired to a genteel lifestyle and polite *mores* on the basis of enhanced rents and more sophisticated country banking.[20] The French Wars of 1793–1815 brought many English farmers high prices and high profits.[21] This, of course, benefited those engaged in the modest service sector of parishes, leaving the parish elite better placed and firmly defining economic relations within the parish in monetary terms. The labouring class subsisted on wages, rather than customary entitlements; and when wages fell or employment ceased, their recourse was to the parish dole, itself in the gift of the parish elite.[22]

In the highly visible, frequently intimate world of the parish, the scope for dissidence was limited. Richard Gough's famous account of the Shropshire village of Myddle in 1701 was organized around reflections on the people and families who occupied the pews in the parish church. The effect is to remind us not just of a society which ordered itself hierarchically in public paces but also of a local community which was highly visible.[23] Gough's wonderfully indiscreet account also reminds us of the centrality of the church both as a meeting place and as a mediating institution in village life. Parishes were defined in a secular and in an ecclesiastical sense and, at its most fundamental level, the English state sought to intermarry church and state. Parish officers repeatedly attempted to police the Sabbath and enforce church attendance. In 1800 the vestry at Dorchester in Oxfordshire launched a vigorous attack on Sunday trading, which it considered 'a wicked practice ... [hindering people from] attending to their public duty on the Lord's day'. Anyone caught trading on the Sabbath, other than those in the 'necessary' trades (butchers, barbers, and bakers) would be prosecuted at the parish's expense. In 1823 the vestry at Finmere adopted the increasingly common expedient of appointing a special constable to 'keep within decent bounds the disposition to play on the Lord's day'. In 1833, 16 parishes in south Oxfordshire petitioned parliament for a stricter enforcement of the Sabbath.[24] If such campaigns were designed forcibly to remind parishioners of primary religious obligations, church rates intruded the costs of religion into the political economy of the village community. Church rates were levied to support the running costs of the parish church and, while in the majority of parishes these were not considerable, they did very explicitly make the established religion a regular public charge in the parish. The responsibility for maintaining the nave of the church lay with the parish and its elected churchwardens, with the clerical tithe going only towards maintaining the chancel, the remainder going into the tithe owner's pocket or, increasingly, his bank account.[25] Nothing, perhaps, did more to distinguish the public culture of rural and urban England in the early-modern period than the relative religious uniformity of rural parishes and the religious diversity of urban communities, where religious Dissent first took root.[26]

Nevertheless, precisely because parochial identities were so closely enmeshed with religious uniformity, anti-clericalism and non-conformity could have an immediate and powerful impact. The growing agrarian prosperity of the eighteenth century translated into considerably enhanced tithe income. The most tangible result of this enhanced prosperity was the new rectories and vicarages which began to spring up from the later eighteenth century. Carefully modelled on gentlemen's residences, these new rectories visibly represented, and probably enhanced, the social distances between incumbents and most of their flock.[27] This visible confirmation of the social standing of the clergy, and the hostility to tithes in communities where agrarian capitalism was beginning to take root, fused with religious individualism to inspire a grumbling anti-clericalism in many rural areas.[28] Much more significant, for the social as well as the religious construction of parish life, was the growth of rural non-conformity. The close alliance between land and church, which was actively supported by most parish officers, gave little formal scope to those Dissenters who wished to forge a distinctive public role within the local community. In this context the advent of Methodism and, to a lesser extent, the

persistence of Old Dissent represented the first intrusion of institutional pluralism into many rural communities.[29] The class
meeting, field preaching, and, eventually, chapel attendance
offered individuals an opportunity to develop institutional affiliations which went beyond the commonplace or the formally
expected. As John Skinner, the gloomy rector of Camerton in
Somerset, saw Methodism, its local leaders offered an alternative
version of religious authority within the parish and modelled different forms of association which at the very least implicitly challenged the traditional public culture of the parish. Meeting two
local Methodist preachers in February 1816, Skinner told them
that 'it would be much better for such ignorant and uninformed
persons as they were to attend to their own business as colliers and
leave me to direct the souls of my parishioners which were committed to my charge; that it was my business and office to do so,
and that they had no place or pretence to take that office from my
hands'.[30] As Methodism moved from field preaching to revivalist
chapels it played a role in dissolving the ideological hegemony of
the local church and parish state. Where it flourished, Old Dissent
could play a similar role. In the Buckinghamshire village of Long
Crendon, for example, the majority community was the local
Baptist Chapel, and the Perpetual Curate, the Reverend Thomas
Hayton, was a beleaguered figure, often forced to work with
Dissenting churchwardens elected by local ratepayers. The public
life of the village was polarized between church shops and chapel
shops, and selective trading became an articulation of sectarian
and social identities.[31] Here and elsewhere, church and chapel
came to constitute powerful polarities within the rural parishes.[32]

It is important that we properly contextualize, and do not exaggerate, the extent of Dissent in rural England. Wherever Dissent
penetrated rural areas, the established church still retained powerful advantages. Most rural elementary schools were church
schools, or subject to strong clerical influence, and in rural
Devon, for example, pupils at church schools attending
Dissenting meetings faced exclusion, punishment, or higher
tuition fees.[33] In Oxfordshire the religious census of 1851 showed
Dissent to be most vigorous in the more urbanized northern parts
of the county around Banbury, while many rural chapels
remained meeting houses rather than purpose-built places of
worship. Nevertheless, in smaller village communities, the cultural

impact of comparatively small Dissenting congregations could be powerful, and in Oxfordshire's smaller villages, comprising 300–500 inhabitants, where a Dissenting congregation was present, it comprised some 40 per cent of the worshipping population. Similar patterns existed in the north Midlands.[34] In the South Lindsey division of Lincolnshire, around 8–9 per cent of the total population were Wesleyan Methodists by 1851, but numbers matter less than distinct forms of sociability, with Methodism serving as a public confession of status and communal association, as well as a private confession of faith.[35] Where they took root, the theology, rituals, and language of Methodism represented a discourse of difference, creating a public idiom which was at once respectable and distinctive; hence, as John Walsh has shown, the fierce resistance to Methodism in rural England.[36] Old Dissent could be rejected with similar violence. On one notorious occasion in 1794, James Hinton, the urbane minister of New Road Baptist Church in Oxford, joined his elders in attending a house meeting in nearby Woodstock. Hinton thought that there might be trouble and vainly sought assurances of safety from the mayor of Woodstock. The meeting was broken up by a crowd of locals, supplemented by troops who happened to be stationed in Woodstock, and Hinton and his elders were chased and, literally, bludgeoned out of the town. Later Hinton protested to the Home Secretary, the Duke of Portland, who thought the matter best forgotten.[37] Hinton's son always maintained that the attack was premeditated and that there was collusion between the mayor, rector, vestry, magistrates, and the crowd – at least to the point of culpable inaction on the part of the authorities.[38] The affair became something of a Dissenting *cause célèbre*, and was taken up by a committee of London congregations who concluded that 'it is a notorious fact that the Peace Officers of Woodstock were very remiss in not affording Protection and Assistance'.[39] But there the matter rested. Sympathy for the rioters extended into respectable Oxford society. Hinton recalled being repeatedly told after the attack that, 'While you continue to preach in Oxford only, we shall respect you; but if you go into the country places, it is so disgraceful a thing, that we cannot be connected with you'.[40] Behind such sentiments lay a sharp distinction between the pluralism acceptable in cosmopolitan centres and the outward conformity expected in rural parts.[41]

Where Dissent was strong, church rates proved increasingly divisive and, on occasions, all but impossible to collect. In closed parishes where Anglicanism retained a monopoly on men's souls, it was assumed to be justifiable that the state religion should remain a civic charge. Elsewhere such imposts were regarded by Dissenters as a sectarian outrage, and by the 1830s Radicals in parliament were encouraged by the chorus of pressure groups outside in their efforts to secure abolition of church rates.[42] The right to levy a church rate on all ratepayers, irrespective of private religious affiliations, was an outward demonstration of the prerogatives and privileges of Establishment. As Edward Stanley told the House of Commons in 1834: 'It is of the very essence of that union between church and state, that the state shall out of the public funds defray the expenses of the religion that it establishes'.[43] The alternative to religion on the rates was the voluntary principle, which explicitly challenged the relationship between parish church and parish state. The Reverend W. C. Risley, the rector of Deddington in Oxfordshire, considered the voluntary system 'utterly inadequate to meet the spiritual wants of our people',[44] while the vicar of nearby Charlbury added a utilitarian gloss by arguing that free religion for the poor was socially useful and therefore a legitimate charge upon public funds.[45] Depriving the church of the financial prop afforded by the rates 'would be nothing short of a suicidal act on the part of the nation'.[46] To Dissenters this was hysterical special pleading, which claimed for Anglicanism a special concern for the poor that had long since evaporated. Where Dissent was strong, Anglican parish officers were compelled to moderate their demands upon ratepayers. In some parishes, while the cost of essential maintenance continued to be covered from the rates, other expenses were met by subscriptions and collections. Organs were installed and minor fabric repairs were funded in this way.[47] Elsewhere, rates were kept low by securing loans against future rates and thus spreading the cost of repairs over a number of years.[48]

In a few parishes the sectarian division was sharply felt. At Enstone in Oxfordshire in 1824 ratepayers clamped down on profligate spending by the church by electing as churchwardens men pledged to reducing expenditure.[49] In Dissenting strongholds such as Witney, Nonconformists demonstrated their hostility by refusing to levy church rates. Where Dissenters held sufficient power in the vestry to block church rates, the fabric of churches could suffer grievous neglect and, as a result of paltry rates, at Witney by the 1830s the roof of the parish church was leaking and structurally unsound. It was only in 1836 with the arrival of an energetic evangelical rector that the Dissenting party relented and agreed to a substantial rate; and this only after the Reverend Charles Jerram offered to put up £500 of his own money towards the cost of repairs, and outflanked the opposition by proposing that all those rated at less than £3 be exempted from church rates.[50] Non-residence, that symbol of Anglican insouciance, regularly led to rates being uncollected and to consequent structural decay.[51] At Henley-on-Thames, Dissenting hostility to rates was sufficiently strong to block repairs to the church in 1827, and an extension of the graveyard shortly after.[52] Although church rates survived until 1868, as Archbishop Thomson confessed to the Lords in that year, the church rates had long since ceased to be a compulsory local tax in numerous parishes.[53]

A more subtle form of sectarianism intruded itself into parish life as the Tractarian movement spread its fondness for Catholic ritual into rural parishes.[54] The evidence of Hanoverian visitation returns suggests that most rural parishes were characterized by liturgical simplicity and infrequent communions, perhaps no more than four times per year.[55] To many in rural parishes in the mid-nineteenth century, Tractarian ritualism was unwelcome, partly because it disturbed established patterns of public worship and partly because it redefined priestly authority, repositioning the priest as the embodiment of a narrowly interpreted religious truth rather than a broader, more inclusive public doctrine. Some clerics rejected and ridiculed Tractarianism. The Reverend John Coker Egerton, of Burwash, chuckled to his diary in April 1867: 'Have you heard that the Bishop of Oxford [Samuel Wilberforce] has now got so high Church that he turns his back upon the people, and reads the lessons from the Rectum!'.[56] In the Bishop's Oxfordshire diocese James Dew, an autodidact and relieving officer at Lower Heyford, fulminated against the Anglo-Catholics. After Wilberforce had taken a confirmation service at Lower Heyford on 25 April 1867, Dew noted that, 'The Bishop is a very clever fellow indeed, & he can clothe his Pusyism in very decent garments, but his clergy have not that power & they show it forth in its worst yet most correct form'. A year earlier a copy of the

Anglo-Catholicly inclined *Church Times* had arrived in Lower
Heyford, and Dew concluded that 'most horrid things are in it'.[57]
Although it would be wrong to see the rural parishes of later
Victorian England as vibrant centres of religious pluralism, they
were undoubtedly more publicly differentiated communities than
they had been in the early eighteenth century.

Alongside what might be termed the official culture of village
communities there was a sometimes veiled and sometimes aggressively public popular culture. For much of the time this was a self-
consciously male culture which located itself around alehouses,
sporting pursuits, and friendly societies; but popular rituals of
village England could also be more comprehensive. Fairs, wakes,
travelling entertainers, *charivaris*, and seasonal celebrations had
appeals which transcended gender, age, and, to some extent at
least, social location. Local magistrates might try to curtail them,
but great fairs such as the annual Wychwood Forest in
Oxfordshire continued to draw crowds of revellers, stallholders,
and entertainers, until the reformed police forces of the mid-
nineteenth century gave the authorities a new capacity to enforce
patrician codes of public decorum. Campaigns were similarly
waged against such traditional sports as prizefighting.
Nevertheless, even the strictures of judges such as Justice Park of
the Home Circuit, who announced that he would treat deaths
from prizefighting as manslaughter, could not prevent plebeians
openly and patricians more circumspectly from continuing to
support illegal prizefighting.[58] Cobbett, in lamenting polite
assaults on popular recreations, caught something of its mascu-
line exuberance: 'Something must be left and something ought to
be left, to the sense and reason and morality and religion of the
people. There were a set of "well-meaning" men in the country,
who would have passed laws for regulating and restraining every
feeling in the human breast, and every motion of the human
frame ... They were hostile to rural and athletic sports; to those
sports which string the nerves and strengthen the frame'.[59]

In 1889 Augustus Jessopp wrote that 'there are scores – perhaps
hundreds – of villages where the inhabitants have absolutely no
amusements of any kind outside the public-house'.[60] Village alehouses had attracted censure for centuries from magistrates,
moralists, clerics, reformers, and those who sought to intrude the
values of polite society into plebeian culture.[61] In 1700 there were

perhaps 58 000 alehouses in England, a ratio of one alehouse per 87 people. By 1830 the combined effects of population growth and stricter licensing policies on the part of magistrates had reduced the total number of alehouses and increased the ratio of alehouses to population to 1 : 282.[62] Symptomatic of magistrates' hostility to the archetypical village alehouse was a Charge to the Grand Jury of Surrey in 1736 which suggested that 'The ancient, true, & Principal Uses of Inns, Alehouses & Victualling-Houses is for the receipt, Relieving & Lodging of Travellers & for the Supply of the Wants of the People ... but was never meant for the Entertainment & harbouring of Lewd & Idle People to spend & consume their Money & their time in a lewd and drunken Manner'. Such attempts to distinguish between the moral world of the inn and the alehouse, and thereby to draw a distinction between commercial and rustic manners, was a magisterial commonplace.[63] Yet the alehouse survived, partly because it adapted and partly because it grew naturally from the rhythms and male popular culture of the parish. Until the 1820s alehouses were not purpose-built public houses but, quite literally, licensed premises. They offered drink and sociability, but gained their particular significance through constituting a focus for many aspects of village life. Friendly societies and other village clubs would generally meet in the more respectable pubs, while by the early nineteenth century distinctive pub games – skittles, draughts, and dominoes – gave a new texture to leisure activities, in the process perhaps further accentuating a gendered separation between the domestic and public spheres of village life.[64]

In the context of the public life of the parish, the extent to which popular rituals empowered parishioners was striking. Many parish officers, in alliance with magistrates, strove in vain to police the Sabbath, ordering constables to prevent those who were playing football or other games during divine service. Constables charged with enforcing Sabbath observance were frequently the subject of abuse and on occasions encountered serious violence.[65] This struggle to define the Sabbath hinged around notions of respectability and divine imperatives on the one hand and claims to leisure and simple freedom of expression on the other. More powerful still could be the collective voice of the village community. 'Rough music' – the practice of a local crowd discordantly serenading individuals or groups who violated popular norms and customs – represented popular indictment, punishment, and ridicule.[66] Most instances of rough musicking went unreported, but extant reports suggest that the victims of popular disapprobation were varied. A random sample includes a Jacobin sympathizer at Thame (Oxfordshire) in 1794, a man cuckolded by his wife in St Albans (Hertfordshire) in 1801, and an unpopular encloser at Bicester (Oxfordshire) in 1815.[67] Adultery often appears to have encountered communal disapprobation in the form of rough music. Flora Thompson (1876–1947) recalled that an affair between a lodger and a married women led to effigies of the pair being made and being 'carried aloft on poles by torchlight to the house of the woman, to the accompaniment of the banging of pots, pans, and coal-shovels, the screeching of tin whistles and mouth-organs, and cat-calls, hoots, and jeers'. The lodger, the woman, and the cuckolded husband soon left the parish.[68] Brutal, participatory, and menacing, 'rough music' reinforced popular solidarities and gave the many in parishes a voice which could influence and constrain.

More striking, if less common, were moments when the polite and the popular in village culture fused in a powerful and idiomatically varied statement of communal priorities. One such episode occurred in the Lancashire village of Astley in 1822 when the vicar of Leigh, the Reverend Joseph Hodgkinson, tried to assert his right to present to the curacy of Astley Chapel. Parishioners at Astley claimed a customary right to elect their incumbent, resisted Hodgkinson's nomination, and held an election. Some 305 householders voted, 287 for Reverend Bowman and a mere 16 for Reverend Birkett, who was Hodgkinson's candidate. A deputation of villagers and sympathetic clerics waited on Hodgkinson and informed him that if he refused to accept their 'elected' candidate, the 287 families voting for Bowman 'have signed their names to a solemn Declaration that they will never enter the door of Astley Chapel' again. Hodgkinson's persisting in his actions would be 'destructive of the peace of the congregation, and injurious to the interests of religion. It will ... fill the meeting-houses of Dissenters'. Hodgkinson did persist, and Birkett was presented. On Sunday 14 July 1822, Birkett was met with a crowd of around one thousand protesting against his installation, and thereafter his progress to his chapel was dogged by parishioners lining his route, beating their pots and pans. Elections and respectable deputations merged into rough music and loud demonstrations, and the noise reached the *Manchester Guardian*, the Bishop of Chester, the Lancaster Assizes, and King's Bench. The parish won its case at Assizes in August 1823 but lost in King's Bench in July 1824. Joseph Hodgkinson was admitted to the Manchester Asylum in January 1823 and died three years later.[69] There were no obvious winners, but such struggles showed the vitality of custom, politics, and parody in village life.

'Rough music' was only one recourse in a large repertoire of popular sanctions. As E. P. Thompson showed in a classic article, crowd interventions in defence of what they took to be just prices or communal rights could be devastatingly effective.[70] At times of shortage and high prices, farmers in particular found themselves intimidated by large crowds who not only demanded food with menaces but might seize grain and sell it off at what they deemed a just price. The logic of collective violence was to deny or over-ride this simple operation of supply and demand. In 1795 at Deddington, Banbury, and Witney, grain about to be shipped out of Oxfordshire was seized and sold off well below the current market price.[71] Price-fixing riots were still more common in the near-famine conditions of 1800–1802.[72] Here urban and rural crowds merged to intimidate the economic elites of local villages. In 1800 a crowd left Oxford to attack Stanford mill, and gathered villagers who were promptly issued with sticks.[73] This willingness to use collective violence to police popular notions of justice was not restricted to economic issues. The game laws, which defined hunting rights very narrowly, engendered bitter hostility.[74] Communities shielded poachers, purchased game from them, and passionately believed this particular law to be an ass. When, in 1808, a special constable arrived at the home of Francis Lancashire at Shipton (Oxfordshire) with a warrant to search for evidence of deer stealing, a crowd forcibly prevented him gaining entry.[75] At such moments the antagonism between the law and officialdom on the one hand and popular morality on the other became explicit.

It would, however, be quite wrong to imply that there was a necessary counterpoint between the polite and popular culture of the parish. Parson Woodforde was alarmed when a parishioner, who had been supplying him with elicit brandy and rum, was discovered and fined. Whether his anxiety concerned the possible interruption to his supply or the possibility of his too being arraigned is unclear, but for some days the matter concerned him grievously. Equally concerned, but less passive, was Thomas Turner who, in 1757, responded with alacrity to Master Paris's request that he draw up a petition on behalf of his sons who had been caught smuggling. After drawing up the petition Turner, a serving parish officer, gave the Paris family 2s 6d not 'so much from the principle of charity as self-interest, having formerly bought some brandy of them'.[76]

Parish elites and the labouring (or perhaps we should say the entrepreneurial) classes were bound together in virtue and well as vice. From the 1760s rural friendly societies became increasingly common, offering the possibility of mutual insurance against ill-health and even unemployment.[77] By 1803 the number of friendly societies in England had reached at least 9347, with an average membership of 72, and by 1831 Devon had as many as 867 friendly societies.[78] These mutual insurance societies generally included the parish elite but reached beyond to include the skilled artisans and skilled labourers. They generally met in a local public house, drinking together on a regular 'club night' and pro-claiming their respectability through an annual 'club day', when their annual feast was preceded by an annual service and sermon. A friendly society was founded at Stonesfield in Oxfordshire in 1765 and was still thriving a century later. By 1860 its member-ship had risen to 88, including 22 agricultural labourers, 12 slate workers, seven masons, four carpenters, four hurdle-makers, four shoemakers, three blacksmiths, three sawyers, two woodmen, a baker, a carrier, a farmer, a shopkeeper, and a wheelwright. The 'Father of the Society' was Edward Davies, the proprietor of the *Black Head*, where members of the society met to drink and social-ize on their club nights. The Stonesfield society's committee included Samuel Hounslow, the parish clerk, and three other members of the parish vestry. This close connection between the friendly society and the vestry had been cemented in 1825 when the society loaned the parish £100 (at 5 per cent per annum) to help fund the rebuilding of the north aisle of the parish church.[79] The close integration of the friendly society into village life was not uncommon. In Bampton in June 1797, the local vestry agreed to make regular subventions to the local friendly society to save it from bankruptcy. The Minute Book records the vestry's firm conviction that the friendly society was 'of the utmost benefit to the parish in general'.[80] Relationships between the friendly society and rector at Burwash were sufficiently cordial for the rector to be able to visit a club meeting and secure signatures for a pro-church rate petition in 1860, while four years earlier the Reverend Drummond Rawnsley of Shiplake had praised the moral effects of friendly societies in his sermon on a society's annual feast day, lauding the 'one great benefit you obtain by belonging to a club – *you keep your independence*'.[81] At Farnborough the annual benefit society dinner was marked by a general wake for the parish, and the children coined the phrase 'a good club' to denote an enjoyable wake.[82] Friendly societies were not without their critics. Some criticized the amount of communal imbibing, which seemed inseparable from the ethos of self-help, and some incumbents pointedly refused to preach at annual feast days.[83] In the main, though, rural friendly societies not only wove themselves into the fabric of the local community but also came to constitute a means through which an elite of parishioners could find security, independence, fraternity, and status.

To the urban mind, the rural parish was striking for, even impoverished by, its institutional and cultural simplicities. It lacked the diversity of places, people, and pastimes which enlivened the world of the town. Where towns had their concerts, in parishes, even when the music wasn't rough, it was rustic. Where urban processions were ordered and orchestrated, parish wakes and festivals were more simply celebratory. In consequence the manners, and even the dialects, of rural England tended to differentiate it from urban England. Having registered the intermittently dichotomous worlds of the village and the town, we would do well not to draw the distinctions too sharply. Many towns were rural market towns, servicing agriculture, heavily influenced by the rhythms of the agricultural year, and owing more to the vernacular of village life than to the elegant artifice of Bath, Cheltenham, and the self-consciously refined manners of the self-consciously elegant town. Moreover, whatever its simplicities, the English rural community had its public sphere. This public life of the parish community – defined by custom, status, function, and parish institutions – found its fullest expression in the political life of the parochial community.

The Parish State

Hitherto historians have paid relatively little attention to the way in which English parishes functioned as political and administrative systems.[84] Partly this is a consequence of the survival of records.[85] Until 1819, vestries were not obliged by law to keep minutes of their meetings, and although minute books for earlier periods do survive for a small number of parishes, a good many vestries clearly only began to keep minutes in a systematic way after they were obliged to do so by law. Following the passage of William Sturges Bourne's Act requiring vestries to keep minutes, the vestry met in the small Oxfordshire parish of South Newington, resolving to meet regularly at 2 p.m. on the first Wednesday in the month and 'that minutes of the Proceedings and Resolutions of every vestry shall be entered in a book to be provided for that purpose'. Many such meetings doubtless took place across England, and the clear implication was that, hitherto, formal minutes had not been kept.[86] The failure to keep formal minutes was not necessarily a manifestation of parish officials' bureaucratic naivety. Most parishes were run by a small elite who occupied, in rotation, the principal offices of overseer, churchwarden, and surveyor of the highways. The political primacy of this elite within local communities was rarely challenged, and they held unquestioned sway within vestry meetings.[87] The governing style in most parishes, therefore, was personal rather than bureaucratic, with word of mouth rather than detailed written records being the essential currency of parish administration. Where parish officers needed to refer to precedent, they generally relied more on the memory of their parish clerks than on an elaborate archive of written records.[88] The style of parish government is reflected in the pattern of archival survival. Overseers' accounts, rate books, and the records of churchwardens' disbursements are much more common than minute books or other records of vestries' decisions in matters of policy. As a result, it is difficult for historians to reconstruct the way in which policy was shaped and implemented within parishes. Occasionally, we encounter parishes which did not fall victim to this archival coyness, and their inner workings are openly displayed in a rich assortment of parish records. In some cases vestries were galvanized by zealous incumbents into formalizing their administrative procedures and maintaining fuller records.[89] Elsewhere, the initiative for more systematic record-keeping came from members of the vestry. But, generally, it seems that the most elaborate bureaucratic procedures were employed in larger parishes, where the sheer complexity of governing the parish demanded greater sophistication.[90]

Until their slow emasculation in the nineteenth century, the political institutions of the parish were representative, participatory, and accountable. The theatre in which the political life of the parish was forged was the vestry, which all ratepayers were entitled to attend and at which each ratepayer enjoyed the right to vote.[91] As with parliament, property and wealth constituted the basis through which participation in the local institutions of the state was regulated. By contrast with parliament, however, the parochial franchise and thus the formal basis of local government was popular. Indeed, in terms of its formal construction, the parish was a ratepayers' republic. Nowhere was this clearer than when parishes were re-valued for rating and ratepayers would pack vestry meetings to protest at new valuations, the relative weights accorded to different types of property, and any transgression of customary entitlements. When Bampton was re-rated in 1831 there was a series of special vestries which dragged on for two years, and fiscal disputes risked crowding out the other business of the parish.[92] Regular vestry meetings punctuated the public life of the parish. By the late eighteenth century, as problems of poverty pressed, many vestries met at least monthly, and some more frequently. Most met in the parish church, either in the vestry room itself or in the body of the church, again confirming the close association of established church and Anglican state; but, as we have seen, this did not prevent Dissenters or even Roman Catholics from playing a substantial role in the political life of the parish.[93] The principal legitimation for public status in the parish was private wealth.

The republican constitution of the parish embodied strong oligarchical tendencies. All ratepayers could meet in vestry, although in practice generally only the principal ratepayers did so. This group of the more substantial, resident ratepayers became the governing elite of the parish. They shared out the major local offices – churchwardens, overseers of the poor, and surveyors of the highways – between them, often serving in rotation. Farmers, respectable tradesmen, and resident incumbents constituted a social elite which became the governing aristocracy of the parish. Occasionally men of greater substance would associate themselves with the day-to-day politics of the parish. Thus Frederick Page, a deputy lord lieutenant of Berkshire and a noted poor law campaigner in the 1820s, was active in his local vestry. J. W. Henley, later Chairman of Oxfordshire Quarter Sessions (1846–63) and the county's MP (1841–78) was active in the Waterperry vestry.[94] But, generally, the gentry sought to influence parish affairs through the administrative and appellate authority of magistrates. A more typical parish officer was Thomas Turner, of East Hoathly, who regularly served as overseer, and brought to the public life of his parish a striking combination of fiscal acumen, political sense, and contempt for those in the parish who had material means but little by way of intellectual refinement.[95] Similarly prominent in the life of Deddington in the later 1830s was William Churchill, a local grocer, who formed a powerful axis with the choleric rector, William Risley, thereby combining local knowledge and local status to considerable political effect.[96]

If local status and visible wealth conspired to create a Venetian oligarchy within the ratepayers' republic, later Hanoverian parliaments were willing, perhaps even eager, to reconstitute the parish in more explicitly oligarchical terms. Thomas Gilbert's famous Act of 1782, which provided for the voluntary association of parishes into unions to erect and run shared workhouses, transferred the management of such workhouses to elected, but more socially selective, Boards of Guardians.[97] Although relatively few Gilbert Unions were formed, such legislation did signal a shift away from the open, plenary, and participatory constitution of the traditional vestry. By 1834 there were probably some 68 unions formed under Gilbert's Act, containing around a thousand parishes and half a million people.[98] A much more decisive repudiation of the traditional constitution of the vestry came in 1819, when William Sturges Bourne steered through his explicitly restrictive Select Vestry Bill. Sturges Bourne had chaired a major enquiry into the operation of the poor laws in 1817, and his report had recommended sweeping legislative changes affecting both the administration of relief and the government of English parishes.[99] In the 1818 and 1819 parliamentary sessions, Sturges Bourne introduced six bills designed to give legislative effect to his committee's principal recommendations. Three bills were lost, but the Select Vestry Bill passed the Commons after some debate.[100] This Act had two principal provisions. First, it enabled parishes to establish a 'select vestry' to administer most aspects of parish government. This was rather more than a standing committee of the vestry because, although annually elected by the whole vestry, the select vestry then appropriated to itself virtually all aspects of policy which would hitherto have been decided in open vestry. In effect, the Act was quite explicitly designed to concentrate power in the hands of the major ratepayers and to this end it instituted its second major provision: a new system of voting which gave householders rated at up to £50 per annum one vote and those assessed at more than £50 an additional vote for each £25 of rateable value, up to a maximum of six votes.[101] The predictable and intended effect was to enable larger ratepayers to outvote the majority of smaller ratepayers. This system of voting, which remained in force until the Parish Councils Act of 1894,[102] ensured that, where parishes adopted a select vestry system, nomination to and generally membership of the select vestry would be dominated by the major ratepayers and their allies. Power, and in particular power over the management of poor relief and parish expenditure, was being placed unequivocally in the hands of the more substantial men of property. By March 1832 some 2234 English parishes had established select vestries, and it seems reasonable to conclude that on the eve of the Poor Law Amendment Act somewhere between one-fifth and one-quarter of the population was governed through select vestries on the model envisaged in the Sturges Bourne reforms.[103]

A parallel trend towards greater sophistication came with the increasing disposition to appoint salaried officials to assist the regular, nominally or actually elected, parish officers. The most common such official was a salaried assistant overseer. Many urban parishes appointed assistant overseers in the eighteenth century, but the practice did not spread to rural parishes on any great scale until the early nineteenth century. Typical of this was Eynsham, which appointed a salaried assistant overseer, accountable to a standing management committee of the vestry, in 1811.[104] There was considerable dispute as to whether existing legislation permitted the payment of regular salaries to non-statutory officers from the rates. The 1817 Select Committee on the Poor Laws had recommended the appointment of assistant overseers and another of Sturges Bourne's Acts, passed in 1819, regularized their appointment.[105] Within three years some 1838 assistant overseers were in post in England and by 1834 this had risen to 3376.[106] Instituting a system of salaried officers, even on a modest scale, rapidly changed the character of parish government. Executive responsibility for the implementation of policy, the assessment of pauper entitlement, and routine financial management passed swiftly from elected overseers to the appointed assistant overseers. The elected members of the select vestry of course retained control over policy, but even here an enterprising assistant overseer could exercise a good deal of influence. Hitherto, the style of government in most parishes had been amateur and authority had been vested in an oligarchy of ratepayers. Now, for the first time, it was becoming possible to make a *career* in parish administration, and thus the age of the professional was in sight. This trend was well exemplified at Bampton, Oxfordshire, in the career of George Frost. In 1821 Frost accepted the unglamorous, but potentially influential office of parish clerk. He seems to have employed his influence to persuade the vestry to adopt a subtle variation of the 'Bread Scales' which were widely adopted throughout rural southern England after 1795.[107] Thereafter his progress was rapid. In April 1823 he accepted the farm of the poor at £1400 per annum, and for good measure also supervised a general smallpox inoculation. The parish abandoned farming the poor two years later, so Frost accepted the post of assistant overseer at an annual salary of £40. Between 1826 and 1829 policy again changed, and Frost resumed the farm of the poor. In December 1829 Frost was appointed schoolmaster and organist, but retained a close interest in and a good deal of influence over local politics. In December 1832, for example, Frost persuaded the vestry to adopt his elaborate labour rate under which major employers were charged a surcharge on their poor rates but were able to offset this by taking on additional labour from amongst the ranks of the able-bodied poor.[108] Adopting Frost's version of the labour rate system was Bampton's last major innovation in poor relief policy before the 1834 Poor Law Amendment Act virtually eliminated vestries' capacity for independent initiative in the local management of poverty.[109] Frost's influence in Bampton was no greater than that of incumbents and traditional parish officers elsewhere, but his enjoying such influence as an employee of the parish hinted at a future in which official status would eclipse social status in the political life of localities.

For most English people their only contact with the world of officialdom and their only experience of political authority came through parish officers. Politicians and theorists might debate the representative nature of parliament, but in most people's lives parliament, and the state authority it embodied, were remote indeed. The immediate structure of authority was that of the parish. The Northamptonshire poet and pauper, John Clare, coined the phrase the 'parish state' to capture the extent and intensity of this perceived authority, which Clare himself had experienced, with bitter resentment, at the hands of the parish officers of Helpston.[110] In the lives of the labouring poor, the parish elite were nothing less than a governing elite. Parish officers had extensive and largely unregulated powers of taxation, and the parish vestry remained responsible for the provision of a wide range of services from welfare and policing through to the maintenance of roads and the church. In most parishes there was a sharp demarcation between a class of office-holders (actual or potential) and the much larger class of lesser ratepayers and the poor who could never aspire to office-holding. This sharp demarcation in social allegiance and political power was highlighted by Clare:

> Churchwardens Constables and Overseers
> Makes up the round of Commons and of Peers
> With learning just enough to sign a name
> And skill sufficient the parish rate to frame
> And cunning deep enough the poor to cheat
> This learned body for debatings meet
> Tho many heads the parliament prepare
> And each one claims some wisdom for its share
> Like midnight with her vapours tis so small
> They make but darkness visible withall[111]

Although parish elites were subject to the appellant authority of magistrates, in practice they enjoyed a good deal of autonomy. This intense localism fostered its own patterns of allegiance, its own parochial pride, and its own local rivalries. In 1802–3 parishes spent a shade under 5 per cent of income from the rates in

litigation over settlements.[112] Magistrates were frequently exasper-
ated at the ways in which parochialism frustrated policy.
Campaigns against vagrancy were undermined when parishes
refused to take responsibility for arresting and conveying vagrants
to county gaols. Parish officers, thinking primarily of local interest, were generally content to continue their usual practice of
instructing constables to 'move on' vagrants.[113] The parish interest extended no further than moving a vagrant off 'their patch'.
There are frequent instances of parish officers compelling known
or alleged fathers to marry women carrying their children. Parson
Woodforde officiated reluctantly at such a ceremony in January
1787, finding it 'very disagreeable for me to marry such persons'.
Revealingly, though, he did not feel able to contradict the will of
parish officers. Thomas Turner as a parish officer could, within a
single day, persuade a magistrate to conduct a bastardy examina-
tion and then compel the named father to marry.[114] Similarly,
parish officers had little hesitation in intervening in the lives of
parishioners, and did so across a positive kaleidoscopic range,
from preventing the poor from keeping dogs to using the law to
end wife beating.[115] From the perspective of the labouring poor
and the parishioner without means, the parish elite was unques-
tionably a governing class.

For parish elites the attraction of the vestry was that it offered
them a framework for political action. By the end of the eighteenth century perhaps as many as 400 000 people (including
some women) regularly attended parish vestries and provided the
pool from which parish officials were elected. Most of these
people did not enjoy a parliamentary franchise and thus were
denied a formal role in electoral politics. Nevertheless, the politics of the parish could provide a satisfying alternative. It would be
misleading to suggest that allegiance to the parish eclipsed other
allegiances. Parish officers were likely to be active in church politics, frequently took a role (even as non-electors) in election campaigns, and many were to the fore in orchestrating celebrations of
national events: of Nelson's victories, of the King's recoveries
from illness, and of George III's golden jubilee. These local elites
also seized opportunities to be active on the wider stage. They vol-
unteered, enlisted in the yeomanry during the French Wars,
joined agricultural societies, and formed prosecution associations.[116] Here too we discover complex patterns of identity and

allegiance, but for many members of these parish elites their networks of allegiance radiated out from the parish which continued to enjoy their primary loyalty. Whether viewed as a social, cultural, or political system, the world of the parish for many had a pleasing sufficiency. Viewed as a public and political institution, the parish was one of the most distinctive and vibrant components of the Hanoverian polity.

NOTES

1.   Paul Langford, *Public Life and the Propertied Englishman 1689–1798* (Oxford, 1991), pp. 377–90.
2.   For a summary, see J. S. Morrill, *The Revolt of the Provinces. Conservatives and Radicals in the English Civil War 1630–1650* (London, 1976), esp. pp. 14–31. See also pp. 15–16 [ch. 1], and 100–2 [ch. 4].
3.   David Cressy, *Bonfires and Bells. National Memory and the Protestant Calendar in Elizabethan England* (London, 1989), pp. 67–92; William Plomer (ed.), *Kilvert's Diary. Selections from the Diary of Rev. Francis Kilvert, 1870–1879*, new edn, 3 vols (London, 1960), i, pp. 45, 86, 142, 145–6, 271, 289, and *passim*.
4.   James E. Bradley, *Religion, Revolution and English Radicalism. Nonconformity in Eighteenth-Century Politics and Society* (Cambridge, 1990), esp. pp. 121–58; Robert Hole, *Pulpits, Politics and Public Order in England 1760–1832* (Cambridge, 1989), pp. 44–53, 95–173; Paul Langford, 'The English Clergy and the American Revolution', in Eckhart Hellmuth (ed.), *The Transformation of Political Culture. England and Germany in the Late Eighteenth Century* (Oxford, 1990), pp. 275–308.
5.   James Hinton, *Vindication of the Dissenters of Oxford* (Oxford, 1792); James Hinton, *Sermon on the Death of His Late Majesty* (Oxford, 1820); James Woodforde, *Diary of a Country Parson 1758–1802*, ed. John Beresford (Oxford, 1978), p. 338.
6.   R. Drummond and B. Rawnsley, *Sermons Preached in Country Churches* (London, 1858), pp. 142–3, 146.
7.   [Thomas Turner], *The Diary of Thomas Turner 1754–1765*, ed. David Vaisey (Oxford, 1985), p. 93.
8.   Ibid., pp. 124–5.
9.   Ibid., pp. 159, 245.
10.   [Carl Philipp Moritz], *Travels of Carl Philipp Moritz in England in 1782*, English trans. 1795 (reprinted London, 1924), p. 138.
11.   William Cobbett, *Rural Rides* [1830], Penguin edn (Harmondsworth, 1967), p. 270; John Coker Egerton, *Victorian Village. The Diaries of the Reverend John Coker Egerton of Burwash*, ed. Roger Wells (Stroud, 1992), p. 70. Egerton was rector of Burwash in the Sussex Weald.
12.   Flora Thompson, *Lark Rise to Candleford*, Penguin edn (Harmondsworth, 1973), p. 210.

13.   Arch, *From Ploughtail to Parliament*, p. 20.

14.   For fuller discussions, see Barry Reay, *The Last Rising of the Agricultural Labourers. Rural Life and Protest in Nineteenth-Century England* (Oxford, 1990), esp. pp. 37–9; Eastwood, *Governing Rural England*, pp. 24–42.

15.   Woodforde, *Diary of a Country Parson*, p. 28; Arch, *From Ploughtail to Parliament*, p. 17.

16.   Ann Kussmaul, *Servants in Husbandry in Early Modern England* (Cambridge, 1981), pp. 40–2; G. E. Mingay, *English Landed Society in the Eighteenth Century* (London, 1964), pp. 239–41.

17.   Cobbett, *Rural Rides*, pp. 226–7.

18.   Arch, *From Ploughtail to Parliament*, p. 30.

19.   Richard Jefferies, *Hodge and his Masters* [1880], new edn, intro. A. M. Richardson (Stroud, 1992), p. 77.

20.   L. S. Pressnell, *Country Banking in the Industrial Revolution* (Oxford, 1956); Audrey M. Taylor, *Gilletts. Bankers at Banbury and Oxford* (Oxford, 1964).

21.   G. Hueckel, 'English Farming Profits during the Napoleonic Wars', *Explorations in Economic History*, 13 (1976), 331–45; A. H. John, 'Farming in Wartime: 1793–1815', in E. L. Jones and J. D. Chambers (eds), *Land, Labour, and Population in the Industrial Revolution* (London, 1967).

22.   George R. Boyer, *An Economic History of the English Poor Law, 1750–1850* (Cambridge, 1990), pp. 9–50; 94–9; K. D. M. Snell, *Annals of the Labouring Poor. Social Change and Agrarian England 1660–1900* (Cambridge, 1985), pp. 104–14; Eastwood, *Governing Rural England*, pp. 166–87; and Ian Dyck, *William Cobbett and Rural Popular Culture* (Cambridge, 1992), p. 72.

23.   Richard Gough, *The History of Myddle*, ed. David Hay (Harmondsworth, 1981), pp. 77–272.

24.   Oxfordshire Archives, MSS D. D. Par Dorchester c.8, Vestry Book 1733–1800, ff. 133–4; MSS D. D. Par Finmere e.1, Vestry Minutes, ff. 90–3; MSS D. D. Par Wheatley e.3, Vestry Minutes, 1829–35, 27 November 1834; *Hansard*, 3rd ser., 1833, xvi, 968–9.

25.   As pointed out by Edward Norman, *Church and Society in England, 1770–1970* (Oxford, 1976), p. 110, church rates could only properly be levied for upkeep of naves and churchyards. This could lead to great difficulties, especially where lay rectors refused to maintain the chancel; see Sir J. H. Seymour, *Plain Statement of Facts, in a Matter in which the Parishioners of Horley are interested* (Banbury, 1839).

26.   A. D. Gilbert, *Religion and Society in Industrial England. Church, Chapel and Social Change 1740–1914* (London, 1976), pp. 3–22, 69–121.

27.   Eric J. Evans, *The Contentious Tithe. The Tithe Problem and English Agriculture 1750–1850* (London, 1976). On the tendency of the established church to become fashionable, visibly respectable, and ostentatiously a church of the more affluent, see [Ellen Weeton], *Miss Weeton's Journal of a Governess 1807–1825*, ed. J. J. Bagley, 2 vols (New York, 1969), i, pp. 122–3.

28. Eric Evans, 'Some Reasons for the Growth of English Rural Anti-Clericalism *c.* 1750 – c.1850', *Past and Present*, no. 66 (1975), 84–109.

29. John Walsh, 'Methodism and the Local Community in the Eighteenth Century', in *Vie Ecclésiale. Communauté et Communautés* (Paris, 1989), pp. 141–51.

30. John Skinner, *Journal of a Somerset Rector 1803–1834*, ed. Howard and Peter Coombs (Oxford, 1984), p. 92.

31. [Thomas Hayton], *The Letters of Thomas Hayton. Vicar of Long Crendon Buckinghamshire 1821–1887*, ed. Joyce Donald, Buckinghamshire Record Society, xx (1979), esp. pp. x–xi.

32. Much the most nuanced local study is James Obelkevich, *Religion and Rural Society. South Lindsey 1825–1875* (Oxford, 1976); but see also Albion M. Urdank, *Religion and Society in a Cotswold Vale. Nailsworth, Gloucestershire, 1780–1865* (Berkeley, CA, 1990).

33. Roger G. Sellman, *Devon Village Schools in the Nineteenth Century* (New York, 1968), pp. 24–6, 44–5.

34. Kate Tiller (ed.), *Church and Chapel in Oxfordshire 1851. The Return of the Census of Religious Worship*, Oxfordshire Records Society, vol. 55 (1987); K. D. M. Snell, *Church and Chapel in the North Midlands: Religious Observance in the Nineteenth Century*, Department of English Local History, Occasional Papers, 4th ser., no. 3 (Leicester, 1991).

35. Obelkevich, *Religion and Rural Society*, pp. 183–219.

36. John Walsh, 'Methodism and the Local Community in the Eighteenth Century', in *Vie Ecclésiale. Communauté et Communautés* (Paris, 1989), pp. 141–51; John Walsh, 'Methodism and the Mob in the Eighteenth Century', *Studies in Church History*, viii (1972), 213–27. See also Snell, *Church and Chapel in the North Midlands*, p. 52.

37. John Howard Hinton, *Biographical Portraiture of the late James Hinton* (Oxford, 1824), pp. 255–63.

38. Ibid., pp. 264–65. Interestingly magistrates were accused of similar collusion in the 'Church and King' riots in Birmingham: see Money, *Experience and Identity*, p. 268.

39. Public Records Office, HO 42/34/189, Edward Jeffries to Portland, 11 March 1795. The staunchly Tory *Jackson's Oxford Journal* had refused even to publish Hinton's allegations, 7 June 1794.

40. Hinton, *Life of James Hinton*, p. 267.

41. See [Mary Smith], *Autobiography of Mary Smith* (London, 1892), pp. 6–8. Mary Smith grew up at Cropredy in north Oxfordshire in the 1820s.

42. W. O. Chadwick, *Victorian Church*, 2 vols (London, 1966), i, pp. 81–9, 148–58; G. I. T. Machin, *Politics and the Churches in Great Britain, 1832–68*, (Oxford, 1977), pp. 45–47, 55–63, 102–7.

43. Quoted in Chadwick, *Victorian Church*, i, p. 87; cf. R. Burn, *Ecclesiastical Law*, 2 vols (London, 1763), i, p. 268ff.

44. W. C. Risley, *Sermon at the Triennial Visitation of the Bishop of Oxford* (Banbury, n.d., ?1838), pp. 17–18.

45. Rev. T. Silver, *Memorial to H. M. Government on the Dangers of Intermeddling with the Church Rates* (Oxford, 1835), pp. 34–35, 38, 55; *idem,*

Letter to the Duke of Marlborough ... on Commutation of Tithes (Oxford, 1842), pp. 33, 46, 68.

46.   Risley, *Sermon*, p. 19.

47.   See Oxfordshire Archives, MSS D. D. Par Bampton c.8., Vestry Book 1792–1858, 11 January 1811, 13 January 1813; MSS D. D. Par Bladon c.5., Parish Book, ff. 11–20.

48.   Oxfordshire Archives, MSS D. D. Par Stonesfield b.8., Rectors Book, 25 July, 30 December 1825.

49.   J. Jordan, *History of Enstone* (London, 1857), pp. 386–93.

50.   [Charles Jerram], *Memoirs and a Selection of the Letters of the late Rev. Charles Jerram*, ed. J. Jerram (London, 1855), pp. 332–5; W. J. Monk, *History of Witney* (Witney, 1894), pp. 170, 213–48. Jerram could afford to be generous: in 1831 the living was worth £1290 per annum: see Diana McClatchey, *The Oxfordshire Clergy, 1777–1869* (Oxford, 1960), p. 57.

51.   M. Dickins, *History of Hook Norton* (Banbury, 1928), p. 151.

52.   Oxfordshire Archives, MSS Par Henley b.2, Vestry Book, 23 October 1833, *et passim; Jackson's Oxford Journal*, 7, 14 and 21 July 1832.

53.   Norman, *Church and Society in England*, p. 216; cf. Chadwick, *The Victorian Church*, i, p. 147; J. Morley, *Gladstone*, 2 vol. edn (London, 1905/6), i, p. 795.

54.   Anthony Russell, *The Clerical Profession* (London, 1980), pp. 39–41, 100–12.

55.   Mary Ransome (ed.), *Wiltshire Returns to the Bishop's Visitation Queries 1783*, Wiltshire Records Society, xxvii for 1971; Arthur Warne, *Church and Society in Eighteenth-Century Devon* (Newton Abbot, 1969).

56.   Egerton, *Victorian Village*, p. 66.

57.   [George J. Dew], *Oxfordshire Country Life in the 1860s: the Early Diaries of George James Dew (1846–1928) of Lower Heyford*, ed. Pamela Horn (Abingdon, 1986), pp. 45, 54.

58.   Bodleian Library, G. A. Oxon 4° 49, Newspaper Cuttings etc., f. 197; *Jackson's Oxford Journal*, 26 August 1826, 1 September 1832; R.W. Malcolmson, *Popular Recreations in English Society 1700–1850* (Cambridge, 1973); W. J. Monk, *A History of Witney* (Witney, 1794); Alun Howkins, *Witsun in Nineteenth Century Oxfordshire* (Oxford, 1973); Sally Alexander, *St Giles's Fair, 1830–1914: Popular Culture and the Industrial Revolution in 19th Century Oxfordshire* (Oxford, 1970).

59.   [William Cobbett], *The Autobiography of William Cobbett*, ed. William Reitzel, new edn (London, 1967), pp. 92–3.

60.   Quoted in Robert W. Malcolmson, 'Leisure', in G. E. Mingay (ed.), *The Victorian Countryside*, 2 vols (London, 1981), ii, p. 606.

61.   The standard study is Peter Clark, *The English Alehouse. A Social History 1200–1830* (London, 1983).

62.   Clark, *English Alehouse*, pp. 45–57.

63.   Anon., *Charge to Grand Jury of Surrey* [Midsummer 1736], printed in Lamonie, *Charges to the Grand Jury*, pp. 285, cf. 290–1, 296, 460; Jefferies, *Hodge and his Masters*, pp. 192–3.

64.   Reay, *Last Rising of the Agricultural Labourers*, pp. 54–5.

65. David Dean (ed.), *St Alban's Quarter Sessions Rolls 1784–1820*, Hertford Record Society Publications, v (1991), 90.

66. E. P. Thompson, *Customs in Common* (London, 1991), pp. 467–531.

67. H. Lupton, *A History of Thame and its Hamlets* (Thame, 1860); *St Albans Quarter Sessions Rolls*, pp. 70–1; Public Records Office, HO 42/146, Henry Walford to Lord Sidmouth, 1 September 1815; HO 42/143, James Lockhart to Sidmouth, 10 March 1815; *Hansard*, 1st ser., xxix, 1227.

68. Thompson, *Lark Rise to Candleford*, p. 140.

69. Florence and Kenneth Wood, *A Lancashire Gentleman. The Letters and Journals of Richard Hodgkinson 1763–1847* (Stroud, 1992), pp. 198–215.

70. E. P. Thompson, 'The Moral Economy of the English Crowd in the Eighteenth Century', reprinted in Thompson, *Customs in Common*, pp. 158–185. There is now a huge literature on popular protest, amongst which one of the most influential works has been John Bohstedt, *Riots and Community Politics in England and Wales 1790–1810* (Cambridge, MA, 1983). Cool and intelligent reappraisals are offered in Adrian Randall and Andrew Charlesworth (eds), *Markets, Market Culture and Popular Protest in Eighteenth-century Britain and Ireland* (Liverpool, 1996).

71. Public Records Office, HO 42/35/366–68, Sir Christopher Willoughby to Thomas Carter, 7 August 1795; Sir F. M. Eden, *The State of the Poor*, 3 vols (London, 1797), ii, pp. 587, 591.

72. Roger Wells, *Wretched Faces. Famine in Wartime England* (Gloucester, 1988), esp. pp. 120–81; *idem*, *Dearth and Distress in Yorkshire, 1793–1802*, Borthwick Paper, no. 52 (1977); *idem*, 'The Revolt of the South West: a Study in English Popular Protest', *Social History*, vi (1977), 713–44; Alan Booth, 'Food Riots in the North West of England 1790–1800', *Social History*, viii (1983), 295–314.

73. Public Records Office, HO 42/51/338, Sir Christopher Willoughby to Duke of Portland, 21 Sept. 1800; HO 42/51/194, Willoughby to Portland, 17 Sept. 1800.

74. Douglas Hay, 'Poaching and the Game Laws on Cannock Chase', in Hay *et al.* (eds), *Albion's Fatal Tree. Crime and Society in Eighteenth-century England*, Penguin edn (Harmondsworth, 1977), pp. 189–254; P. B. Munch, *Gentlemen and Poachers* (London, 1981).

75. Bodleian Library, Oxford, MSS Top. Oxon d. 441–4, W. J. Oldfield, 'Abstract of Oxfordshire Quarter Sessions', 4 vols, n.d., iii, Michaelmas 1808.

76. Woodforde, *Diary of a Country Parson*, pp. 421–4; Turner, *Diary*, p. 122.

77. Eric Hopkins, *Working Class Self-help in Nineteenth Century England* (London, 1995), pp. 9–26; P. H. J. H. Gosden, *The Friendly Societies in England 1815–1875* (Manchester, 1961), pp. 1–70.

78. *Abstract of the Answers and Returns Relative to the Expense and Maintenance of the Poor*, P[arliamentary] P[apers], 1803–4, xii (175); *Report on Friendly Societies*, P.P., 1831/32, xxvi, 297–8.

79. Oxfordshire Archives, Ston. 1/ii/b/1, Stonesfield Friendly Society Club Book 1766–1854; Ston. 1/ii/b/2, Stonesfield Friendly Society Club

Book 1854 onwards; Ston. 111/i/1, Stonesfield Friendly Society Rules; MSS D. D. Par Stonesfield b.8, Rector's Book entry for 13 July 1825; David Eastwood, 'The Benefits of Brotherhood: The First Century of the Stonesfield Friendly Society, 1765–1865', *Oxfordshire Local History*, ii (1986), 161–8.

80.   Oxfordshire Archives, MSS D. D. Par Bampton b. 10, Surveyor's Book, 11 June 1797.

81.   Egerton, *Diaries*, 58; Rawnsley, *Sermons Preached in Country Churches*, 200; Simon Cordery, 'Friendly Societies and the Discourse of Respectability in Britain, 1825–1875', *Journal of British Studies*, xxxiv (1995), 35–58.

82.   George Sturt, *William Smith, Potter and Farmer, 1790–1858*, new edn (Firle, Sussex, 1978), p. 184.

83.   F. M. Eden, *Observations on Friendly Societies, for the Maintenance of the Industrious Classes, during Sickness, Infirmity, Old Age and other Exigencies* (London, 1801); T. R. Malthus, *An Essay on the Principle of Population* [1803 edn], 2 vols, ed. T. H. Hollingsworth (London, 1973), ii, p. 243; *Report from the Select Committee on the Laws Respecting Friendly Societies*, P.P., 1825, iv (522), 330; B. E. Supple, 'Legislation and Virtue: an Essay in Working Class Self-help in the Early-nineteenth Century, in N. McKendrick (ed.), *Historical Perspectives: Studies in English Thought and Society* (London, 1974), pp. 211–54; J. M. Baernreither, *English Associations of Working Men* (London, 1889), 5; Arch, *Ploughtail to Parliament*, p. 34.

84.   The classic account remains S. and B. Webb, *The Parish and the County* (London, 1906), esp. pp. 9–103, 146–276. The principal defect in the Webbs' treatment was their deep-seated hostility towards what they regarded as the corruption and structural inefficiencies of the vestry system. Bryan Keith-Lucas, *The Unreformed Local Government System* (London, 1980), pp. 75–107, offers a somewhat more sympathetic overview. W. E. Tate, *The Parish Chest*, 3rd edn (Cambridge, 1969) remains useful, but lacks analytical subtlety. The arguments sketched briefly here are explored more fully in Eastwood, *Governing Rural England*, pp. 24–42, 166–87; and David Eastwood, 'The Republic in the English Village: Parish and Poor at Bampton, 1780–1834', *Journal of Local and Regional Studies*, xii (1992), 18–28.

85.   Where records do survive, excellent work can be done. See, for example, Keith Wrightson's immensely penetrating discussion of the political culture of English parishes in the seventeenth century in *English Society 1580–1680*, pp. 39–65, 149–82.

86.   Oxfordshire Archives, MSS D. D. Par South Newington d.2, Vestry Minutes 1821–68, pp. 1–2. The Act in question was 58 Geo. III c. 69, which required vestries to keep minute books.

87.   See William Wing, *Changes in Farming and the Rural Economy during the Fifty-five Years, 1826–1880* (Oxford, 1880), p. 7; *Jackson's Oxford Journal*, 19 December 1818.

88.   Jordan, *History of Enstone*, p. 200; P. H. Ditchfield, *The Parish Clerk* (London, 1907).

89. As at Finmere in Oxfordshire: see Oxfordshire Archives, MSS D. D. Par Finmere e.1, Vestry Minutes 1815–27; J. C. Bloomfield, *History of Finmere* (Buckingham, 1887), pp. 26–7, 54–68.

90. The vestry at Henley-on-Thames was divided into quite distinct 'interests' (brewing, agriculture, trade, 'independent inhabitants', and parish officials), and its elaborate decision-making procedures were designed to give due weight to each distinct interest: see Oxfordshire Archives, MSS D. D. Par Henley-on-Thames b.1, Vestry Minutes 1725–1816, 14 October. 1814 and *passim*.

91. R. Burn, *The Justice of the Peace and the Parish Officer*, 28th edn, 6 vols (London, 1837), vi, pp. 131–7.

92. Oxfordshire Archives, MSS D. D. Par Bampton c.8, Vestry Book 1792–1858.

93. Eastwood, *Governing Rural England*, pp. 38–9.

94. J. M. Davenport, *Oxfordshire Annals* (Oxford, 1869); Mark Neuman, *The Speenhamland County. Poverty and the Poor Laws in Berkshire 1782–1834* (New York, 1982), pp. 80–1 and *passim*; Eastwood, *Governing Rural England*, p. 38.

95. Turner, *Diary*, pp. 35, 148.

96. 'Diary of Rev. William Cotton Risley', Bodleian Library MSS D. D. Risley, c. 66, *passim*.

97. 22 Geo. III c. 83; see also S. and B. Webb, *English Poor Law History: Part 1. The Old Poor Law* (London, 1927), pp. 170–2, 272–6; Geoffrey W. Oxley, *Poor Relief in England and Wales 1601–1834* (Newton Abbot, 1974), pp. 82–7; Anne Digby, *Pauper Palaces* (London, 1978), pp. 34–47.

98. Felix Driver, *Power and Pauperism. The Workhouse System 1834–1884* (Cambridge, 1993), pp. 42–7. A further 125 incorporations were created under local acts between 1647 and 1833.

99. *Report of the Select Committee on the Poor Laws, Parliamentary Papers*, 1817, vi (462). See also J. R. Poynter, *Society and Pauperism. English Ideas on Poor Relief, 1795–1834* (London, 1969), pp. 244–6, 285–9; and David Eastwood, 'Rethinking the Debates on the Poor Law in Early Nineteenth-century England', *Utilitas*, vi (1994), pp. 97–116.

100. *Hansard*, 1st ser., xxxviii (1818), pp. 534–5, 574.

101. 59 Geo. iii c. 12.

102. John Prest, *Liberty and Locality. Parliament, Permissive Legislation, and Ratepayers' Democracies in the Mid-nineteenth Century* (Oxford, 1990), pp. 10–11.

103. *Abstract of Moines Levies in Counties of England and Wales, P.P.*, 1833, xxxii, pp. 349–50.

104. Oxfordshire Archives, MSS D. D. Par Eynsham, e. 1, Vestry Book, 19 April 1811.

105. *Report from Select Committee on Poor Laws, P.P.*, 1817, vi (462); 59 Geo. III c.12, 59 Geo. III c. 8.

106. *Report from Select Committee on Poor Rate Returns, P.P.*, 1822 v (556), 547; *Abstract of Returns [Poor Laws], P.P.*, 1835, xlvii (284), 453.

107. Oxfordshire Archives, 'List of Paupers and Bread Scale', MSS D. D. Par Bampton, b. 15.

108.   Oxfordshire Archives, MSS D. D. Par Bampton c.8, Vestry Book 1792–1858.

109.   Labour rates were common throughout rural England from the 1820s: see *Report from the Select Committee on Relief to the Able-bodied, P.P.,* 1828, iv (494), pp. 144–6; E. Hampson, *Poverty in Cambridgeshire, 1597–1834* (Cambridge, 1934), p. 202 *et seq.* Labour rates were legalized in 1831 by 2 & 3 William IV c. 96 but roundly condemned in an early report of the Poor Law Commission: see *Report of the Royal Commissioners on the Labour Rate, P.P.,* 1833, xxxii (619); Eastwood, *Governing Rural England,* pp. 155–60.

110.   John Clare, *The Parish. A Satire,* ed. Eric Robinson (Harmondsworth, 1985), p. 63, line 1289. The poem was written between 1823 and 1827.

111.   Clare, *The Parish,* p. 62, lines 1220–9. A similar perception of social order and political allegiance within parish communities emerges from Joseph Mayett's autobiography. Mayett's autobiography offers a rare insight into the thoughts and attitudes of an agricultural labourer and frequent claimant for parish poor relief: see *The Autobiography of Joseph Mayett of Quainton 1783–1839,* ed. Ann Kussmaul, Buckinghamshire Records Society, xxiii (1986), pp. 72–9, 92–5.

112.   *Abstract of the Poor, P.P.,* 1803–4, xiii (175).

113.   J. Hewitt, *Guide for Constables and Peace Officers* (London, 1779), pp. 16–17; Newman, *The Speenhamland County,* pp. 110–43.

114.   Woodforde, *Diary of a Country Parson,* p. 295; Turner, *Diary,* pp. 118–19, 148.

115.   Oxfordshire Archives, MSS D. D. Par Wheatley e.1, Vestry Minutes 1829–1835, 21 July 1829; MSS D. D. Par Spelsbury e.2, Minutes of Select Vestry 1822–28, 28 October. 1824; *St Albans Quarter Sessions Rolls,* 1808, 107.

116.   Kate Watson, 'Liberty, Loyalty, and Locality: the Discourse on Loyalism in Britain, 1790–1815', Ph.D. thesis, Open University (1995); Eastwood, *Governing Rural England,* pp. 230–3.

3   Civic Ideals and the Life of Towns

The Urban Community: Definitions, Defenders, and Detractors

Historians are fond of describing urbanization in terms of the growth of towns. At one level this kind of analysis satisfies by constructing a positivist language through which to map a conceptually complex process. If we define a town as a settlement with over 2500 inhabitants, urbanization seems both impressive and ineluctable. In 1700, 18.7 per cent of the population of England and Wales lived in towns. By 1750 this had risen to 22.6 per cent and by 1801 it reached 30.6 per cent. In the nineteenth century urban growth, thus measured, was still more striking, with 54 per cent of the population living in towns by 1851 and 78 per cent by 1901.[1] But such figures distort as much as they describe. In 1700 some settlements that we might regard as characteristically urban contained fewer than 2500 inhabitants, while by 1900 many settlements of 2500 were hardly towns at all. Viewed in another light, these figures reveal the profoundly rural character of large areas of England and Wales until well into the Victorian period. As late as the census of 1871, agriculture was the largest single employer of male labour, and only after this census did the population of rural England begin to fall in absolute terms.[2] What gave Victorian towns and cities their increasing cultural and political power was not that they were home to a majority of England's people but, rather, that they were home to England's new wealth and economic elites. Economic well-being fostered civic self-confidence.

Thus, urban identities are more complex than mere demography might suggest. If size was insufficient in itself to distinguish 'town' from 'village', neither were formal institutions. Until the passage of the Municipal Corporations Act of 1835, many

57

settlements that in terms of either economic and social construction were palpably urban were nevertheless still governed by the
same formal institutions as the village. Birmingham, Bolton,
Bradford, Manchester, Salford, and Sheffield, with a combined
population of 545 000 in 1831, retained their parish vestries and
parochial officers until the late 1830s and early 1840s, while settlements which were little more than large villages, such as Howden,
Tarporley, and Woodstock, were governed through the formal
apparatus of a borough corporation.[3] Moreover, in industrial
cities such as Leeds, although formally incorporated in 1661, the
Corporation exercised little real power until its remodelling after
the passage of the Municipal Corporations Act of 1835.[4] Similarly,
in Nottingham the Corporation was politically and ceremonially
active in the eighteenth and early nineteenth centuries, but it
construed its public responsibilities narrowly and did not attempt
to develop wider regulatory or policy-making powers.[5] Nor was
there a distinctive culture which systematically distinguished town
and country. The life of the spas, unimpeachably 'urban' in its
textures and rhythms, was sharply differentiated from that of
market towns, industrial towns, commercial ports, university
towns, or even of London itself. There was, however, a pattern of
public life which, although varied and modulated by quite different modes of economic activities, marked off the world of the
town from that of the village. Towns possessed, developed, and
cherished cultural, institutional, and ideological forms which in
turn constituted characteristically urban identities. These urban
communities forged a civic experience which was at once distinctive and fragile: distinctive for its richness, diversity, and sense of
place; fragile because, more perhaps than in rural communities,
the civic life of towns was constantly being made and unmade.
Demographic pressures, political change, and economic energy
constituted persistent challenges to the public life of urban
England, distinguishing the eighteenth-century town from the
nineteenth-century city, and the modern metropolis. The counterpoint to rural nostalgia was urban restlessness.

   The distinctive character of urban England lay in its cultural
pluralism and institutional diversity. Both actually and ideologically, the public space of urban England was more expansive
than that of rural villages. Dissenting chapels, local newspapers,
clubs, reading rooms, schools, and political associations nurtured

competing and complementary public cultures. Social relations were, by function of size and spatial separation, less personal and more obviously structural. Towns had a richer language of social description which reflected the complexity and fluidity of their social composition. Thus in the eighteenth century linguistic usage was casting around for terms which precisely described urban social location, and the terminology of social stratification oscillated between reference to 'classes', 'sorts', 'ranks', and 'degrees'. Those whom the later nineteenth century might happily describe as working class were, in the eighteenth century, described variously as the 'lower kind' (Henry Fielding), 'lower class' (Earl of Waldegrave), 'industrious class' (Norwich Corporation), 'lower classes' (Jonas Hanway), and 'workman' and 'labouring poor' (Adam Smith). Meanwhile, an increasingly visibly commercial, professional, and leisured class could be celebrated as the 'middling sorts' or 'middling classes' or denounced, inelegantly, as the 'middlocrats'.[6] Only in the nineteenth century, and then gradually, did new ideological presumptions reconfigure maps of social analysis in terms of overarching discourses of social class.[7] If the languages of orders, ranks, or classes might have separated classes linguistically, urban geography came increasingly to separate social classes spatially. Towns had quarters, zones in which different social groups proclaimed and fostered their distinctive character. In Manchester, according to Friedrich Engels in 1845, the Irish were crowded into the New Town area, which rapidly became known as 'Irish Town'. The indigenous working class inhabited high-density, often jerry-built houses close to the town's industrial centre. Beyond lay increasingly distinct suburban gentility: 'Th[e] area of workers' houses includes all Manchester proper, except the centre [and some small districts] ... Beyond this belt of working-class houses or dwellings lie the districts inhabited by the middle classes and the upper classes. The former are to be found in regularly laid out streets near the working-class districts. The villas of the upper classes are surrounded by gardens and lie in the higher and remoter parts of Chorlton and Ardwick or on the breezy heights of Cheetham Hill, Brougham and Pendleton'.[8] This pronounced social geography was by no means confined to Manchester and the other great industrial centres of the Midlands and North. John Glyde's 1850 history of Ipswich combined new languages of social description and a sharp sense of social geography in describing the district in which Ipswich's common lodging houses were located as the area in which 'the dangerous classes are to be found'.[9]

The associational life of urban England was more voluntaristic than that of the rural village. There was no equivalent of the parish church, demanding allegiance and arbitrating cultural orthodoxy and self-proclaimed heterodoxy. The relationships between priest and parish were necessarily constructed quite differently in a large urban parish.[10] In the main urban parishes were larger and this, coupled with the greater anonymity of urban life, made the incumbent a more distant figure. Indeed, the Anglican church did not reach Duckinfield near Manchester until 1841, when the population had already exceeded 10 000 and the town had 17 Dissenting chapels.[11] In towns social bonds were forged less by shared residence than by shared activities. Church, chapel, the friendly society, the mechanics' institutes, the political club, and even tea rooms, coffee houses, pubs, and reading rooms were forged through complex patterns of voluntary association, translating urban individualism into social solidarities. As John Glyde put it in 1850, 'The tendency to associate is one of the great characteristics of the age'.[12] For many, association, improvement, and cultural diversity gave towns their moral texture. Robert Vaughan, the great nineteenth-century apologist for urbanization, saw towns not simply as driving cultural development but also as engines of moral improvement: 'The facilities [for education] are greater in towns, partly on account of greater wealth, and their greater freedom from prejudice; and partly in consequence of their more general sympathy with popular improvement, and their comparative freedom from the discountenance or control of powerful individuals or classes. Towns are not like villages, subject, it may be, to the oversight and guidance of a single family, or of a single clergyman. They possess greater means and greater liberty, and, a stronger disposition to use both in favour of education, even on behalf of the children of the poorest'. From this disposition to improvement the associational life of urban England arose, and with it cultural forms which were distinctively urban.[13]

Nineteenth-century urbanists such as Robert Vaughan were fond of juxtaposing an urban moral dynamism and rural social inertia. They perceived in village life a habitual monotony, an absence of social ambition, and patterns of defence which were antithetical to improvements and innovation. The ancient fabric of village life persisted because cultural modernization had yet to take root. By contrast, the rhythms of urban life were energizing and creatively subversive: 'The shop, the factory, or the market-place; the local association, the news-room, or the religious meeting, all facilitate this invigorating contact of mind with mind'.[14] This kind of argument draws contrasts too starkly, and wilfully ignores the dramatic transformation of rural England through enclosure, agricultural innovation, and the transport revolution. Nevertheless, less schematically formulated, there is something of significance here. If we are to explain the self-consciously 'improving' civic culture of Hanoverian towns, we should see improvement not simply as a means of employing superior means to confront more acute social problems, but also as a dynamic cultural expression which embodied a quite distinctive notion of what constituted, or what might constitute, 'the public'.[15]

Cultural definitions are notoriously elusive, and even contemporaries differed sharply in their assessments. Hanoverian Bath, for example, was elevated by some as the paradigm of refined gentility and despised by others for effete luxury and for degrading public manners.[16] Critics of urban culture ranged from the prejudiced to the perceptive. William Cobbett is best placed at the prejudiced – but robustly entertaining – end of this spectrum. Passing through Cheltenham in the 1820s, his spleen exploded: 'CHELTENHAM, which is what they call a "*watering place*"; that is to say, a place, to which East Indian plunderers, West Indian floggers, English tax-gorgers, together with gluttons, drunkards, and debauchers of all descriptions, *female* as well as male, resort, at the suggestion of silently laughing quacks, in the hope of getting rid of the bodily consequences of their manifold sins and inequities'.[17] Nevertheless, even Cobbett's anti-urbanism contained some substance. His vilification of London as 'the Great Wen' is well known; less well-known is his characterization of all towns, or at any rate all towns deriving their wealth from commerce, as 'wens'. His point was that the wealth of many non-manufacturing towns was parasitic on local agriculture. Tax revenues, from local rates most notably, tended to flow from agricultural to urban England, and fundholders, government pensioners, and public officials predominantly resided in towns and disposed of their not inconsiderable incomes there: 'The land is now used to raise food and drink for the monopolizers and the tax-eaters and their purveyors and lackeys and harlots; and they get together in WENS'.[18] In so far as any systematic economic critique undergirded Cobbett's anti-urbanism, it was a boldly etched physiocratic faith in the primacy of agriculture. Other agricultural writers certainly shared this, and articulated it in more economically refined terms. Arthur Young warned against the dangers posed to rural property by the over-expansion of towns and their tendency to suck in rural labour in good times and release it back to the rural poor law in slack periods.[19] The poet and evangelical, William Cowper, offered not an economic but a moral critique of urbanization. In *The Task* (1785), urban money begat moral enervation, and the visible sewerage of the city became a metaphor of the deeper pollution of the mind:

> But though true worth and virtue, in the mild
> And genial soil of cultivated life
> Thrive most, and may perhaps thrive only there,
> Yet not in cities oft, – in proud and gay
> And gain-devoted cities; thither flow
> As to a common and most noisome sewer,
> The dregs and faeculence of every land.
> In cities foul example on most minds
> Begets its likeness. Rank abundance breeds
> In gross and pamper'd cities sloth and lust,
> And wantonness and gluttonous excess.[20]

Defenders of urban culture responded at a variety of levels. For some, of course, the cultural primacy of the urban world was self-evident. Whereas the rhythms of village life were rude and insistent – traditional pastimes, vulgar celebrations, and sports which delighted in physical indulgence and physical violence – town life was better-regulated, decorous, and substituted self-conscious leisure for rough recreations.[21] John Price, chronicling 'public amusements' in Hereford in 1796, captured something of the social tone of urban leisure: 'In winter there are card and dancing assemblies, which can engage the attention of elegant society. In summer, frequent excursions in parties on the Wye, which are now so fashionable ... and favourite walks in the neighbourhood of the city are the principal amusements of the company which resort to this town'.[22] Half a century later, John Glyde found that steam was as morally purifying as walking, lauding the ways in which 'The facilities for *excursions*, offered by steam boats and railways, have tended very much to purify the character of our amusement at the holiday periods'.[23] Purifying the character of public amusement was central to many urban communities' self-image. At Stroud in 1824 magistrates, sensible of the reputation of their town, sought to end the annual rolling of flaming tar barrels which enlivened celebrations on 5 November. A riot ensued, and imprisonments followed. But this was the last explosion of a great popular festival. On 5 November 1825 no barrels rolled, and bonfires were erected by public subscription.[24] The Stroud incident is a fine, if late, example of a much broader Hanoverian project aimed at reordering the urban cultural environment. The characteristic Georgian emphasis on 'police', with its overtones of general regulation rather than uniformed patrol, produced, in many towns, a new civic decorum.[25]

Urban histories in the eighteenth century grew in number and popularity, partly celebrating and partly defending the public life of towns. In the 40 years after 1780, some 129 histories of English towns were published. This efflorescence of urban history can be seen as part of the complex process through which urban identities were contested and constructed. Significantly, many urban histories strove to demonstrate that provincial town life was no mere imitation of metropolitan life, but rather had a vibrancy and character of its own. London provided a standard, not a model, for provincial town life thus imagined. This was important, for much of the moral critique of urban life took London as its paradigm. Sobriety, virtue, and philanthropy in provincial towns were presented as a counterpoint to the vice, crime, and dissipation of London life. Simultaneously, urban histories could contest the ways in which towns were ordered and governed. Thus Joshua Toulmin's 1791 *History of the Town of Taunton* was a defence of religious liberty and independence, presenting the moral vitality of local opposition to political oligarchy. Similarly, while J. Brand's *History and Antiquities of the Town and County of Newcastle-upon-Tyne* (1789) celebrated Newcastle's civic government, J. Baillie's significantly titled *Impartial History of the Town and County of*

Newcastle-upon-Tyne and its Vicinity (1801) offered a much fuller account of the commercial life of Newcastle and launched a fierce assault on local political oligarchies.[26] Reflecting on the contemporary literature on towns well illustrates the extent to which urban identities were constructed ideologically as well as architecturally. More profoundly, perhaps, than villages, towns were imagined cultural communities, the identities of which were made and remade by those who sought to shape, control, inhabit, and reform them.

Urban Improvement and Civic Virtue

Central to this imagined urban vision was the notion of improvement. Urban histories and town guides were, in part, celebrations of Hanoverian England's sense of a new richness in the textures of urban life. J. H. Plumb has painted the cultural landscape of late-seventeenth-century England in stark colours: 'The cultural poverty of late seventeenth century England was vast – no newspapers, no public libraries, no theatres outside London, no concerts anywhere, no picture galleries of any kind, no museums, almost no botanical gardens and no organized sports'.[27] This picture of a cultural wasteland is almost certainly overdrawn, ignoring for example the vitality of sacred music and private and corporate music-making. Henry Purcell's *Dido and Aeneas*, the greatest of all English operas, was possibly written for, and certainly first publicly performed in, a girls' boarding school in Chelsea in 1689. Nevertheless, Plumb does point to the profundity of the transformation in public culture in Hanoverian England and, as Peter Borsay has demonstrated, an 'urban renaissance' was crucial to this cultural transformation.[28] As late as 1726, a provincial centre such as Lincoln had no local newspaper, local news and advertisements being proclaimed by the crier or by word of mouth. There was no coffee house, no library, no theatre, no public assembly rooms, and social gatherings were confined to private houses and inns.[29] The transformation of cultural expression was at once central in redefining the urban and celebrating its vitality. If we remain for a moment with music, the most enduring and one of the most influential provincial music festivals, the 'Three Choirs Festival' centred on Worcester, Hereford, and

Gloucester, was established in 1715. From 1737 the Three Choirs Festival was conducted by none other than William Boyce, whose contemporary reputation as a composer was surpassed only by that of Handel. Between 1757 and 1760 a music festival was held annually in Bristol, while in 1768 the Birmingham Music Festival began, followed two years later by the Norwich festival. By the end of the century no city of ambition and self-respect was without its music festival.[30] Meanwhile, provincial choral societies were already flourishing, to the extent that Warrington alone had three rival choral societies by 1834.[31] By the late eighteenth century, while London developed the richest repertoire of public concerts of any European capital, the Handel cult had transformed music making in provincial England and, for more than a century, the oratorio enjoyed a remarkable popularity. Certainly from the Handel Commemoration of 1784 to Mendelssohn's premiering *Elijah* in Birmingham in 1846, English choirs and provincial audiences regarded the oratorio as the highest, and perhaps most distinctively English, of musical forms.[32] Mendelssohn's massive Birmingham performances were far removed, culturally, musically, and idiomatically, from the fashionable courtly semi-operas of the late seventeenth century.

The cultural transformation of Hanoverian England was driven by a powerful synergy of changes in private taste and public cultural amenities. This revolution in private taste is represented most vividly in the rise of the novel, especially in its picaresque, urbane, delightfully contrived forms.[33] Similarly, the continuing evolution of the novel as a form is indicative not only of changes in aesthetic idiom but also of developments in public taste. The fact that Henry Fielding stands at one end of our period and Charles Dickens at the other tells us something about changes in taste and moral sense in urban drawing rooms; the popularity of Samuel Richardson in the 1740s and Mrs Oliphant in the 1860s may tell us even more. More publicly visible was the development of theatre in the provinces. Between 1730 and 1830 over 100, and perhaps as many as 150, theatres were built outside London. Public theatres became characteristic of all manner of towns. Theatres were erected in provincial centres such as Colchester (1764), Stamford (1768), and Salisbury (1777); in ports such as Bristol (1764–6), Hull (1768), and Boston (1777); and in manufacturing centres such as Birmingham (1774) and

Manchester (1775). Assembly rooms, libraries, and reading rooms were opened with similar rapidity in the last quarter of the eighteenth century. The cost of provincial theatres was considerable, with buildings in Liverpool (1772) costing £6000, in Brighton (1806), £12 500, and in Bury St Edmunds (1819) £5000. The impressive capital sums certainly reflected a commitment to new patterns of leisure and culture, but also indicated a willingness to commit very considerable sums of public and private capital to reconstructing and reordering the built environment of English towns. New theatres, libraries, and assembly rooms took their place alongside hospitals, asylums, schools, and workhouses in urban landscapes in which public buildings were assuming a striking prominence.[34]

Perhaps the most characteristic civic institution of eighteenth-century England was the improvement commission. Established under local acts of parliament, improvement commissions constituted more than executive agencies for the remodelling of the urban environment: they provided a new political framework for local government and civic action. Whereas the formal institutions of the English state continued to proscribe Dissenters and Recusants, or admit them only on unequal terms, the constitution of improvement commissions generally reflected the ecumenism of urban life, enabling Dissenters most notably to enjoy a richer *public* life. As Paul Langford has argued, the eighteenth century saw 'the power of statute used radically to revise and expand the membership of Britain's governing body', and nowhere was this augmentation of the governing class more apparent than in the towns of Hanoverian England.[35] Between 1760 and 1799, some 427 new improvement commissions had been established by statute, giving commissioners new and considerable powers to improve the policing, lighting, paving, water supply, and fabric of towns. This momentum was maintained into the nineteenth century, and in the years 1800–45 almost 400 Local Improvement Acts were passed, covering building regulation and sanitary provision in 208 English and Welsh towns.[36] At Exeter, Improvement Acts passed in 1806 and 1810 gave fresh momentum to urban renewal, leading one local directory to speak of Exeter being under the thrall of the 'exhilarating hand of improvement'.[37] At different times, and in different places, a tendency towards greater religious comprehension in the public institutions of urban England might either unify or fissure urban communities. The sectarianism still latent in this pattern of civic administration is well exemplified in Bury St Edmunds, where the Corporation retained its Anglican exclusivity and, by the early nineteenth century, was riven by personal and party rivalries. Meanwhile Bury's affluent Dissenters were active in the vestry, and on the Court of Guardians, the Improvement Commission, and the Guildhall Feoffment Trust.[38] Similar sectarian divisions appeared in eighteenth-century Bristol. Nevertheless, as Jonathan Barry has argued, sectarian divisions should be understood as a constituent element in an associational urban culture through which individual towns, especially those such as Bristol with means and status, created strong, distinctive, and increasingly bourgeois civic identities.[39]

The interaction between traditional institutions and urban improving commissions is nicely illustrated in late Hanoverian Cheltenham, a traditional market town seeking to build on the new-found reputation of its water. The competition between late-eighteenth-century spa towns was considerable, and Cheltenham emerged as a leading beneficiary of this new form of civic commerce. Until the passage of its first improvement act in 1784, Cheltenham possessed what might be termed a rudimentary unitary authority, the parish vestry. Cheltenham's expansion amply demonstrated the limitations of the vestry system, and the response was the typical urban strategy of creating a multi-agency framework of improvement commissions and private initiatives. Relations between the vestry and the improvement commissions remained generally harmonious, with the vestry always construing itself as the superior *representative* institution and the Commission serving as a powerful executive agency. In 1786 a local act for the paving, repairing, cleansing, and lighting of Cheltenham established an improving Commission of 58 local inhabitants on a property qualification of real estate to the value of £400 or an annual income of £40 or greater. The Commission appointed a salaried town surveyor and salaried local scavengers, and began construction programmes. A further act of 1806 increased its membership to 72 and gave the Commission powers of compulsory purchase. Later acts passed in 1826 invested the Commission with considerably enhanced authority to regulate building and provide sanitation. Meanwhile, a private gas company was established in 1818 to supply the town and a private act of 1834 established a sewers company. In the 1820s the Commission began to employ a regular police force of beadles and a night watch and, from 1823, the force was led by a former Bow Street Runner. This institutional fusion of private, public, and corporate initiatives was wholly typical, and in Cheltenham it continued until incorporation in 1876.[40]

Although incorporated, Cheltenham's most immediate competitor, Bath, relied on a similar improving partnership between individual and civic enterprise. By 1727 the Avon was made navigable from Bristol to Bath, bringing in an annual toll income of £1200, which was in turn ploughed back into further improvements. In 1769 some 72 shareholders subscribed £23 000 to build the New Assembly Rooms. Meanwhile, an improvement act was passed in 1766, and used to facilitate the building of new pump rooms and baths in the 1780s. The corporation's debt rose from £3110 in 1765 to £26 400 in 1783 as it strove to maintain Bath's image and market lead. In the midst of a new building boom, a further improvement act was passed in 1789. Over the century as a whole, somewhere in the region of £3 million had been invested in improving, expanding, and developing Bath into a large town of 33 000.[41] The whole ensemble delighted Richard Hodgkinson, an estate steward from Lancashire, who visited Bath in 1794: 'I was perfectly amazed at everything I saw. It is impossible to give an idea of Bath to any person who never saw it. The most common streets are superior to anything I ever saw in London. The Houses are built of Free-stone which gives them a most grand appearance, particularly those lately erected, which is the case with the greatest part of Bath, it having doubled in size within the last seven Years'.[42] Where statutory authority, political will, and public opinion were in harmony, improvement schemes could mobilize resources on a huge scale. In 1801 the Lincoln Drainage Commissioners reported in favour of a complete embankment of the river. The works were completed during the Napoleonic Wars, but only after two additional local acts were secured, in 1808 and 1812, to augment the commissioners' powers to tax lands within the trust and to raise tolls. In their way, improvement commissioners were able to carry through public works schemes which were every bit as impressive as the improvement schemes sponsored by the reformed municipalities of mid-Victorian England.[43]

It is, perhaps, misleading to dwell over-long on the precise institutional means through which urban improvement was undertaken. Contemporaries were less concerned with agency than with effectiveness. They worked with tools which came to hand, and only when they found themselves bereft of instruments which might be refashioned for improving purposes did they embrace structural innovation. Thus whereas some urban elites chose to promote public health through separate statutory commissions, others found that existing Municipal Corporations could be persuaded to use existing powers to novel effect. In November 1766, for example, Leominster Corporation directed the town cryer to make a weekly proclamation ordering all persons to remove rubbish and nuisances from their doors, and that the Corporation would prosecute those who failed to comply. In 1788 the Corporation ordered the surveyor to undertake major paving works, again without seeking any additional powers.[44].

It would therefore be misleading to make too much of the distinction between incorporated and unincorporated towns. The more important distinction was between those boroughs in which the Corporation was genuinely active and those in which it had atrophied. In boroughs such as Banbury and Buckingham, the Corporations survived until 1835, but did so only as oligarchical electoral colleges, which made the boroughs' parliamentary returns and provided an occasional ceremonial descant to civic life. Here powerful aristocratic patrons bent the Corporations to do their political bidding and, in the process, created a civic space in which other agencies could exercise local power.[45] In many other smaller boroughs, Corporations had lost their political primacy; partly, no doubt, as a result of local struggles between local elites, but partly because the rating powers of Corporations were less explicit and more open to challenge than those enjoyed by vestries.[46] There is, however, little doubt that an active Corporation could mobilize resources and develop a local governmental infrastructure of far greater reach and sophistication than that available to vestries. The Cheshire borough of Congleton was administered by a Corporation of eight aldermen and 16 capital burghers, and this Corporation annually appointed some 40 borough officers, including four inspectors of wood cutting, four market-lookers, four scavengers, four lookers of commons, four lookers of wells, four inmate lookers (to prevent illegal settlements), four swine catchers, two leather sealers, two fire-lookers, two overseers of weights and measures, two takers of tolls; and a tender of town wood, a bellman, a dog whipper, and an ale taster.[47] Even allowing for political favouritism (especially, perhaps, in this last appointment), this list suggests an impressive ability to regulate urban life and a corporate ambition to police civic space.

The pace of change in urban communities was generally far more rapid than in rural areas. In part, of course, developments in paving, lighting, police, and public health were driven by demographic imperatives and by the superior economic resources available to urban communities. Nevertheless, cultural factors played at least as prominent a role as material circumstances in shaping patterns of urban improvement. The most visible manifestations of complex urban civic cultures were town halls. Function and fashion combined to determine their scale, style, and situation. Many town halls were rebuilt less to house a new urban bureaucracy than to proclaim the majesty, authority, and political aspirations of local governing elites.[48] Village vestry-men might be content to meet in the aisles of churches, in church vestries, or even in local inns, but borough corporations and powerful commissions aspired to meet in circumstances which at least confirmed, if not enhanced, their sense of dignity and status. The town hall in Congleton was rebuilt in 1804 and again in the mid-1860s, while northern civic pride was, by the Victorian period, almost invariably proclaimed in the gothic or classical splendour of their town halls – although few could muster the million pounds that Manchester invested in the 1870s in Alfred Waterhouse's masterpiece.[49] In the 1840s the *Leicester Chronicle* conceded that 'laurels were only to be won by the builder of Town Halls' and, acerbically, consoled those readers worried by fever and cholera, suggesting they raise their eyes from mundane medical apprehensions to the urban aesthetics: 'Have you not a great Market Place and a beautiful Town Hall to look at?'.[50]

Civic pride reached well beyond a grandly imagined civic landscape. Private philanthropy, public resources, and associa-tional energy also combined to promote – and even to impose – distinctively urban patterns of public culture, in which educa-tion, health, and secular respectability played an increasingly

salient part. The activities of one generation in Tewksbury
(Gloucestershire) illustrate this well. In 1789 a new market house
was opened; three years later a Road Club was founded to
improve local highways; and in 1796 a new workhouse was completed under a local act at a cost in excess of £7000. War slowed
but did not subvert improvement, and in 1806 a lying-in charity
was established. In 1812 a branch of the Auxiliary Bible Society
was established and a British School opened. In the following year
local Anglicans responded by opening a National School. In 1815
a dispensary was established to improve local medical facilities,
and two years later economic recession led to the formation of a
charity to provide blankets for the poor. Religious enthusiasm
continued to infuse Tewksbury's public life, with the establishment of local branches of the Society for the Propagation of
Christian Knowledge (1820), The Auxiliary Religious Tracts
Society (1821), and the Church Missionary Society (1826).[51] In
many civic projects the moral ambitions were clear. Doubtless,
too, economic ambitions played a part, but towndwellers' resistance to urban elites' improving plans could be economically as
well as morally frustrating. At Stroud (Gloucestershire) in 1831, a
Mr Parker constructed an elaborate complex of public rooms,
intended for public meetings, lectures, exhibitions, and balls.
Although the hustings for the 1832 and 1859 elections were held
there, the rooms never made money and were eventually con-
verted into shops and houses. Almost simultaneously, the Stroud
Subscription Rooms were built, opening in 1837, and intended
for public meetings, literary, scientific, and philosophical meetings, and concerts. The rooms cost some £2500 and were funded
by public subscription. The project was never intended to make a
profit, but by the 1850s dividends were being paid and sub-
scribers' shares were being openly traded. By contrast, the Stroud
Library, which opened in 1835 with a collection of 2000 volumes,
never covered its running costs, and by 1844 was closed, the town
having refused to purchase the library for a relatively paltry £150.
The Stroud Mechanics' Institute flourished briefly in the 1830s
but closed in 1841. A year later a new Mechanics' Reading Room
was opened, but the Mechanics' Institute fractured – interestingly,
given that these were the years of Chartism – over a proposal to
purchase a copy of Paine's *Rights of Man*. Seceders formed the
Stroud Young Men's Improvement Society, but neither venture

lasted much beyond a year. Undeterred *soi-disant* improvers
founded the Young Men's Mental Improvement Society in 1845,
and the local MP, G. P. Scrope, served as president of the Stroud
Athenaeum founded in 1847. Scrope donated some 150 volumes,
but this venture too collapsed in 1853. Meanwhile the Stroud
Dispensary, founded in 1750, continued to thrive under voluntary
management, treating 849 patients in 1867, with an annual
budget of £612. The sometimes sisyphean labours of Stroud's civic
leaders suggests that the spirit of improvement proved resilient
and mutable, even when locals' enthusiasm for being improved
waned swiftly.[52]

Urban life promoted and rewarded civic virtue. John Heathcoat
caught something of this when the borough of Tiverton presented him with his portrait in 1843 as a gesture of gratitude for
generous benefactions to the town. Heathcoat's response was to
argue that 'To contribute to the comfort of the town one lives in
is but to secure one's own, and to attribute merit to a man for so
doing would be almost as inconsistent as to be surprised at his
endeavouring to make his own house comfortable'.[53] One of
Heathcoat's much-praised acts of philanthropy was to open a
factory school attached to his lace factory in 1832. In so doing he
joined a small army of private patrons of education. A wide variety
of motives – private, philanthropic, entrepreneurial, spiritual, and
practical – issued in diverse educational provision within many
towns. Charity schools, public grammar schools, factory schools,
and the much-derided dame schools offered different kinds of
educational experience to those of different means, aptitudes,
and social ambitions. Similarly, from the 1780s, the Sunday
School movement combined the teaching of basic skills with the
inculcation of Christian virtue.[54] Again, while it would be misleading to exaggerate the range and quality of the education thus provided, there is a tendency to take the indictments of educational
reformers of the nineteenth century too literally. Voluntary provision in many towns expanded rapidly. In Ipswich, for example,
there were 26 schools in 1781 and 74 by 1833. The number of
pupils in day schools rose from 1395 in 1818 to 3980 by 1850.
According to one contemporary calculation, some 5314 of the
7350 children aged between five and 15 had received formal
instruction in day schools.[55] As Edward Baines's survey of 1843
suggests, the situation in Ipswich was probably not untypical.

Macclesfield in Cheshire, for example, in 1843 had 31 dame schools, 22 private schools, and five public schools, with a total of 2864 children in day schools.[56]

Nor was the voluntaristic educational effort confined to the young. The establishment of Mechanics' Institutes from the 1820s was an attempt to create a systematic, voluntaristic, adult educational movement. Most larger towns established a Mechanics' Institute in the 1830s and 1840s. By 1850 there were 113 institutions and 18 000–20 000 members affiliated to the Yorkshire Union of Mechanics' Institutes, and many more remained unaffiliated.[57] Not all Mechanics' Institutes succeeded in their popular mission, and a good number became institutions of genteel culture.[58] Nevertheless, irrespective of their precise social constituency, Mechanics' Institutes did play a central role in thickening the culture textures of Victorian towns. In 1849 The Warrington Mechanics' Institute lent a total of 4480 books, including 2485 works of fiction and poetry, 800 historical works, and 781 dictionaries and magazines. In the same year the Ipswich Mechanics' Institute boasted a library of 5000 volumes and subscription to 32 newspapers and reviews. In 1849 some 10 722 loans were made. Alongside lending libraries, reading rooms, and booksellers, Mechanics' Institutes helped the complex process of translating literacy into reading habits. In a way which was not typical of rural England, the towns of later Hanoverian and Victorian England were developing a reading public.[59]

Political Culture and Political Reform in Urban England

Behind these sometimes frenetic attempts to develop urban cultural infrastructures lay a strong sense that what distinguished urban life was urban amenities. R. J. Morris and Richard Rodger have recently suggested that 'In 1750 there were very few towns and cities which had a regular newspaper, an adequate trade directory, or an accurately surveyed map. By 1850 there were very few without all three'.[60] If this was the trinity that defined urban life by the nineteenth century, the head of the trinity was undoubtedly the local newspaper. A developing print culture, of which newspapers were a crucial component, helped to shape and define the public domain of urban England. In the eighteenth century over 220 provincial papers were established, and while some quickly foundered, others wove themselves closely into the fabric of local communities.[61] Newspapers mattered to urban life because they helped lend coherence to what might otherwise be disparate and fissiparous communities.[62] Less perhaps in their reporting than in their listing of local events, their advertising of local services, and their publicizing the decisions of local government and quasi-governmental agencies, newspapers were the medium through which the activities that defined the local community were most apparent. Newspapers mattered, too, for what they said. By the postwar period, many towns had not one but two or more newspapers, representing different strands in local politics and contributing to the process of ideological contestation through which urban identities were being reformed. The radical Manchester journalist, Archibald Prentice, bought the *Manchester Gazette* in 1824, believing that the *Manchester Guardian's* Whiggism was so diluted as to make it almost indistinguishable from Toryism, a view hardly shared by the avowedly Tory Manchester newspapers, the *Mercury, The Chronicle*, the *British Volunteer*, and the *Exchange Herald*. The *Guardian* and the *Gazette* between them enjoyed a circulation of nearly 4000.[63] Similarly, by 1815 Nottingham was served by the Tory *Nottingham Journal* and the radical, Nonconformist *Nottingham Review*. By 1833 their combined weekly sales exceeded 2000 copies.[64] This vigorous and partisan local press was not confined to the major cities. A modest-sized town such as Banbury had, by the 1860s, the impeccably Liberal *Banbury Guardian*, the militantly Dissenting *Banbury Advertiser*, and the genteelly Conservative *Banbury Herald*.[65] Moreover, although the provincial press might have begun as the poor relation of the London press, dependent on London newspapers for national news and political coverage, by the late eighteenth century a self-confident, distinctive provincial press had emerged. The *Leeds Mercury* was established as early as 1718. By 1801 it had a circulation of approximately 800, and the average number of words in each copy was 21 736. By 1829 sales had reached 5000, and the fall in stamp duty boosted sales to 9000 in 1836. By 1848 the average number of words per copy (including a weekly supplement) had risen to 180 000.[66] The cultural and political significance of a provincial press of such scale and sophistication was as much national as local.

The press was crucial to the broader political movement which took root in urban England. Towns, especially the new or newly expanding towns of the new industrial areas, came to claim to be able to mobilize and represent public opinion in a unique and uniquely authoritative way. Perhaps the last reformist movement in which there was a genuine partnership between urban and rural England was the Association Movement of 1779–85, and even here the York press played a key role.[67] From the 'English Jacobinism' of the 1790s onwards, towns played a central role in cradling reformism. The first genuinely popular radical political society was formed in Sheffield in 1791, and the Sheffield Society for Constitutional Information anticipated the formation of the London Corresponding Society. English Jacobinism was impressive precisely because of its strong base in provincial towns, with radical societies formed in places as geographically diverse as Manchester, Birmingham, Nottingham, Leicester, and Norwich.[68] This tradition of active provincial radicalism put down deep roots, and it was no coincidence that the Chartist National Convention adjourned to Birmingham, Feargus O'Connor was elected MP for Nottingham in 1847, and the movement's unity was proclaimed and maintained by the *Northern Star*.[69] Indeed, as reformers rested their case on an appeal to 'public opinion', they were, in the main, appealing to advanced urban opinion, fanned and trumpeted by urban newspapers. Archibald Prentice's history of Manchester between 1792 and 1832 was a study which almost embedded the national in the local: Manchester's triumphant struggle to rescue its civic life from an anti-reforming, counter-revolutionary civic culture would become Britain's history, and local struggles were replayed on a national stage. And, for men such as Prentice, what justified this shift in the social distribution of power was the many demonstrations within urban public opinion of the fitness of new social groups to assume and exercise public power. Prentice's narrative, an urban morality tale, thus ran from the attempted suppression of reform in Manchester in 1792 to the passage of the Reform Act in 1832.[70] Read in this way, through the agencies of the Birmingham and Manchester political unions, the passage of the 1832 Reform Act represented the enfranchising of urban opinion.[71]

Editors of provincial newspapers might be partial spectators, vindicating themselves by vindicating the power of opinion in the provinces. Nevertheless, they were at the heart of a movement which helped to remodel the British polity and public life in the nineteenth century. By the 1820s provincial England had a formidable repertoire of instruments available through which national policy might be shaped. Full use was made of traditional modes of influencing parliament, notably through resolutions of county and town meetings and through petitioning. Parliamentary select committees constituted increasingly important conduits through which ideas and policies generated in the provinces might find their way into parliamentary discussion.[72] Under Pitt the Younger a parliamentary session in which 30–40 petitions were presented was striking: by the 1817 parliamentary session over 700 petitions were presented and some 62 per cent of these came from the Midlands, Lancashire, Cheshire, and Yorkshire, where public opinion was weakly represented in terms of parliamentary seats but strongly represented in newspapers and public meetings. Similarly, in the crucial days between 8 and 23 May 1832, when it appeared that Tory peers and an Ultra Tory ministry might thwart a Reform Bill the perceived intention of which was to make parliament more representative of public opinion, some 290 petitions in support of the Bill came flooding in.[73] Many petitions were no more than special pleading by specific interests, but others did mobilize provincial opinion in truly impressive ways. The 1823 Yorkshire petition in support of parliamentary reform contained the signatures of 17 083 freeholders. A petition from Leeds supporting parliamentary reform in 1831 contained around 17 000 signatures and similar petitions from Manchester and Bristol each carried around 12 000 signatures.[74] Older public discourses which, for example, defended the 'unreformed' electoral system by arguing that it represented a settled distribution of property and property rights, were now overwhelmed by the claims of provincial property and the clamour of provincial opinion. Reflecting on the passage of Catholic Emancipation, Parliamentary Reform, the abolition of slavery, and Corn Law Repeal, Edward Baines Junior remarked in 1851 that, 'thanks both to the democratical and aristocratical parts of our institutions, the provinces share very largely with London the influence, and often originate and sustain the movements that decide national policy'.[75] Provincial political influence, of course, was not new. What was new was a shift in the centre of gravity of provincial opinion towards new towns, new wealth, and new provincial elites. The contours of public opinion, and the distribution of power and influences in the English provinces, were quite different in the England of Lord Grey, Thomas Attwood, Richard Cobden, and the *Leeds Mercury*, than they had been in the England of Pitt the Younger, Christopher Wyvill, the county association movement, and the *York Chronicle*.

If the passage of Parliamentary Reform in 1832 could be construed by urban partisans as a victory for urban public opinion, the Repeal of the Corn Laws in 1846 seemed, to the Manchester-based Anti-Corn-Law League at least, to be a vindication of their attempt to place Manchester at the vanguard of public opinion.[76] From its origins in Manchester in 1838, Richard Cobden and the League's leaders built a national organization, the power base of which was in the new urban areas. From 1844 onwards, urban wealth was deployed on a large scale to buy up rural freeholds and amplify the voice of free-trading urban England through the political voices of a new army of forty-shilling freeholders.[77] By 1846 some 70 per cent of the League's larger contributions, donations over £100, came from Lancashire.[78] The leading organs of the provincial press, most notably the *Manchester Guardian* and the *Leeds Mercury*, became passionate organs of an uncompromising free trade orthodoxy. It is certainly possible that Peel would have carried Corn Law Repeal without Cobden and the League, but in a sense such high-political counter-factuals are immaterial. What was material was that Peel chose to bestow credit for repeal on 'the Honourable Member for Stockport' (Richard Cobden) and thus, by implication, on the League itself.[79] Equally significant was that what emerged from repeal was a new liberal economic ideology, centred on free trade, manufacturing prosperity, and international co-operation, which became known as 'The Manchester School'.[80] What Manchester was thinking today, the rest of Britain might be persuaded or coerced into thinking tomorrow. Or, as John Bright put it to a celebratory meeting in Manchester on 2 July 1846, when Repeal had passed and the League was dissolving itself:

> it is in this and a neighbouring county that the greater element of power in this country is henceforth to be found. Lancashire, the cotton district, and the West Riding of Yorkshire, must govern England. I don't mean that they must of themselves assert a superiority of other parts of the kingdom, like that

which the rural and agricultural counties have asserted over us in time passed [sic]; but I say that the vast population of those counties, with their interests, their morality, their union, that all those must exercise an immense influence upon all future legislation in this kingdom.[81]

Although the campaign for Corn Law Repeal came close to uniting urban manufacturing England, public opinion in the towns was always fissured by politics, religion, and competing social discourses. The municipal politics of Maidstone was vigorously contested, and notably partisan, in the second half of the eighteenth century.[82] The development of a partisan urban press and the emergence of more explicitly representative municipal institutions after 1835 served to intensify, and even institutionalize, ideological conflict within urban public culture. Political clubs became an increasingly prominent feature of urban life. Many towns in postwar England boasted Pitt and Fox clubs, and a modestly sized town such as Colchester could boast some twenty political clubs.[83] The Tory elite that controlled Manchester politics from the 1790s through to the 1820s emerged from and consolidated itself through the local Pitt Club, John Shaw's Club, and the Association for Preserving Constitutional Order.[84] In York, the polarities of local and national politics were constantly reinforced by the whiggish *York Herald* and the passionately Tory *Yorkshire Gazette*. Alongside this, political clubs flourished, notably the York Whig Club established in September 1818, and serving as a model for similar clubs elsewhere.[85] The York Whig Club's most public triumph was in securing the return of a Reformer, Marmaduke Wyvill, as York's second Member at the 1820 General Election. Contested elections offered oxygen which often helped to sustain local partisanship. In a quite explicit sense, elections confronted local communities with the responsibility of returning members to represent that community, and in so doing created a framework within which competing local interests were invested with specific political meanings. Simultaneously, they offered a mechanism through which constituencies could demonstrate their autonomy and political self-confidence.

Partisanship in urban life was not confined to clubs and elections; it could infuse relationships within and between urban insti-

tutions. In Bury St Edmunds in 1798 separate Grand Balls were
held to celebrate Nelson's naval victories: one was attended by the
Corporation and the Anglican establishment, and the other by
leading Dissenters and the 'trading community'.[86] A similar
tension between the Corporation and a large Dissenting community existed in Banbury, resulting by the 1820s in a sectarian separation of bankers – the Gilletts for the Tories and the Cobbs for
the Whigs – and a similar distinction along political and sectarian
lines amongst the borough's solicitors. The struggle between a
Tory Corporation, dominated by the Earl of Guilford, and
Banbury's new wealth culminated in electoral violence in 1831
and an acrimonious Liberal ascendancy after 1832. Even this was
not without its vicious ironies. In 1837, for example, Banbury
Liberals accused local Tories of treating poverty as 'a crime' by
implementing the New Poor Law, itself (of course) a Whig
measure.[87] Municipal reform, the New Poor Law with its elections
for Poor Law Guardians, and annual registration battles following
the 1832 Reform Act all conspired to intensify local political rivalries. Registration, with its provisions for objection to a would-be
voter's qualifications, opened the door to mass objections. In
practice, therefore, voters were registered by local Conservative or
Liberal committees and relied on political agents to protect them
from vexatious objection.[88] Thus conducted, registration etched
local alignments into the electoral registers.

Money, in its customary way, proved the most compelling currency for disputing between private well-being and the public
good. Even before the mid-nineteenth century, and to some
extent even thereafter, towns enjoyed relatively weak fiscal
powers.[89] In theory, through parish vestries, the fiscal powers
invested in improvement commissions, and through corporations
themselves, most urban communities could muster revenue-
raising prerogatives which, on paper, looked impressive. In practice, though, local fiscal instruments were increasingly ill-adapted
and the political constraints on raising local taxes were formidable. Local rates were levied predominantly on fixed property –
land and houses – and the most prosperous section of many
urban communities, the commercial and manufacturing sectors,
made a distinctly modest contribution to local expenditure. In
1841–2, for example, rates in England totalled £6 009 564. Of this,
£3.1 million was levied on landed property, £2.3 million on

dwelling houses, and a mere £0.6 million on moveable property, commercial premises, and profits of stock. Indeed, in 1840 the Melbourne administration had passed an Act clarifying the legal position and formally exempting stock-in-trade from rateable assessments.[90] The urban improvement schemes, therefore, rested heavily on the right to mortgage the rates, granted under improving local acts and, more systematically, under the Public Health Act of 1848. In Congleton, local Liberals happily dubbed themselves the 'Cheap Party' and their Tory opponents the 'Dear Party'. Exeter Liberals made similar claims to fiscal probity, but became mired in disputes over local finances and lost control of the Corporation in 1840.[91] These kinds of disputes with Corporations, and between reformed Corporations and their electors, were common. Attempts to use commercial rather than fiscal mechanisms to fund municipal improvement were equally contentious. Faced with the expense of paying for lighting and paving, the Police Commission in Manchester, which controlled the municipal gas company, used the profits from supplying gas to underwrite the costs of other improvements to the urban infrastructure. By the 1820s this system of thinly disguised progressive taxation of affluent gas consumers was being strongly challenged. Consumers objected, attributing high gas prices less to the costs of improvement than to the politics of oligarchy, and both the composition of the Police Commission and the pricing policy for municipal gas were modified.[92] Only with the mid-Victorian boom, and then only briefly, could civic pride and public services be purchased from the small change of urban wealth.

Ultimately, the improving framework of the Hanoverian town worked most efficiently in moderately sized towns which were growing moderately quickly. The quickening pace of urbanization in the nineteenth century, coupled with the long-run consequences of sustained urban growth, saw many towns beginning, quite literally, to outgrow their existing public institutions.[93] In unincorporated towns the absence of a general unitary authority became increasingly problematic. Manchester well illustrates both the scope and the limitations of the Hanoverian system. In 1792 the Manchester Police Act established a new police commission, with powers over watching, lighting, traffic, public health, and fire-fighting. All inhabitants with a rateable liability of £30 per annum or more were eligible to serve as commissioners. The

Police Commission, coupled with Manchester's stipendiary magistrates, provided a functioning governmental structure under which measures of urban improvement were effected. Nevertheless, by the 1820s Manchester was approaching something like governmental stasis, partially because of political conflicts between local institutions – vestries, the Police Commission, water companies, and lesser commissions – and partly because of growing political rivalries. A new Improvement Act of 1824 did little to ease the situation, and the pressure was increasing for city-wide representative authorities.[94] It is important to understand the circumstances surrounding municipal reform in the 1830s. It is too easy to embroider the findings of the *Royal Commission on Municipal Corporations*, which reported in 1835, into a general indictment of what became known as the 'unreformed' system of municipal government. Hardly surprisingly, the Commissioners found myriad examples of inefficiency, institutional decay, oligarchy, and petty corruption. For political reasons of their own, the Commissioners saw fit to concatenate examples of abuse in their report. Reformers seized on this with glee and, as a result, historians peering through the lens of the Royal Commissioners' *Report* have found their perspective on the public life of municipal England distorted.[95] The structure of urban government, which was substantially reordered in 1835, should be understood not as a system which was inherently defective, but rather one which evolved through quite specific historical processes and which, for much of the eighteenth century at least, was operating with some flexibility and efficiency.[96]

The reforming imperative is best understood in political terms. Tory-dominated borough corporations, viewed from the moral high ground of the Reformed House of Commons in 1833, resembled the unreformed electoral system all too closely. The fact that they provided something of a Tory bastion lent urgency and political piquancy to the reforming project. In Lincoln Tory members of the Corporation chided lessees of Corporation property, 'many of whom have assisted to bring on this measure by your wild advocacy of the Reform Bill'.[97] The victors of 1832 were to be victorious again. In June 1833 the Royal Commission was named. It reported swiftly, in the twilight of Peel's 'Hundred Days'. The Whigs legislated on the basis of the report, establishing elected municipal authorities and providing for unincorporated towns to petition for borough status and incorporation. The protestations of Tory Corporations such as Leicester that the Whigs were relying on an 'illegal commission', the report of which was 'partial and unjust', were as predictable as they were unavailing, although amply testifying to the political significance of the issues at stake.[98] At Lincoln the old Corporation conceded defeat, but in a final act of despairing partisanship sought to frustrate its successor body by rapidly selling off property at between 20 and 25 per cent of gross rental.[99] Under the Municipal Corporations Act, the franchise was extended to ratepayers with three years' residence and new corporations were given extensive new powers, including the obligation to establish borough police forces. Revising barristers, under the indefatigable Joseph Parkes, were compiling registers of eligible ratepayers even before the Bill passed (thereby fuelling suspicion that the principal beneficiaries of most reforming initiatives of the 1830s were lawyers). The Lords was appalled by the wholly elected character of the new councils and sought to interpolate an amendment which would have provided for a quarter of the aldermen on any council holding officer for life. The Commons rejected this attempt to preserve something of the aristocratic principle in municipal government, settling instead for a senatorial compromise whereby one-third of the council was indirectly elected (by councillors) for six years. With a flurry of activity, and a whirlwind of barristers' fees, elections for the reformed corporations were held in December 1835.[100]

The possibilities of reform were quickly appreciated, and its limitations sometimes darkly shadowed. Richard Cobden, leading the campaign for incorporation in Manchester, clearly perceived new political possibilities. Incorporation would fully integrate a liberal class of small capitalists into urban government, heralding a decisive tilt in the balance of urban politics. The language of incorporation was unflinchingly a language of politics and class. Cobden's pamphlet, *Incorporate your Borough*, captured the nuance of this discourse, as well as prefiguring the language of the struggle for corn law repeal:

> The Lords of Clumber, Belvoir and Woburn, although they can no longer storm your towns and ransack your stores and shops at the head of their mailed vassals, are as effectually plundering your manufactures and their artizans ... And you must tamely

submit to the pillage, or, like your ancestors of old, will you not resist the aristocratic plunderers? If the latter, then imitate your forefathers by union and cooperation; amalgamate all ranks in your town, by securing to all classes a share in its government and protection; give unity, force, efficiency to the intelligent and wealthy community of Manchester, and qualify it by organization, as it is already entitled by numbers, to be the leader in the battle against monopoly and privilege. In a word, INCORPORATE YOUR BOROUGH.[101]

An avalanche of new incorporations followed, including Manchester and Birmingham (1838), Bolton (1842), Sheffield (1843), Salford (1844), Bradford (1847), Warrington (1847), and Wakefield (1848). In Lincoln local Reformers initially promised non-party elections, but swiftly conducted a secret canvass, realized that they were well ahead, and established local causes which carried them to victory in every seat; while in the newly incorporated boroughs of south-east Lancashire, textile masters were around one-third of all councillors in the period 1835–60.[102] In a profound sense, Cobden was right. By building on the political foundations of the Municipal Corporations Act and the economical foundations of new wealth, the manufacturing cities of industrial England did initiate a revolution in the social and a spatial distribution of power in nineteenth-century Britain.

Yet if the 1835 Act provided a framework through which civic ambition could be translated into political reality, the Act was in some respects surprisingly limited. The municipal franchise appeared more representative than the parliamentary borough franchise, giving the vote to all ratepayers rather than those paying rates at or over £10 per annum. But the three-year residence requirement proved a surprisingly effective check on the real expansion of the urban electorate. In a number of places, the 'reformed' municipal electorate was smaller than the old corporation electorate. The old Norwich Corporation was elected by 2221 freemen, of whom 1123 were not rated at all and 315 were paupers, and in Macclesfield, too, the new municipal franchise emerged as more restrictive than the old franchise.[103] What the Act created in practice was not a ratepayer franchise, but an electorate of the respectable, settled, and stable urban middling sorts. For better or worse, the social distribution of urban power was shifting decisively. Radicals such as the Chartist Thomas Cooper lamented the way in which an empowered urban middle class had abandoned its radicalism:

> How eloquently abusive was the prevailing Whig strain about 'nest of corruption' and 'rotten lumber' and 'impositions and frauds and dark rogueries of the self-select'. And how the scale has turned since, in the greater share of boroughs, where the poor and labouring classes threw up their hats for joy at 'municipal reform' – and now mutter in discontent at the pride of upstarts become insolent oppressors ... recreant [sic] middle classes whom municipal honours have drawn off from their hot-blooded radicalism, and converted into cold, unfeeling, merciless wielders of magisterial or other local power.[104]

The Whig diarist Thomas Creevey invested the same process with quite different political and moral meanings, construing the Municipal Corporations Act as nothing less than a grand _coup:_ 'It marshals all the middle classes in all the towns of England in the ranks of Reform; aye, and gives them monstrous power too'.[105] Urban improvement was now entrusted, politically, to a self-consciously improving bourgeoisie. The equally self-conscious architectural grandiloquence of Victorian towns and cities is an aesthetic bequest from this political victory. More generally, urban public space was now remodelled after the bourgeois social vision: parks, libraries, sanitation, and public amenities represented the fruits of this new civic order.[106]

NOTES

1. P. J. Corfield, _The Impact of English Towns 1700–1800_ (Oxford, 1982), p. 9; Robert Woods, _The Population of Britain in the Nineteenth Century_, new edn (Cambridge, 1995), p. 15; Kathleen Wilson, _The Sense of the People. Politics, Culture and Imperialism in England, 1715–1785_ (Cambridge, 1995), p. 7.
2. Jose Harris, _Private Lives, Public Spirit: Britain 1870–1914_, Penguin edn (Harmondsworth, 1994), pp. 41–3.
3. For a complete listing, see Frederic A. Youngs, _Guide to the Local Administrative Units of England_, 2 vols, London, Royal Historical Society (1979/91).

4. S. and B. Webb, *The Manor and the Borough* (London, 1908), pp. 414–23; Brian Barber, 'Municipal Government in Leeds 1835–1914', in Derek Fraser (ed.), *Municipal Reform and the Industrial City* (Leicester, 1982), pp. 62–110; R. J. Morris, *Class, Sect and Party: the Making of the British Middle Class, Leeds 1820–1850* (Manchester, 1990).

5. Malcolm I. Thomis, *Politics and Society in Nottingham 1785–1835* (Oxford, 1969), pp. 4–5, 114–42.

6. Penelope J. Corfield, 'Class by Name and Number in Eighteenth-century Britain', in Corfield (ed.), *Language, History and Class* (London, 1991), pp. 101–30; Corfield, *Impact of English Towns*, pp. 134–8.

7. A. Briggs, 'The Language of "Class" in Early Nineteenth-Century England', in A. Briggs and J. Saville (eds), *Essays in Labour History: in Memory of G. D. H. Cole* (London, 1960), pp. 43–73; Dror Wahrman, *Imagining the Middle Class. The Political Representation of Class in Britain, c. 1780–1840* (Cambridge, 1995).

8. Friedrich Engels, *The Condition of the Working Class in England*, trans. and ed. W. O. Henderson and W. H. Chaloner (Stanford, CA, 1968), pp. 55, 65. A similar sense of Manchester's social topography emerges in Peter Gaskell, *Artisans and Machinery: the Moral and Physical Condition of the Manufacturing Population* (London, 1836).

9. John Glyde, *The Moral, Social and Religious Condition of Ipswich in the Middle of the Nineteenth Century* (Ipswich, 1850), p. 59.

10. Jonathan Barry, 'The Parish in Civic Life: Bristol and its Churches, 1640–1750', in S. J. Walsh (ed.), *Parish, Church, and People: Local Studies in Lay Religion, 1350–1750* (London, 1988), pp. 152–78.

11. Hugh McLeod, *Religion and the Working Class in Nineteenth-century Britain* (Basingstoke, 1984), p. 18.

12. Glyde, *Ipswich*, p. 168. See also R. J. Morris, 'Voluntary Societies and British Urban Elites, 1780–1850', *Historical Journal*, xxvi (1983), pp. 95–118; and *idem*, 'Clubs, Societies, and Associations', in F. M. L. Thompson (ed.), *The Cambridge Social History of Britain 1750–1950*, 3 vols (Cambridge, 1990), iii, pp. 395–443.

13. Robert Vaughan, *The Age of the Great Cities: or, Modern Society Viewed in its relation to Intelligence, Morals, and Religion* (London, 1843), pp. 152–3. Vaughan (1795–1868) was a congregationalist minister and intellectual, whose influence has not yet been fully appreciated by historians, but see the perceptive discussion in Andrew Lees, *Cities Perceived. Urban Society in European and American Thought, 1820–1940* (Manchester, 1985).

14. Vaughan, *Age of the Great Cities*, pp. 146–58, quotation at p. 152.

15. Rogers, *Whigs and Cities*, esp. pp. 133–342; Dickinson, *The Politics of the People*, pp. 93–124.

16. See Peter Borsay's suggestive article, 'Image and Counter-image in Georgian Bath', *British Journal for Eighteenth-century Studies*, xvii (1994), 165–79.

17. Cobbett, *Rural Rides*, p. 401.

18. Ibid., p. 395; cf. pp. 183, 320, 396.

19. Arthur Young, *General View of the Agriculture of Oxfordshire* (London, 1813), pp. 326–7.

20.   William Cowper, *The Task* [1785], printed in Bruce Coleman (ed.), *The Idea of the City in Nineteenth-century Britain* (London & Boston, 1973), pp. 24–5.
21.   W. B. Daniel, *Rural Sports*, 4 vols (London, 1812–13); Malcolmson, *Popular Recreations in English Society.*
22.   John Price, *An Historical Account of the City of Hereford* (Hereford, 1796), p. 74.
23.   Glyde, *Ipswich*, p. 55.
24.   Peter Hawkins Fisher, *Notes and Recollections of Stroud [1871]*, new edn, ed. N. M. Herbert (Gloucester, 1986), pp. 70–1.
25.   This process has been explored in Peter Borsay, 'The English Urban Renaissance: the Development of Provincial Urban Culture *c.* 1680 – *c.* 1760', in Borsay (ed.), *The Eighteenth Century Town. A Reader in English Urban History 1688–1820* (London, 1990), pp. 159–87. See, however, Jonathan Barry's important critique in his 'Provincial Town Culture, 1640–1780: Urbane or Civic', in Joan H. Pittock and Andrew Wear (eds), *Interpretation in Cultural History* (London, 1991), pp. 198–234.
26.   In this paragraph I am heavily indebted to Rosemary Sweet's soon-to-be-published doctoral thesis, 'The Writing of Urban Histories in Eighteenth-century England', D. Phil. thesis, University of Oxford (1993).
27.   J. H. Plumb, 'The Public, Literature and the Arts in the Eighteenth Century', in Paul Fritz and David Williams (eds), *The Triumph of Culture: Eighteenth Century Perspectives* (Toronto, 1972), pp. 27–48, here at pp. 30–1.
28.   See Peter Borsay's rich and subtle *The English Urban Renaissance. Culture and Society in the Provincial Town, 1660–1770* (Oxford, 1989).
29.   Francis Hill, *Georgian Lincoln* (Cambridge, 1966), p. 51.
30.   Reginald Nettel, *The Orchestra in England. A Social History* (London, 1946), pp. 66–7; Borsay, *English Urban Renaissance*, pp. 121–7.
31.   W. B. Stephens, *Adult Education and Society in an Industrial Town: Warrington 1800–1900* (Exeter, 1980), p. 35.
32.   Simon McVeigh, *Concert Life in London in the Age of Haydn and Mozart* (Cambridge, 1993); William Webber, *The Rise of Musical Classics in Eighteenth-century England: a Study in Cannon, Ritual, and Ideology* (Oxford, 1992); Christopher Hogwood, *Handel* (London, 1984), pp. 232–65; Philip Radcliffe, *Mendelssohn*, 3rd edn (London, 1990), pp. 45–8.
33.   Isobel Rivers (ed.), *Books and their Readers in Eighteenth-century England* (Leicester, 1982); W. A. Speck, *Society and Literature in England 1700–60* (Dublin, 1983), pp. 186–98.
34.   C. W. Chalkin, 'Capital Expenditure on Building for Cultural Purposes in Provincial England, 1730–1830', *Business History*, xxii (1980), pp. 51–70; Roy A. Church, *Economic and Social Change in a Midland Town. Victorian Nottingham 1815–1900* (London, 1966), pp. 11, 16.
35.   Langford, *Public Life and the Propertied Englishman*, pp. 207–87, quotation at p. 209.
36.   E. L. Jones and M. E. Falkus, 'Urban Improvement and the English Economy in the Seventeenth and Eighteenth Centuries', in Peter Borsay (ed.), *The Eighteenth Century Town. A Reader in English Urban History*

1688–1820 (London, 1990), pp. 116–58, here at p. 139; Richard Rodger, *Housing in Urban Britain*, new edn (Cambridge, 1995), p. 26.
37. Robert Newton, *Eighteenth Century Exeter* (Exeter, 1984), pp. 127–8.
38. Jane Fiske (ed. and intro.), *The Oakes Diaries. Business, Politics and the Family in Bury St Edmunds 1778–1827*, 2 vols, Suffolk Record Society, xxxii–xxxiii, (1990/1991), i, pp. 138–94.
39. Jonathan Barry, 'Bourgeois Collectivism? Urban Association and the Middling Sort, 1500–1800', in Barry and Christopher Brooks (eds), *The Middling Sort of People. Culture, Society and Politics in England 1550–1800* (London, 1994), pp. 84–112.
40. Gwen Hart, *A History of Cheltenham*, 2nd edn (Stroud, 1990), pp. 237–313.
41. Phyllis Hembry, *The English Spa 1560–1815. A Social History* (London, 1990), pp. 118–30. See also R. S. Neale, *Bath: a Social History* (London, 1981).
42. Wood, *Letters and Journals of Richard Hodgkinson*, p. 73.
43. Hill, *Georgian Lincoln*, p. 177.
44. George Flyer Townsend, *The Town and Borough of Leominster* (Leominster, [1863]), p. 193.
45. Trinder, *Victorian Banbury*, pp. 52–3; Richard W. Davies, *Political Change and Continuity 1760–1885. A Buckinghamshire Study* (Newton Abbot, 1972), pp. 22–4; O'Gorman, *Voters, Patrons and Parties*, pp. 38–43, 47, 169–70.
46. Webbs, *Manor and Borough*, pp. 703–4; Hill, *Georgian Lincoln*, pp. 241–3. This important point is often overlooked.
47. W. II. Semper, 'Local Government and Politics since 1700', in W. B. Stephens (ed.), *History of Congleton* (Manchester, 1970), p. 83.
48. For the construction of a civic landscape and its political meanings, see James Vernon, *Politics and the People. A Study in English Political Culture c. 1815–1867* (Cambridge, 1993), pp. 49–63.
49. Semper, 'Local Government and Politics', 88, 102; P. J. Waller, *Town, City, and Nation. England 1850–1914* (Oxford, 1983), pp. 78, 82.
50. Cited in Derek Fraser, *Urban Politics in Victorian England. The Structure of Politics in Victorian Cities*, new edn (London, 1979), pp. 168–9.
51. James Bennett, *The History of Tewksbury* (Tewkesbury, 1830), pp. 219–27, 281.
52. Fisher, *Notes and Recollections of Stroud*, pp. 162–89.
53. W. Gore Allen, *John Heathcoat and His Heritage* (London, 1958), p. 133.
54. Gillian Sutherland, 'Education', in F. M. L. Thompson (ed.), *The Cambridge Social History of Britain 1750–1950*, 3 vols (Cambridge, 1990), iii, pp. 119–69, esp. pp. 119–32; T. W. Lacquer, *Religion and Respectability: Sunday Schools and Working Class Culture 1780–1850* (New Haven, 1976).
55. Glyde, *Ipswich*, pp. 139–53.
56. Edward Baines, Jr., *The Social, Educational, and Religious State of the Manufacturing Districts*, 2nd edn (London, 1843), p. 45.
57. Edward Baines, *The Life of Edward Baines* (London and Leeds, 1851), pp. 127–30.

58.   Church, *Victorian Nottingham*, p. 215.
59.   Stephens, *Adult Education in Warrington*, p. 60; Glyde, *Ipswich*, pp. 170–82.
60.   R. J. Morris and Richard Rodger (eds), *The Victorian City. A Reader in British Urban History 1820–1914* (London, 1993), p. 8.
61.   Hannah Barker, 'Catering for Provincial Tastes: Newspapers, Readership and Profit in Late Eighteenth-century England', *Historical Research*, lix (1996), 42–61; Jeremy Black, '"Calculated upon a Very Extensive and Useful Plan". The English Provincial Press in the Eighteenth Century', in P. Issac (ed.), *Six Centuries of the Provincial Book Trade in Britain* (Winchester, 1990), pp. 61–72; R. M. Wiles, 'Provincial Culture in Early Georgian England', in Paul Fritz and David Williams (eds), *The Triumph of Culture: Eighteenth Century Perspectives* (Toronto, 1972), pp. 49–68.
62.   Jonathan Barry, 'The Press and the Politics of Culture in Bristol 1660–1775', in Jeremy Black and Jeremy Gregory (eds), *Culture, Politics and Society in Britain 1660–1800* (Manchester, 1991), pp. 49–81.
63.   Archibald Prentice, *Historical Sketches and Personal Recollections of Manchester. Intended to Illustrate the Progress of Public Opinion from 1792–1832*, 2nd edn (London, 1851), pp. 245–8, 262.
64.   Church, *Victorian Nottingham*, p. 18.
65.   Barrie Trinder, *Victorian Banbury* (Chichester, 1982), p. 5.
66.   Baines, *Life of Edward Baines*, pp. 37, 41, 50–1, 146, 224.
67.   Hannah Barker, 'Press, Politics and Reform: 1779–1785', D. Phil. thesis, University of Oxford (1994); Ian R. Christie, *Wilkes, Wyvill and Reform. The Parliamentary Reform Movement in British Politics 1760–1785* (London, 1962), pp. 68–221.
68.   John Stevenson, 'Sheffield and the French Revolution', in David Williams (ed.), *1789: the Long and the Short of It* (Sheffield, 1991), pp. 159–86; Goodwin, *Friends of Liberty*, pp. 136–70; A. Temple Patterson, *Radical Leicester. A History of Leicester 1780–1850* (Leicester, 1954), pp. 63–78; Thomis, *Nottingham*, pp. 169–94.
69.   R. C. Gammage, *History of the Chartist Movement 1837–1854* [1854], new edn (London, 1894), pp. 109, 285; Thompson, *The Chartists*, pp. 45–56, 68–9; Church, *Victorian Nottingham*, pp. 128–57.
70.   The subtitle of Prentice's *Historical Sketches and Personal Recollections of Manchester* indicated that the book was 'intended to illustrate the progress of public opinion from 1792 to 1832'.
71.   Prentice, *Historical Sketches of Manchester*, esp. pp. 1–19, 353–417; Carlos Flick, *The Birmingham Political Union and the Movements for Reform in Britain 1830–1839* (Folkestone, 1978), pp. 17–92; Asa Briggs, 'The Background of the Parliamentary Reform Movement in Three English Cities (1830–1832)', *Cambridge Historical Journal*, x (1952), 293–317.
72.   David Eastwood, '"Amplifying the Province of the Legislature". The Flow of Information and the English State in the Early Nineteenth Century', *Historical Research*, lxii (1989), 276–94; Adam Ashforth, 'Reckoning Schemes of Legitimation: on Commissions of Inquiry as

Power/Knowledge Forms', *Journal of Historical Sociology*, iii (1990), pp. 1–22.

73.   John Cannon, *Parliamentary Reform 1640–1832* (Cambridge, 1973), pp. 171–2, 238.

74.   Baines, *Life of Edward Baines*, p. 119; Michael Brock, *The Great Reform Act* (London, 1973), p. 160.

75.   Baines, *Life of Baines*, p. 7.

76.   Donald Read, *The English Provinces* c. *1760–1960. A Study in Influence* (London, 1964), pp. 131–51.

77.   John Prest, *Politics in the Age of Cobden* (London, 1977), pp. 72–102; Norman McCord, *The Anti-Corn Law League 1838–1846*, 2nd edn (London, 1968).

78.   Anthony Howe, *The Cotton Masters 1830–1860* (Oxford, 1984), pp. 212–13.

79.   John Morley, *The Life of Richard Cobden*, new edn (London, 1903), pp. 387–414; Donald Read, *Peel and the Victorians* (Oxford, 1987), pp. 230–41.

80.   Nicholas C. Edsall, *Richard Cobden. Independent Radical* (Cambridge MA and London, 1986), pp. 173–268.

81.   Quoted in Read, *The English Provinces*, p. 148.

82.   John A. Phillips, 'Municipal Politics in Later Eighteenth-century Maidstone', in Eckhart Hellmuth (ed.), *The Transformation of Political Culture. England and Germany in the Late Eighteenth Century* (Oxford, 1990), pp. 185–203.

83.   O'Gorman, *Voters, Patrons and Parties*, pp. 290, 329–32; James J. Sack, *From Jacobite to Conservative. Reaction and Orthodoxy in Britain* c. *1760–1832* (Cambridge, 1993), pp. 89–90, 99–103.

84.   M. J. Turner, 'Gas, Police and the Struggle for Mastery in Manchester in the Eighteen-twenties', *Historical Research*, lxvii (1994), pp. 301–17, here at 307.

85.   Peter Brett, *The Rise and Fall of the York Whig Club 1818–1830*, University of York, Borthwick Papers no. 76 (1989).

86.   Fiske (ed.), *The Oakes Diaries*, i, p. 370.

87.   Bodleian Library, G. A. Oxon b. 101, Banbury Election Cuttings, Poster dated 24 July 1837.

88.   John A. Phillips, *The Great Reform Act in the Boroughs. English Electoral Behaviour 1818–1841* (Oxford, 1992), pp. 228–33; Prest, *Politics in the Age of Cobden*, pp. 23–71.

89.   Hill, *Georgian Lincoln*, pp. 241–3; Church, *Victorian Nottingham*, p. 10.

90.   *Return on Real Property*, *P.P.*, 1842, xxvi (235), 665; Edwin Cannan, *The History of Local Rates in England*, 2nd edn (London, 1912), pp. 97–101.

91.   Semper, 'Local Government and Politics', 94; Robert Newton, *Victorian Exeter* (Leicester, 1968), pp. 34–59.

92.   M. J. Turner, 'Gas, Police, and the Struggle for Mastery in Manchester'; Prentice, *Historical Sketches and Personal Recollections of Manchester*, pp. 310–27; V. A. C. Gatrell, 'Incorporation and the Pursuit of

Liberal Hegemony in Manchester 1790–1839', in Derek Fraser (ed.), *Municipal Reform and the Industrial City* (Leicester, 1982), pp. 15–60.

93.   This was not a new process. Industrial towns had begun to experience a tension between antique institutions and economic change in the early modern period. See David Levine and Keith Wightson, *The Making of an Industrial Society: Whickham 1560–1765* (Oxford, 1991).

94.   For the terms of the Manchester Acts, see 32 George III c.69 and 5 George IV c.83. See also Turner, 'Gas, Police, and the Struggle for Mastery in Manchester'.

95.   *Report from the Royal Commission on Municipal Corporations, Parliamentary Papers*, 1835, xxiiii (116); Webbs, *Manor and the Borough*, pp. 712–37 offers a balanced assessment. See also G. B. A. M. Finlayson, 'The Politics of Municipal Reform, 1835', *English Historical Review*, lxxxi (1966), 673–92.

96.   Langford, *Public Life and the Propertied Englishman*, pp. 437–509.

97.   Cited in Hill, *Georgian Lincoln*, p. 254.

98.   G. A. Chinnery (ed.), *Records of the Borough of Leicester. Hall Books and Papers 1689–1835* (Leicester, 1965), pp. 512–14. Interestingly, the Corporation were as concerned at the appropriation of the Corporation's corporate property as they were at its political emasculation.

99.   Hill, *Georgian Lincoln*, pp. 254–5.

100.   Joseph Redlich and Francis W. Hirst, *The History of Local Government in England*, 2nd edn, ed. Bryan Keith-Lucas (London, 1970), pp. 116–38; Webbs, *Manor and the Borough*, pp. 748–55.

101.   Richard Cobden, *Incorporate your Borough* (Manchester, 1837), p. 2; cf. Edsall, *Richard Cobden*, pp. 52–4.

102.   Francis Hill, *Victorian Lincoln* (Cambridge, 1974), p. 38; Howe, *Cotton Masters*, pp. 142–6.

103.   John A. Phillips and Charles Wetherell, 'Parliamentary Parties and Municipal Politics: 1835 and the Party System', *Parliamentary History*, xiii (1994), 48–85, here at 58; C. Stella Davies (ed.), *A History of Macclesfield* (Manchester, 1961), p. 176.

104.   Thomas Cooper, *Wise Saws and Modern Instances* (1845), ii, pp. 11–12, cited in Hill, *Victorian Lincoln*, p. 42.

105.   [Thomas Creevey], *The Creevey Papers. A Selection from the Correspondence and Diaries of the Late Thomas Creevey, M.P.*, (ed. Herbert Maxwell, 2 vols (London, 1904), ii, p. 308.

106.   Davies, *History of Macclesfield*, pp. 285–7.

4 County Communities and Patterns of Power

Imagining the County

By their very nature, towns and villages projected a public identity. Here residence created an immediate sense of belonging, while political and social hierarchies were persistent and generally visible. Such communities were animated by a public and political life which, intentionally or incidentally, gave substance to parochial and civic identities. The English counties, by contrast, commanded no real presence. Everyone lived in a county, but this was sensed, if at all, through processes of incomplete revelation. Some counties might have reached their *frontiers naturelles*, with the Tamar marking off Devon from Cornwall and the Thames elegantly defining the boundary between Berkshire and Oxfordshire. Other county boundaries were altogether more ambiguous. Lancashire and Yorkshire met on Pennine uplands; and the vigorous walker might move from Hampshire, to Wiltshire, and into Devon without the physical landscape so much as hinting that important boundaries were being traversed. Writers who entertained the public with accounts of their travels rarely commented on the passage from one county to another, but almost always remarked on the towns and even the villages through which they passed. Accents might change, but did so incrementally, and like dialects acted as markers for loosely defined regions rather than tightly-mapped counties. Passing from Suffolk into Norfolk in 1784, the young and perceptive French traveller, François de la Rochefoucauld, stopped at Thetford and noticed how little separated the counties, with Thetford standing 'in an extremely shallow valley on a little stream which divides the counties'. The gentle ambiguity of the topography was reflected in ambiguities in the decaying town's location. The puzzled Frenchman mused that

91

'as three-quarters of the houses are on the Norfolk side, I reckon the town as being in the county'. On leaving Thetford, little changed and the 'road continued across country as barren as that we had passed in the morning'.[1]

In so far as England's county divisions reflected coherent organizing principles, those principles were historical rather than administrative. The principal territorial divisions of England emerged from the dialectic of medieval administrative imperatives and patterns of local lordship. By the early eleventh century England was divided into 32 counties. Six of the seven remaining historic English counties (Cornwall, Lancashire, Cumberland, Westmorland, Durham, and Northumberland) would soon be created with the incorporation of those areas into the Anglo-Norman state. Only Rutland was intruded into the pattern of shires established in the Anglo-Saxon period, and in territorial terms, this was hardly a substantial intrusion.[2] The territorial subdivision of the English polity into a settled pattern of counties might have been precocious and the system of county power elaborated from it impressive. It was, however, far from being uniform. Cheshire and Lancashire were to become county palatinates with distinctive liberties, while Yorkshire and Lincolnshire were trisected into ridings and trithings respectively. All counties were subdivided into hundreds, but again local lordship and custom determined the pattern of administrative organization. This Sussex emerged subdivided into rapes and 65 hundreds, Kent into 60 hundreds, Hampshire into 38, Dorset into 33, and Devon into 32. Characteristically, midland and northern counties had fewer hundreds, with Warwickshire and Westmorland each divided into four hundreds, Cumberland and Durham into five, Derbyshire and Leicestershire into six, and Lancashire into seven.[3] By the time of the first census in 1801, English counties differed enormously in both acreage and population. Yorkshire covered some 3 669 510 statute acres, Lincoln 1 663 850, Devon 1 636 450, and Lancashire 1 117 260. By contrast, Rutland was a mere 97 500 acres, Middlesex 179 590, Huntingdon 241 690, and Bedfordshire 297 632.[4] Variations in county population were similarly vast too, from Middlesex's 1 088 000 and Lancashire's 673 000; to Huntingdon's 38 000 and Rutland's 16 000. Irrespective of physical size and population density, the political infrastructures which made counties work might seem remarkably distant from most peoples' lives.

If we acknowledge that all political communities are, in some fundamental sense, imagined communities, we might still conclude that envisioning the county was a more abstract process than most. There were, however, institutional and cultural aids to imagining the county as a political and social entity. Over the eighteenth century, county-wide institutions began to develop. County agricultural associations formed, met, and drew considerable numbers into their activities. The Oxfordshire Agricultural Association not only promoted the spirit of improvement, but offered prizes ranging from awards for innovation through to monetary rewards for the virtuous poor who managed to escape having to apply for parish relief.[5] Kent's agricultural society was formed in 1793 under the patronage of the county's two Members of Parliament. A year later an agricultural society was founded in Berkshire, with eight district subcommittees, and an over-elaborate county-wide infrastructure of control.[6] Similarly, some of the prosecution associations that sprang up in England in the later eighteenth and early nineteenth centuries were organized, at least nominally, on a county-wide basis. Nevertheless, given patterns of crime and the benefits of locally associating, the parish or the hundred was generally seen as a more appropriate unit of organization for such initiatives. Thus in one listing of 196 prosecution associations, only six were organized on a county-wide basis.[7] In Lincolnshire, with its far-flung geography and subdivision into trithings, a short county season was developing by the late eighteenth century. Lincoln races began the festivities, with plays, balls, and concerts offering evening epilogues during race week. The annual Stuff Ball might draw as many as 300 from throughout the county.[8] Elsewhere, too, the races drew together the cream of county society, as did some hunts, and grand balls.[9] After attending one ball in 1851, a Bedfordshire squire confided to his diary that he had 'met all the County there'.[10] Nevertheless, in so far as the county existed as a social entity it existed for the social elite, and then only fleetingly.

Perhaps the county, as a cultural entity, was most frequently represented in the pages of the county press. By 1800 many of the 68 extant provincial newspapers functioned in part as county newspapers, carrying increasing amounts of local news as well as advertisements for the concerts, theatrical performances, races, lectures, and agricultural shows.[11] Some local papers did not merely advertise the county's cultural life but helped constitute it by carrying poems, essays, and extensive correspondence.[12] With a growing number of circulating libraries, increasing book sales, and the rise of the novel, the fashion for county newspapers should be seen as part of a wider print culture that helped to give counties a sense of local identity while simultaneously binding them into a much richer national print culture.[13] As Kathleen Wilson has argued, provincial newspapers played a crucial role not only as the 'central instruments in the social production of information', itself a powerful motor of politicization, but also by constituting the prism through which local experiences were verified and national events translated into meaning hierarchies of importance.[14] Of course, even 'county' newspapers circulated well beyond the confines of a single county and their advertising could reflect a regional rather than a county circulation. Thus in 1789 the *Birmingham Gazette* was circulating as far afield as Chester, Shrewsbury, Worcester, Warwick, Leicester, and Derby; while the *Hereford Journal* found its way to Shrewsbury, Gloucester, Bath, Bristol, and Carmarthen.[15] Moreover, the tendency of print cultures is always towards the cosmopolitan rather than the local, and in so far as newspapers contributed to defining county identities, they did so for a literate elite. The institutions which were to articulate counties with a popular, partisan edge – county teams and leagues in general, and county cricket clubs in particular – were products of new patterns of leisure, rapid popular communications, and thus of the later nineteenth century and beyond.

The Political Home of the Gentry

In Hanoverian England the county had meaning because it was the power base of the English gentry. Whereas aristocratic estates might be widely scattered across many counties, gentry estates – at least their core estates – tended to be concentrated within particular counties. The English gentry was the landowning class *par excellence*, committed to agriculture and estate life long after the aristocracy had begun to diversify economically into new speculations and commercial ventures, and socially into the London season and metropolitan culture.[16] Typical of the Hanoverian gentry were men such as William Henry Ashhurst of Oxfordshire,

Sir George Onesiphorous Paul of Gloucestershire, and Henry Zouch of the West Riding of Yorkshire. In this context the career of Paul is especially revealing. Born Onesiphorous Paul, heir to a baronetcy and valuable estates, his youth was devoted to London Society, the Grand Tour, balls, concerts, and the races. In the process he comfortably overspent his annual allowance of £1000. His succession to his title and estates promoted a major change in habits and lifestyle. In 1780 he was pricked as high sheriff of Gloucestershire, and took the new name of George, a titular patriotism which came to betoken a deeper patriotism. His library boasted an impressive collection on local government and advanced penal theory, and the cycle of balls, races, and gaming halls gave way to Quarter Sessions, prison visits, and appearances before Select Committees of the Commons. His funerary inscription highlighted individual achievement and county status: 'For to the object of this memorial it is to be ascribed that *this county* has become the example and model of the best system of criminal discipline in which provident regulation has banished the use of fetters and health has been substituted for contagion, thus happily reconciling humanity with punishment, and the prevention of crime with individual reformation'.[17]

In a polity in which property was the basis of power and prerequisite for political participation, landownership led naturally to nomination to the Commission of the Peace. The formal requirement for being named for the Commission of the Peace lay in possessing landed property within the county to the value of at least £100 per annum. This property qualification was established by an Act of 1732, which disappointed Tories who had been lobbying long and loudly for a much higher property qualification to quarantine the social exclusivity of the bench.[18] Although, as the Tories implied, a higher property qualification would have been required formally to confine the bench to the gentry, in practice social conventions, political practice, and habits of governance were, by the later Hanoverian period, effectively confining membership of the Commission to the gentry and a relatively small number of clerics. In Hampshire in 1821 there were around 900 who possessed landed property of sufficient value to qualify them to become a justice. In fact, only 238 were named on the Commission of the Peace, and of these only 152 were qualified to act.[19] The Commissions of the Peace, which generally ran to more than 200 names, circumscribed but did not define the active magistracy. Anyone whose name appeared on these lists could take out their *dedimus potestatem*, which formally qualified them to act as a magistrate. In general, rather fewer than one-third of those named on the Commissions actually did this. Thus what defined the magistracy as a political and judicial force was individuals' willingness to commit themselves to the judicial and secular administration of their counties. In this crucial sense, the magistracy was a self-constituting political elite.[20]

The formal prerequisite for becoming a magistrate might have been the possession of landed property, but the practical prerequisite was residence. Active magistrates operated in two distinct, but related, theatres of authority. They were generally present at the Quarter Sessions, the quarterly meeting of magistrates to hear cases and transact the administrative business of the county. More routinely, they were active in their own localities, localities which became more formally defined as petty sessional districts.[21] By 1831 English counties were formally divided into 523 petty sessional divisions, and these recently revised administrative units better reflected population densities and local political geography than did the old hundreds.[22] At petty sessional level magistrates heard cases, dispensed summary justice, committed suspects to higher courts, inspected overseers' accounts, heard appeals against parish officers, licensed innkeepers and others engaged in the drink trade, attempted to regulate weights and measures, and acted as the crucial points of contact between parish, county, and parliament. The proper discharge of these responsibilities demanded that magistrates were both available and visible in their localities.[23] This pattern of authority implied a lifestyle which sat uneasily alongside a deep involvement in the politics of Westminster and the consumption of metropolitan culture, but which was wholly consonant with estate management, rural improvement, and country pursuits. The politics of the gentry and of magisterial power had a very precise social location.

Gentry power was predicated on a very distinctive language of social description. French writers, Tocqueville most notably, perceived the ideological significance of the word 'gentleman'. The absence of a French correlate was, for Tocqueville, not so much a matter of linguistic peculiarity as of politico-cultural impoverishment.[24] A class of *privileged commoners*, oxymoronic in the context of European political culture, was peculiarly potent in the English polity. Tocqueville's compatriot, Hippolyte Taine, puzzled over precisely this strangely English social formation:

> I have been trying to get a real understanding of that most essential word 'a gentleman'; it is constantly occurring and expresses a whole complex of particularly English ideas ... The class is fully recognised as a fact: a workman, a peasant, or a shop-keeper would not try to cross the line of demarcation ... The gentry, the squires, the barons, feudal chiefs did not, as under Louis XV, become simply privileged individuals, ornamental parasites ... No; here they kept in touch with the people ... and they have remained a ruling class, or at least the most influential class in both parish and State.[25]

The English, too, employed a political vocabulary which both distinguished and privileged the gentry. Perhaps the most expansive eighteenth-century formulation comes in William Blackstone's *Commentaries on the Laws of England* (1765–9), but the socially and politically distinctive position of the gentry was elaborated and defended in works ranging from Francis Hutcheson's *System of Moral Philosophy* (1755), through William Paley's highly influential *Moral and Political Philosophy* (1785), to William Marshall's *On the Landed Property of England* (1804).[26] Similar sentiments, differently expressed, persisted in a vulgar language which defined the gentleman and legitimated his public role. In her most influential 'Cheap repository' tract, *Village Politics* of 1793, the evangelical conservative Hannah More had the loyalist blacksmith Jack Anvil declare to the Jacobinical mason Tom Hod that he was 'indeed as good as another man. But are all men fit for all kinds of things? ... I am a better judge of a horse-shoe than Sir John; but he has a deal better notion of state affairs than I; and I can no more do without him than he can do without me'. This popular language of socio-political legitimation took root, and Flora Thompson heard its resonance a century later in her village on the Oxfordshire/Northamptonshire border. The local rector still exhorted his congregation to faith in the great chain of being in which status and public duties were beneficially co-terminus: 'A gentlemen might seem to some of his [the rector's] listeners to have a pleasant, easy life, compared to theirs at field labour; but he had his duties and responsibilities, which would be far beyond their capabilities. He had to pay taxes, sit on the bench of magistrates, oversee his estate, and keep up his position by entertaining. Could they do these things? No. Of course they could not; and he did not suppose that a gentleman could cut as straight a furrow or mow or thatch a rick as expertly as they could'.[27] Any irony here, for the speaker if not for the redactor, was unintended and all the more revealing for that.

Something of the social character and public life of the gentry can be gleaned from its less publicly prominent members. The young Charles Fothergill quietly celebrated members of the Yorkshire gentry in his account of a tour in 1805. Passing through Richmond he noted that John Yorke (1732–1813) had an income of £20 000 per annum, and had built a folly on a rocky precipice in Netherdale, but nevertheless regularly spent the greater part of his income 'in ameliorating the condition of the indigent poor and indeed the whole lower class of community ... it is said that he merely reserves from his income sufficient to support his own family'. John Hutton (1774–1841) of Marske was similarly lauded as 'a man of great talents by nature and tolerably well cultivated, a great lover of books, a sportsman and an agriculturalist, fond of his bottle and good cheer, no pride, no ostentation; has about £5000 per annum from a paternal estate and is a good specimen of the compleat English Squire'. His public patriotism was exemplified in service as Lieutenant Colonel of the Loyal Dales Volunteers.[28] A Bedfordshire gentleman of a later generation, John Thomas Brooks of Flitwick, was assiduous in keeping a diary in the 1840s and 1850s. He not only spoke, but felt the local patriotism typical of the English gentleman, noting in February 1853 that 'I can safely say that even in the wider bounds of Merrie England, an ancestral Estate more compact, prettier, or more profitable is, for its extent, not to be found ... I am very fond of it, and well I may be'. Much time was lavished on the administration of this estate, and Brooks moved constantly between the private and public domains, happiest with his family, and in his active cultural life which embraced a sophisticated aesthetic, ranging from Scott's novels to Rossini's *Stabat Mater*. Brooks clearly had no great ambition for public power, but was diligent in public service, chairing the Amphill Board of Guardians, attending parish meetings, sponsoring emigration schemes, visiting the poor, distributing annual prizes for a local friendly society, accepting the obligation of service on special or grand juries; and quietly sponsoring the cultural life of the county, taking shares in the Bedford Assembly Rooms and serving on the committee of the Bedfordshire Archaeological Society, founded in 1848. From Brooks's own translation of private status into public action to his two sons taking a commission in the Indian army and orders in the Church of England, this was Merrie England at its most quietly resilient.[29]

The system of county government which emerged from the local political primacy of gentry elites was described by the mid-nineteenth-century Prussian jurist, Rudolph von Gneist, as 'magisterial self-government'.[30] As aphorisms go, this will serve better than most, but we need to define the nature and development of magisterial power with considerable care. The formal basis of county government remained 'local government at the King's command', and for much of the later Stuart period, these commands were frequent, intrusive, and above all partisan. Commissions of the Peace were constantly remodelled as kings and ministers sought to build power bases and frustrate opposition in the counties. Between 1680 and 1715 the Commissions of the Peace were remodelled no fewer than twelve times, and in Kent some 128 magistrates were removed in the first eighteen years of the eighteenth century.[31] The effect of such intrusions of the centre into the affairs of the localities was at once to destabilize and discourage the regular work of county government. In this context, Professor Plumb's 'growth of political stability' had a quite particular meaning for the public and political life of English counties. As the apparently neurotic interventions of the centre diminished, membership of the Commissions of the Peace stabilized, and active justices seized the opportunity to develop both the institutional structure and the policy agenda of county government. As Norma Landau has shown, Kentish magistrates developed an elaborate structure of petty sessions, policy subcommittees, and adjourned (i.e. business) meetings of the Quarter Sessions from the early eighteenth century. Similar developments occurred in most counties during the eighteenth century, and by the early nineteenth century most counties were run by an inner cabinet of senior magistrates, under the direction of a regular Chairman of Quarter Sessions, and served by a virtually full-time Clerk of the Peace.[32]

Throughout the Hanoverian period, then, the county was a real presence in the lives both of county elites and of the parish officers who were subject to their jurisdiction. Debates have raged in early-modern historiography over the nature and meaning of the 'county community'. A 'school' of historians of the early-modern county community has been portrayed as suggesting that, by the period of the Civil War at least, counties had become 'politically independent states', that actively sought disengagement from national politics and national struggles. The politics of the county, like its culture, values, and institutions, were inward looking.[33] It is probably true that, in rediscovering the 'county community', a generation of historians including Alan Everitt and John Morrill exaggerated counties' introspection and political quietism.[34] But there is no necessary tension between arguing for the distinctiveness of county communities and the development of a national political culture. The process was dialectical rather than dissonant. Different social groups found their political identities in different regions of the nation's political culture. The power base of the gentry was the county, but from that base they participated freely and decisively in the public lives of parishes, manorial courts, hundreds, petty sessions, voluntary bodies, the professions, and parliament itself.[35]

So much, at least, is clear for the later Hanoverian period. When the Grand Juries of Presentment gathered at Quarter Sessions and Assizes, contemporaries were conscious of a defined 'county community' being gathered. Henry Jodrell told the Grand Jury of Norwich in January 1793 that 'The power is in you to look around the several districts to which you belong; for which purpose you are directed to be summoned from various parishes and different hundreds, that by bringing, in your persons, *the whole county to one spot,* you may be able to redress what, in your private capacities, you have had occasion, individually, to complain of'.[36] The common practice of publishing the *Charge* delivered to the Grand Jury further substantiated this sense of a moment at which the county was formally constituted and powerfully tangible. When Grand Jurors were dismissed, they were dismissed as men of substance within the county community who, in their persons and through other agencies and institutions, could realize policy and priorities agreed by the county at Quarter Sessions. This empanelling of a Grand Jury of Presentment was only one part of an elaborate set of interlocking rituals through which the county was constructed. Constables were summoned to the Sessions, and were expected to make presentation on behalf of their parishes, often embodying a curious ceremony during which the constable presented white gloves as an emblem of the purity and peace of his parish.[37] High Constables made similar presentations for their hundreds. Numerous parish officers arrived as appellants or defendants in cases relating to their parishes. Petty jurors were empanelled to try cases and enjoy a fleeting fame. Magistrates hurried between transacting judicial and administrative business, while the Clerk of the Peace and his Deputies generated ever greater volumes of paper. The formal meeting of the Sessions might last only two or three days, but they were days in which power was exercised with an administrative intensity and judicial ostentation which gave symbolic and substantive authority to the political life of the county.[38]

As business, paper, and committees began to proliferate, magistrates were increasingly disposed to emulate corporations and invest public money in a county hall which combined administrative utility with a symbolic architecture of power. Meeting in a large inn, or sharing quarters with a city corporation, might have been conducive to the economy of county government but was increasingly ill-suited to its sense of dignity. The Bedford Sessions House was opened in 1753 to serve the Assizes, the Quarter Sessions, and the borough sessions; while Oxfordshire magistrates erected a substantial County Hall in 1840, the castellated gothic of which left little room to doubt magistrates' sense of the significance of the county.[39] The axis between political power and social status was reflected in the mini-season which began to develop around the Quarter Sessions. Balls were often held on the opening evening of the Sessions, touring theatres might well arrive in town, and by the 1830s some Conservative Associations were holding their meetings and balls to coincide with the Sessions.[40] Paul Langford captured something of the essence of the county community when he suggested that 'the county was a group of people rather than a physical location'.[41]

In the county calendar, the Sessions were eclipsed only by the bi-annual Assizes, when a circuit judge arrived to preside at the highest court in the county. The sheriff, invariably a leading member of the county gentry pricked for an annual term of office, led a procession of javelin men, local worthies, and a judicial retinue into the county town. By the 1830s the costs of the sheriff's ceremonial duties were becoming prohibitive, and parliamentary intervention gave them greater access to the county rates to defray expenses.[42] Even so, ceremony did not come cheap, and Barbara Charlton recalled that delight at her father-in-law's being pricked as the first modern Catholic High Sheriff of Northumberland in 1837 was moderated by 'the extra expenses of the office, with outriders, trumpeters and robes of state, coming to at least £800'. But as the formal power of the sheriff declined, ceremony was all, and the sheriff's Assize rituals orchestrated the subtle marriage of county authority and central power.[43] An Assize sermon was preached, normally by a local incumbent and invariably by a member of the established church. County magistrates might license Dissenting places of worship, but they had no desire to listen to their ministers, still less to inflict them on judicial dignitaries. Prisoners were tried, justice was ritualized and dispensed, and the county revelled in its ceremonial splendour. A Frenchman, Charles Cottu, in 1822 described Assize judges arriving 'with bells ringing and trumpets playing, preceded by the sheriff's men, to the number of twelve or twenty, in full dress, armed with javelins. The trumpeters and javelin-men remain in attendance on them during the time of their stay, and escort them every day to the assize-hall, and back again to their apartments'.[44] In the evening the High Sheriff would dine judicial and county dignitaries, often at vast expense to himself but at some advantage to his social reputation.[45] This weaving of show and parade with the power of life and death at the Assizes demonstrated unequivocally the interconnectedness of symbolic and substantive power which was wholly characteristic of the public culture of Hanoverian England.

County Politics

Counties were invested with a specific political meaning as parliamentary constituencies. Until the Grampound redistribution in 1821 gave Yorkshire two additional seats, each English county returned two members to parliament. Within the pre-1832 electoral system, county representation played an important and

distinctive role. Whereas borough constituencies varied profoundly in terms of their franchise, political character, and representative capacity, county constituencies were elaborated around a
uniform franchise and a clearly delineated association between
members and electors. Borough electorates were constructed
through franchises as varied as the highly populist scot-and-lot – a
ratepayer franchise, in effect – and the potentially highly restrictive freeman and burgage boroughs.[46] County constituencies, by
contrast, were constructed around a clearly defined propertied
franchise, and the forty-shilling freeholder was the only kind of
county elector. Freeholders might, of course, also be tenants, and
were certainly part of larger communities within which complex
patterns of clientage and deference prevailed.[47] Nevertheless, in
all but a few exceptional English counties, these were political
relationships constructed around relatively settled or only slowly
changing patterns of landownership and landholding. The precise
political meaning of landed politics varied from county to county.
In some, such as Northamptonshire, the nobility was powerful and
the gentry enmeshed in networks of clientage.[48] Writing of north
and south Durham in the years after 1832, Professor Nossiter has
suggested that 'The polls leave no doubt that the disposition of
the great estates constituted the political geography of England'.[49]
A comparison of Nossiter's emphasis on the political primacy of
landed elites in mid-nineteenth-century Durham with Professor
Namier's strikingly similar analysis of mid-eighteenth-century
Shropshire suggests deep continuities in prevailing patterns of
rural politics. From a very different premise, Professor Moore con-
curred, solemnly proclaiming the electoral politics of nineteenth-
century rural England a 'politics of deference'. Moore went on to
construct a sociology of the electoral politics of the English counties which robbed them of much of their colour, interest, and
unpredictability.[50] Much hinges here on the manner in which we
believe the electoral geography of rural England to have been
constituted, and the ways in which we believe the electoral
influence of land to have been constructed and mediated. In
other counties the gentry held sway, or came to hold sway. In
Oxfordshire, for example, a ruinously expensive contest in 1754
had led to an agreement between the Duke of Marlborough and
the local gentry, whereby the Duke nominated to one county seat
and the gentry to the other. In 1815, in the person of William

Henry Ashhurst, this arrangement was challenged and the Duke's nominee, his grandson Lord Sunderland, was defeated at a by-election.[51] The dominant language throughout this contest was a language of county patriotism which elevated the idea of an independent gentry. One of Ashhurst's election posters captured the nuance of this local patriotism, with its strong sense of distinctiveness of county politics: 'There is a spirit of resistance in this County, which will not submit to bend its neck to the yoke of the Nobility, or to suffer the County of Oxford to be again assimilated to a rotten Borough'.[52]

In a very real sense, county elections were county events. Even uncontested returns were accompanied by a ritualized political incarnation of the county. The High Sheriff was charged with making a return, speeches were made to nominate and second candidates, and the return was noisily acclaimed by assembled electors and non-electors. After a decisive Nomination the successful candidates might be chaired by parties of supporters, again embracing both electors and non-electors. Contested returns constructed the county in far more dramatic, sophisticated, and ambiguous ways. At one level a contested return shattered the image of an harmonious, politically united county community; but at another it created a massive participatory process in which an active, politicized county contested its priorities and identities. Press advertisements and press coverage, from the mid-eighteenth century onwards, carried news of county contests to the remoter regions of the constituency, and themselves constituted theatres of political contestation. Electors were canvassed, and these massive, county-wide canvasses, involving impressive numbers of electoral agents, volunteer committees, and candidates traversing the county, not only created a county-wide electoral machinery but also promoted myriad negotiations between candidates and voters, between landlords and tenants, and even between traders and customers, which dramatized the extent to which politics were comprised by individual negotiations and identities. The sheer scale of these activities is well exemplified in the sums that could be expended, from the prodigious £250 000 on the great Yorkshire contest of 1807 to the near £240 000 spent in Northumberland in 1826 on a by-election and a general election.[53] The climax of a contested election literally brought the political county together in the poll. Electors were transported to the county town to vote; candidates and their committees fed, watered, and fêted the voters as men of substance; and flags, songs, and flysheets ensured that county contests climaxed in a moment of carnivalesque exuberance.

The sheer size of the county electorate invested county members with a particular kind of authority. Well into the nineteenth century, the parliamentary vernacular continued not only to describe but also to conceive of county members as 'knights of the shire'.[54] The connotations here were of social standing, constitutional antiquity, and representative distinctiveness. In part, of course, the reference was to ways in which representation was personated, but parliamentary practice and representative theory accorded particular standing to the county constituencies being so represented. In 1831 the English county electorate totalled somewhere in the region of 225 900 and was represented by some 82 knights of the shire. Each pair of county members thus represented around 2755 electors, whereas their borough member counterparts represented only an average of 536 electors.[55] In fact, some county electorates were very large indeed. As many as 23 007 electors voted in the Yorkshire election of 1807, and 6300 in the Somerset poll in the same general election. In Kent, in 1802, 8848 freeholders voted, and 7251 cast a vote in Norfolk in the same election.[56] Significantly, late-eighteenth-century parliamentary reformers were committed to reforming projects which would enhance the representation of the county. The Association Movement, which flourished between 1779 and 1785, was in significant measure a county reforming movement. Its committee structure reflected and respected county identities. County meetings were employed in order to encourage county constituencies to petition for parliamentary reform. In the event some 29 counties petitioned in support of parliamentary reform, and the Marquis of Rockingham estimated that the petitions as a whole contained 'upwards of 60,000' signatures.[57] Moreover, the Association Movement's reform proposal would have enhanced county representation by 100 seats.[58] This programme, with its strong sense of county identity and county representation, was embodied in William Pitt's 1785 proposals for parliamentary reform, which would have transferred 72 seats from the boroughs to the counties. In addition, Pitt proposed extending the franchise to copyholders in the counties, in the belief that more counties and a more extensive representation of property within the counties 'would give an additional energy to representation'.[59] While it would be misleading to reduce the Association Movement to a county reform movement, the tensions within the movement between moderate reformers in the county associations and metropolitan radicalism are only intelligible when due weight is accorded both to the strength of the counties as political institutions and to the vibrancy of political reformism within those county communities.

If the failed parliamentary reform movement in the late eighteenth century aimed to enhance the representative role of the county, the successful nineteenth-century reform movement reconstructed and deconstructed the county in important ways. The 1832 Reform Act respected the propertied basis of county constituencies, retaining the forty-shilling freeholder as the paradigmatic rural elector, and buttressing the power of landowners by extending the franchise to customary tenants (the so-called 'fifty pound tenants-at-will') and holders of long leases.[60] In the years after 1832, the dominant political language in county constituencies hovered uneasily between one that rested power on social standing and one that did not flinch from the politics of party. Thus when a by-election occurred in Bedfordshire in 1851, John Thomas Brooks attended 'a Meeting of the County Gentlemen of Bedford to consider who *we* should send as County Members ... The meeting decided unanimously on Col. Gilpin'. Exactly a week later he attended a Tory party caucus to promote Gilpin's election.[61] As the politics of the gentry became the politics of Conservative Associations and Protectionist societies, the very basis of that politics was becoming transformed. It was less that Brooks's 'county gentlemen' were becoming the committee men of the Conservative Associations than that the county gentlemen were losing confidence in the old politics of the county community.[62] Other developments contributed to this process, including the formal political redefinition of the counties themselves. The 1832 Reform Act divided all but 13 English counties, creating 52 new political units that intruded a new political ambiguity into the imagined public community of the county. It was no coincidence that counties were largely divided for the purposes of political representation in 1832 and for the purposes of poor law administration after 1834. The liberal architects of reform in the

1830s had little fondness for the county as a political, cultural, and social unit, and Edwin Chadwick cherished a vision of a new territorial division of the English polity around newly constructed poor law unions.[63] And what the 1830s began the 1880s would complete, by creating uniform single-member constituencies in the Third Reform and Redistribution Acts of 1884–5, and by remodelling county government in the County Councils Act of 1888.[64]

Personal Power and Public Policy

In the Hanoverian period, the vitality of the county community and the vibrancy of its political and social life had given it a pivotal position in the public life of the nation. The business of county government caused it to look both inwards and outwards: inwards to the affairs of the parishes, to problems of crime, punishment, and poverty within the county, and to the discharge of magistrates' appellant and regulatory responsibilities; and outwards to parliament, which created the statutory framework within which magistrates operated, to national priorities, and to the Home Office which, from its creation in 1782, came to constitute the most fruitful point of contact between centre and locality.[65] Unambiguously, magistrates saw themselves as part of a national polity. In times of crisis their priorities were the nation's priorities. Throughout the Revolutionary and Napoleonic Wars, the counties sustained militias, raised volunteer forces, and played their role in conscription.[66] Simultaneously, they sought to counter massive food shortages and savage poverty, notably in 1795–6, 1800–2, and 1811–13, by revising the operation of the poor law, by discouraging the baking of refined bread, and by attempting to police the grain market.[67] Similarly, in their participation in the campaign against wartime subversion, postwar radicalism, and rural revolt in the 1830s, county authorities in general, and magistrates in particular, played a key role in national policy.[68]

Moreover, the counties did not simply respond to a national agenda: they played a crucial role in forging that agenda. Magistrates' influence over poor law policy, and their role in developing income support and sliding scales of family allowances, notably after 1795, is well known. Less well known, but equally important, is the role of magistrates in the revolution in penal policy that occurred in England from the last third of the eighteenth century. John Howard's investigation of prison conditions was undertaken after he had taken on the responsibility of prison inspection during his terms as High Sheriff of Bedfordshire in 1773. Howard's contacts were pre-eminently with fellow magistrates.[69] The great model prisons were built by county magistrates, sanctioned by local acts of parliament, and driven on by men such as Sir Christopher Willoughby and Thomas Butterworth Bayley, chairmen, respectively, of the Oxfordshire and Salford Quarter Sessions in the late eighteenth century.[70] The most influential figure to appear before the Select Committees on goals and penitentiaries in 1810–11 and 1819 was not the retrospectively celebrated Jeremy Bentham but the Gloucestershire gentleman magistrate and Chairman of Gloucestershire Prisons Committee, Sir George Onesiphorous Paul.[71] The revolution in prison architecture, the huge prison building plan that led to almost all counties building or rebuilding gaols between 1770 and 1840, was undertaken at the county rather than the national level.[72] To be sure, central government came to play an important regulatory role from the Gaols Act of 1823 onwards, but what was being regulated was a penal infrastructure and regime that the counties had constructed.

The architects of public policy in the English counties corresponded, exchanged information, and pooled ideas. Individual counties would embark on their own penal projects, secure local acts for prison improvement and enhanced rating powers; but they would do so in the full knowledge of policy being pursued elsewhere. The Gloucestershire Gaol Act of 1785 constituted something like a model Act for other counties redeveloping their county gaols.[73] Meanwhile, in Oxfordshire, Sir Christopher Willoughby was persuading magistrates to embark on an ambitious penal experiment which sought to develop reformatory penal regimes within the new county gaol while reserving transportation as a powerful deterrent for those criminals who proved resistant to the moral reconstruction that lay at the heart of Oxfordshire's penal policy in the 1780s and 1790s.[74] This Oxfordshire experiment was widely known and led to Willoughby's gaining influence as an advisor to central government in penal policy. Men such as Bayley, Paul, and Willoughby were evidently known to each other and to colleagues elsewhere.[75]

Moreover, other bodies, notably the Proclamation Society between 1787 and the later 1790s, made considerable use of county meetings and sought to invoke both the support and the energy of the counties for its programmes to enhance the policing of public morality. The Proclamation Society's campaigns for the better regulation of vagrancy, for the stricter enforcement of Sabbath observance, for more rigorous implementation of regulations relating to weights and measures, and for a general enhancement of what they were wont to regard as public virtue, depended crucially on collaboration with county authorities.[76]

The importance of the county lay in its being a pivotal political constituency within the English polity. It constituted the framework through which the potentially disparate policies pursued in individual parishes could be lent coherence and placed within some sort of regulatory regime. Moreover, through magistrates' statutory powers of inspection, oversight, and appellate jurisdiction, the Quarter Sessions developed an independent capacity for policy-making. In the Hanoverian period at least, the principal responsibility for policy in key areas such as poor relief, police, penal policy, and social policy lay with magistrates as an agency and the Quarter Sessions as an institution.[77] By the 1830s, of course, Reformers were fond of pointing out that, in a strict constitutional sense, the magistracy and the Quarter Sessions were 'irresponsible': accountable to no-one and elected by no-one. The Royal Commission on the Poor Laws, which reported in 1834, helped to set the tone. More than once, it inverted the traditional social arguments in favour of the authority of a landed magistracy, hinting that 'there are strong grounds for thinking that the present magistrates are not the best persons to be entrusted' with power over determining public expenditure and pauper entitlements because 'they are men of fortune, unacquainted with the domestic economy of the applicants for relief'.[78] The consequence was that 'in the great majority of instances ... the magistrates have exercised the powers entrusted to them by the Poor Laws – not wisely, indeed, or beneficially ... but [this] was, in part, the necessary consequence of their social position'.[79] In similar vein, John Stuart Mill condemned magistrates for 'holding their important functions ... virtually by right of their acres'; while the Royal Commission on County Rates, reporting in 1836, insisted that county rates lacked legitimacy because they were levied on ratepayers not by 'their representatives' but by an unelected, unaccountable magistracy.[80] Ernest Jones, the Chartist and proto-socialist, offered a similarly intentioned critique; although here the political agenda, only perhaps implicit in the reports of reforming committees and commissions in the 1830s, was made explicit:

> There is not a greater curse to a community than a set of men who proffer to administer the law for nothing. There are generally an average of three hundred members of the house of commons who are magistrates, and who put themselves to all the trouble of magisterial duties, lazily, and infamously performed, for the sake of the power, tyranny, and extortion, which it vests in their order.[81]

It is important to understand this critique, which would ultimately be fatal to the power and status of the county gentry, as having a very precise ideological and temporal context. As a political community, the county had developed through royal dispensations and crown authority. It was, in effect, a key component in the political geography of 'local government at the King's command'. Moreover, the sphere and capacity of county government had been augmented through parliamentary statute, and through the landed elite's willingness to use local and general acts to extend the authority of magistrates. Landownership, social status, and a political self-confidence born of political activism legitimized the power and position of the county gentry in Hanoverian England. As the language which legitimated public power began to shift, from a social language of power to a political language of representation, the institutions of the county and the gentry and their social allies began to lose power – not dramatically, not suddenly, but persistently and decisively from the 1830s onwards. English counties would persist, of course, but increasingly as a 'tier' of government rather than as self-constituting political communities. Reforming legislation in the nineteenth, and particularly in the twentieth centuries, would treat 'historic' county boundaries not as fundamental divisions within a territorial constitution, but as sufficiently plastic to yield to reforming convenience or administrative fashion. The 1834 Poor Law Unions cut across county boundaries, the 1888 County

Councils Act created 'county boroughs', and the twentieth century has increasingly been given to dalliance with 'single-tier authorities'.[82] What has been created has differed fundamentally from the county communities from Hanoverian England. Those communities gave political expression to the power which a propertied polity invested in landownership; they developed their authority from persistent public intervention by a resident landed class; and they achieved a degree of social coherence by developing patterns of association at county level. Crucially, though, these were county communities within a broader political community. Constitutionally, they were suspended between parliament and parishes. These wider political relationships were negotiated formally through moments such as elections, Assizes, and petitioning; and informally through travel, cultural association, and common frameworks of education and belief. According the county a local and a cosmopolitan identity might look like having your cake and eating it, but that was precisely why the county appealed so strongly to the landed gentry who dominated its public and political spaces.

NOTES

1. François de la Rochefoucauld, *A Frenchman in England in 1784*, ed. Jean Marchand, trans. S. C. Roberts (Cambridge, 1933), pp. 211–12. By the eighteenth century, two of Thetford's parishes in fact remained in Suffolk, the remainder, as Rochefoucauld rightly divined, being in Norfolk.

2. Gneist, *History of the English Constitution*, pp. 37–9, 113–26; Jewell, *English Local Administration in the Middle Ages*.

3. Data from Youngs, *Local Administrative Units of England*. Even nomenclature was not consistent, with Cumberland, Durham, and Westmorland having wards, not hundreds, and Lincolnshire and Yorkshire wapentakes. See also V. D. Lipman, *Local Government Areas 1834–1945* (Oxford, 1949), pp. 18–24. The Lonsdale hundred of Lancashire was subdivided into two divisions.

4. *Return on Real Property*, P.P., 1842 xxvi (235), 665.

5. *Jackson's Oxford Journal*, 3 August 1811.

6. William Marshall, *Review and Abstract of the County Reports of the Board of Agriculture*, 5 vols (York, 1818), v, pp. 75, 427. Most agricultural associations were organized on a local rather than a county-wide basis.

7. David Philips, 'Good Men to Associate and Bad Men to Conspire: Associations for the Prosecution of Felons in England, 1760–1860', in

Douglas Hay and Francis Synder (eds), *Policing and Prosecution in Britain 1750–1850* (Oxford, 1989), pp. 152–60.

8.   Richard Olney, *Rural Society and County Government in Nineteenth Century Lincolnshire* (Lincoln, 1979), pp. 13–14; Hills, *Victorian Lincoln*, p. 79.

9.   Church, *Victorian Nottingham*, p. 14.

10.   Richard Morgan (ed.), *The Diary of a Bedfordshire Squire (John Thomas Brooks of Flitwick 1794–1858)*, Bedfordshire Historical Records Society, vol. 66 (1987), 150.

11.   Barker, 'Press, Politics and Reform: 1779–1785', 272–86.

12.   Wiles, 'Provincial Culture in Early Georgian England', 49–68.

13.   Plumb, 'The Public, Literature and the Arts in the 18th Century'; Terry Belanger, 'Publishers and Writers in Eighteenth-century England', in Isobel Rivers (ed.), *Books and Their Readers in Eighteenth-century England* (Leicester, 1982), esp. pp. 11–13.

14.   Wilson, *The Sense of the People*, pp. 29, 40.

15.   Barker, 'Catering for Provincial Tastes', 54. See also Jeremy Black, 'The Development of the Provincial Newspaper Press in the Eighteenth Century', *British Journal for Eighteenth-Century Studies*, xv (1991), 159–70.

16.   J. V. Beckett, *The Aristocracy in England 1660–1914* (Oxford, 1986), pp. 362–73; G. E. Mingay, *The Gentry. The Rise and Fall of a Ruling Class* (London, 1976), pp. 80–164; F. M. L. Thompson, *English Landed Society in the Nineteenth Century* (London, 1963), pp. 109–50.

17.   E. A. L. Moir, 'Sir George Onesiphorous Paul', in H. P. R. Finberg (ed.) *Gloucestershire Studies* (Leicester, 1957), pp. 195–224; my italics.

18.   5 Geo. II c. 18. For the Act, see W. C. Costin and J. Steven Watson (eds), *The Law and the Working of the Constitution: Documents 1660–1914*, 2 vols (London, 1952), i, pp. 130–1; and, for a judicious discussion of its context, Langford, *Public Life and the Propertied Englishman*, pp. 420–1, 440.

19.   Foster, *The Politics of County Power*, p. 27.

20.   *Return of the Number of Justices of the Peace Qualified*, P.P., 1831/2, xxxv (39); J. M. Beattie, *Crime and the Courts in England 1660–1800* (Oxford, 1986), pp. 59–63; L. K. J. Glassey and Norma Landau, 'The Commission of the Peace in the Eighteenth Century: A New Source', *Bulletin of the Institute of Historical Research*, xlv (1972), 247–65; Eastwood, *Governing Rural England*, pp. 76–81.

21.   H. J. Pye, *Summary of the Duties of Justices of the Peace out of Sessions* (London, 1827). The most perceptive account of the development of petty sessions is Norma Landau, *The Justices of the Peace, 1679–1760* (Berkeley, CA, 1984), pp. 209–39.

22.   Lipman, *Local Government Areas*, pp. 22–3.

23.   The petty sessional and summary activities of justices are well illustrated in Elizabeth Crittal (ed.), *The Justicing Notebooks of William Hunt 1744–1749*, Wiltshire Record Soc., xxxvii (1981); Alan F. Cirket (ed.), *Samuel Whitbread's Notebooks 1810–11, 1813–14*, Bedfordshire Historical Records Soc., 1 (1971).

24.   Seymour Drescher, *Tocqueville and England* (Cambridge MA, 1964), pp. 45–6, 208–9.

25.   Taine, *Notes on England*, p. 144.

26.   In addition to the works cited in the text, see Thomas A. Horne, *Property Rights and Poverty, Political Argument in Britain, 1605–1834* (Chapel Hill, NC, 1990), pp. 77–87; H. T. Dickinson, *Liberty and Property, Political Ideology in Eighteenth-century Britain* (London, 1977); Langford, *Public Life and the Propertied Englishman*, esp. pp. 28–34, 377–410.

27.   Hannah More, *Village Politics* (Canterbury, 1793), p. 8; Thompson, *Lark Rise to Candleford*, p. 212.

28.   Charles Fothergill, *The Diary of Charles Fothergill 1805*, ed. Paul Romney, Yorkshire Archaelogical Society, cxlii (1982), 83, 158.

29.   Morgan (ed.), *Diary of a Bedfordshire Squire*, pp. 2, 34, 50–1, 86–7, 112, 120, 134, 152, 154, 159, 180, and *passim*.

30.   Gneist, *History of the English Constitution*, p. 640.

31.   Lionel K. J. Glassey, *Politics and the Appointment of Justice of the Peace, 1675–1725* (Oxford, 1979), pp. 262–8; Landau, *Justices of the Peace*, pp. 69–95.

32.   The fullest discussion of this process is Eastwood, *Governing Rural England*, pp. 50–75; see also Edgar Stephens, *The Clerks of the Counties, 1360–1960*, Society of Clerks of the Peace, Warwick (1961).

33.   The case against the 'county community' school has been put most pugnaciously by Clive Holmes in 'The County Community in Stuart Historiography'.

34.   Everitt, *The Community of Kent and the Great Rebellion*; Morrill, *Cheshire 1630–1660*; Morrill, *The Revolt of the Provinces*.

35.   The process has been carefully explored in the historiography of eighteenth-century Wales: see Jenkins, *The Making of a Ruling Class*; David W. Howell, *Patriarchs and Parasites. The Gentry of South-West Wales in the Eighteenth Century* (Cardiff, 1986). For England, see J. D. Chambers, *Nottinghamshire in the Eighteenth Century. A Study of Life and Labour under the Squirearchy* (London, 1932), esp. pp. 45–75, 211–330.

36.   Henry Jodrell, *A Charge to the Grand Jury of Norfolk … Jan. 16, 1793*, printed in Lamonie, *Charges to the Grand Jury*, p. 478; my italics.

37.   William Man Godschall, *General Plan of Provincial and Parochial Police* (London, 1787), pp. 33–5.

38.   For fuller accounts, see Dowdell, *A Hundred Years of Quarter Sessions*; Webbs, *Parish and County*, pp. 238–386; Eastwood, *Governing Rural England*, pp. 43–75.

39.   Joyce Godber, *History of Bedfordshire 1066–1888* (Bedford, 1969), pp. 323, 371, 433, 463; Oxfordshire Archives, County Hall Oxford (plans), QSE 18.

40.   Bodleian Library, MS D. D. Risley c. 66, 'Diary of Rev. William Risley', vol. iv, 17 January 1837.

41.   Langford, *Public Life and the Propertied Englishman*, p. 383.

42.   *Report from the Select Committee on the Office of High Sheriff, P.P.*, 1830, x (520); *Return of Sheriffs Accounts, P.P.*, 1835, xlvi (204); W. H. Watson, *Practical Treatise on the Office of Sheriff*, 2nd edn (London, 1848).

114   *Government and Community, 1700–1870*

43.   Barbara Charlton, *The Recollections of a Northumbrian Lady 1815–1866* ed. L. E. O. Charlton (London, 1949), p. 148.
44.   Cited in Douglas Hay, 'Property, Authority and the Criminal Law', in Douglas Hay *et al.*, *Albion's Fatal Tree. Crime and Society in Eighteenth-century England*, Penguin edn (Harmondsworth, 1977), pp. 17–63, here at p. 27.
45.   *Jackson's Oxford Journal*, 26 July 1806.
46.   For authoritative accounts, see O'Gorman, *Voters, Patrons and Parties*, pp. 27–67; Brock, *The Great Reform Act*, 15–49.
47.   This is explored more fully in David Eastwood, 'Contesting the Politics of Deference', in Miles Taylor and Jon Lawrence (eds), *Party, State and Society: Electoral Behaviour in Modern Britain* (Aldershot, 1996). See also Richard Olney, *Lincolnshire Politics 1832–1885* (Oxford, 1973).
48.   E. G. Forrester, *Northamptonshire County Elections and Electioneering 1695–1832* (London, 1941).
49.   T. J. Nossiter, *Influence, Opinion and Political Idioms in Reformed England. Case Studies for the North East 1832–1874* (Hassocks, 1975), p. 47.
50.   Lewis Namier, *The Structure of Politics at the Accession of George III*, 2nd edn (London, 1957), pp. 235–98; D. C. Moore, *The Politics of Deference, A Study of the Mid-nineteenth Century English Political System* (Hassocks, 1976); D. C. Moore, 'The Matter of the Missing Contests: Towards a Theory of the Mid-nineteenth century British Political System', *Albion*, vi (1974), 93–119.
51.   David Eastwood, 'Toryism, Reform and Political Culture in Oxfordshire, 1826–1837', *Parliamentary History*, vii (1988), 98–121; David Eastwood, 'The Triumph of Toryism in Oxfordshire Politics, 1754–1815', *Oxoniensia*, liv (1989), 355–62.
52.   Bodleian Library, G. A. Oxon b.15 (63), Election Poster, 21 August 1815.
53.   R. I. Wilberforce and S. Wilberforce (eds), *The Life of William Wilberforce*, 5 vols (London, 1838), iii, 316–37; E. A. Smith, 'The Yorkshire Elections of 1806 and 1807', *Northern History*, xi (1967), 69–90; Peter Burroughs, 'The Northumberland Elections of 1826', *Parliamentary History*, x (1991), 86–97.
54.   K. Roberts, 'English County Members of Parliament 1784–1832', B.Litt. thesis, University of Oxford (1974).
55.   Needless to say, these are very crude calculations, which make no allowance for the huge differences in the size of constituencies. Figures are derived from Cannon, *Parliamentary Reform 1640–1832*, pp. 290–1. They are adjusted upwards by 20 per cent to allow for the difference between electoral turnout and the maximum theoretically qualified electorate: see O'Gorman, *Voters, Patrons and Parties*, pp. 178–80.
56.   Cannon, *Parliamentary Reform 1640–1832*, p. 291.
57.   Christie, *Wilkes, Wyvill and Reform*, 97n.
58.   E. C. Black, *The Association. British Extraparliamentary Political Organization 1769–1793* (Cambridge MA, 1963), p. 52.
59.   *Parliamentary History*, xxv (1785–6), 447.

60. Brock, *The Great Reform Act*, pp. 227–9; Moore, *Politics of Deference*, pp. 164–8.

61. Morgan (ed.), *Diary of a Bedfordshire Squire*, p. 150; my italics.

62. Eastwood, 'Toryism, Reform and Political Culture in Oxfordshire', 107–15.

63. S. E. Finer, *Edwin Chadwick* (London, 1952), pp. 77, 184–5; R. A. Lewis, 'William Day and the Poor Law Commissioners', *University of Birmingham Historical Journal*, ix (1964), 172–87; Edwin Chadwick, *County Government* (London, 1879); Driver, *Pauperism and Power*, pp. 37–42.

64. J. P. D. Dunbabin, 'The Politics of the Establishment of County Councils', *Historical Journal*, vi (1963), 226–52; J. P. D. Dunbabin, 'British local government reform in the nineteenth century and after', *English Historical Review*, xcii (1977), 777–805; Charles Seymour, *Electoral Reform in England and Wales. The Development and Operation of the Parliamentary Franchise 1832–1885*, new edn (Newton Abbot, 1970), pp. 456–518.

65. R. R. Nelson, *The Home Office, 1782–1801* (Durham, NC, 1969), pp. 102–13; Clive Emsley, 'The Home Office and its Sources of Information and Investigation' *English Historical Review*, xciv (1979), 532–561; A. P. Donajgrodzki, 'The Home Office, 1822–1848', D.Phil. thesis, University of Oxford (1973); and for the later period see Christine Bellamy, *Administering Central–Local Relations. The Local Government Board in its Fiscal and Cultural Context* (Manchester, 1988).

66. Richard Glover, *Britain at Bay. Defence against Bounaparte, 1803–14* (London, 1973), pp. 125–48; Clive Emsley, *British Society and the French Wars 1793–1815* (London and Basingstoke, 1979), pp. 38–40, 99–112, 144–6; J. W. Fortescue, *The County Lieutenancies and the Army, 1803–14* (London, 1909); Eastwood, 'Patriotism and the English State'.

67. W. F. Galpin, *The Grain Supply of England during the French Wars* (New York, 1925); Neuman, *The Speenhamland County*; Eastwood, *Governing Rural England*, pp. 107–65.

68. E. J. Hobsbawm and George Rudé, *Captain Swing*, Penguin edn (Harmondsworth, 1973), pp. 71–139, 215–25; John Stevenson, *Popular Disturbances in England 1700–1870* (London, 1979), pp. 205–18; F. O. Darvell, *Popular Disturbances and Public Order in Regency England*, new edn intro. Angus Macintyre (Oxford, 1969).

69. J. Howard, *The State of Prisons in England and Wales* (Warrington, 1777); J. B. Brown, *The Public and Private Life of John Howard, Philanthropist* (London, 1818); J. B. Brown, *Memoirs of John Howard* (London, 1823); Eric Stockdale, *A Study of Bedford Prison 1660–1877*, Bedfordshire Historical Record Society, vol. 56 for (1977), 66–83.

70. Anon., *Biographical Memoirs of Thomas Butterworth Bayley* (Manchester, 1802); Margaret de Lacy, *Prison Reform in Lancashire, 1700–1850. A Study in Local Administration*, Manchester, Chetham Society, xxxiii (1986), 70–94; Eastwood, *Governing Rural England*, 244–50.

71. *[First] Report from the Committee on the Laws Relating to Penitentiary Houses*, P.P., 1810–11, iii (199); *Report from the Select Committee on the State of Gaols*, P.P., 1819, vii (579).

72.   Michael Ignatieff, *A Just Measure of Pain. The Penitentiary in the Industrial Revolution* (London, 1978), pp. 80–113; Sean McConville, *A History of English Prison Administration, Volume 1: 1750–1877* (London, 1981), pp. 218–62; R. Evans, *The Fabrication of Virtue: English Prison Architecture 1750–1840* (Cambridge, 1982), pp. 236–76 and *passim.*
73.   25 Geo. III c.10; G. Holford, *Thoughts on the Criminal Prisons of this Country,* (London, 1821), pp. 1–4; S. and B. Webb, *English Prisons Under Local Government* (London, 1922), p. 42.
74.   Eastwood, *Governing Rural England,* pp. 249–51; W. R. Ward, 'County Government, 1660–1835', *Victoria County History, Wiltshire,* v (1957), 170–94, here at 185–6.
75.   Oxfordshire Archives, Willoughby Collection, Wi x/1–33.
76.   Joanna Innes, 'Politics and Morals. The Reformation of Manners Movement in Later Eighteenth-century England', in Eckhart Hellmuth (ed.), *The Transformation of Political Culture. England and Germany in the Late Eighteenth Century* (Oxford, 1990), pp. 57–118.
77.   Dorothy Marshall, 'The Role of the Justice of the Peace in Social Administration', in *British Government and Administration. Studies Presented to S. B. Chrimes,* ed. H. Hearder and H. R. Loyn (Cardiff, 1974), pp. 155–68.
78.   The Commissioners' Report is most easily accessible in the edition by S. G. and E. O. A. Checkland, *The Poor Law Report of 1834* (Harmondsworth, 1974), here at p. 21.
79.   Ibid., p. 241.
80.   J. S. Mill, *On Representative Government,* in *The Collected Works of J. S. Mill,* ed. J. M. Robson *et al.,* 33 vols (Toronto, 1981–91), xviii, p. 537; *Report from the Royal Commission on County Rates, P.P.,* 1836, xxvii (58), 48.
81.   From the *People's Paper,* 23 September 1854, reprinted in John Saville, *Ernest Jones: Chartist. Selections from the Writings and Speeches of Ernest Jones* (London, 1952), p. 176.
82.   *Royal Commission on Local Government in England 1966–1969,* Cmnd. 4040, HMSO (1969), i, pp. 25–8, 65–75, 161.

5 Public Policy in Provincial England

Personal Power and Local Patriotism

Public authority in Hanoverian England consisted in a careful play on the symbolic and the substantial. Where formal powers were relatively weak or ill-defined, symbols that impressed, or simply dignified officials were instrumental in the social construction of power. Thus, civic rituals in provincial towns, notably mayoral processions or meetings of municipal sessions, ordered the urban community while simultaneously dignifying the exercise of authority. Typical was the inauguration of the Mayor of York on St Blaise's day (3 February) in a ceremony which moved impressively between the council chamber, the Guildhall, and the new mayor's residence. Elaborate oath-taking rituals were *hors-d'œuvres* to drinking three gallons of wine at Pavement's Cross and then proceeding to a lavish dinner.[1] In early-nineteenth-century Boston, the Mayor's Procession began with bells which summoned townsfolk to observe the robed corporation, led by a silver oar and maces, accompanied by a band, and treading over cowslips carefully strewn by children of the Blue Coat School.[2] Without such rituals, corporate authority would have appeared less definitive and more remote. Indeed, even the routine exercise of personal power was enacted in ways which dramatized social authority. When magistrates dispensed summary justice and administrative law from their back parlour, as men such as Samuel Whitbread did, they carefully combined personal convenience, the visible authority of the county seat, and the uncertain and therefore extensive power that flowed from highly personalized judicial and administrative forms.[3] In a much more modest but equally unambiguous way, the richer farmers rebuilt their houses, gentrified their own parlours, excluded the farm servants who hitherto had shared meals at their tables, and translated greater economic power into visibly greater social distances.[4] From the ritualized splendour which greeted Assize judges through to rectors' wives who expected other village women to curtsy to them in church, the public life of provincial England was punctuated by moments that translated social status into visible dramas of recognition.[5]

Such rituals did not make power in provincial England; rather, they enhanced it by making authority visible and tangible. The substantive bases of power were social and statutory. The symmetry between social status and political power, both in urban and in rural England, was striking. Village vestries were dominated by the major local employers. Urban elites similarly dominated local corporations and improvement commissions. For much of this period, county government was the untrammelled preserve of the active gentry, and when the Whigs opened up the Commission of the Peace to new wealth in the 1830s, they succeeded only in introducing commercial and manufacturing plutocrats who were relatively easily assimilated into county establishments.[6] If the governing elites of provincial England were largely self-defining, their public powers and extensive discretionary authority were underwritten by statute. Large areas of public policy, from poor law administration, wage regulation, highway regulation, and licensing of places to worship, through to policing, punishment, and licensing of places to drink, were entrusted by parliamentary statute to local government. Within this statutory framework, the public life of provincial England was still subject to local self-government. Local elites thus had ample justification in imagining themselves to be governing elites rather than executive functionaries within a strongly centralized state.

Yet this careful distribution of power in later Hanoverian England, like the social and statutory structures that underpinned it, was fragile. Explicit ideological challenges came from the democratic revolution of the late eighteenth century; while, virtually simultaneously, economic and demographic changes were reconfiguring the political and economic geography of England, with an ineluctability which was all the more striking because its processes were at best imperfectly understood. Certainly public authorities in provincial England were inclined to resist both the democratization that the French Revolution heralded and the social redistribution of power that the Industrial Revolution implied. For a time, this disposition to resist, coupled with a belief in the resilience of England's territorial and antique constitution, looked as if it might succeed. Eventually, and sometimes imperceptibly, an old provincial order passed, and new forms, new policies, and new anxieties emerged. In the process, reliance on status and symbols yielded to surveillance.

It is at least arguable that the territorial constitution was at its most resilient when it was threatened most directly. England, as is well known, greeted the outbreak of Revolution in France with relaxed interest. Edmund Burke's hysteria aside, majority English opinion either saw the Revolution as either unfortunate for France while insignificant for Britain, or as a useful fillip for the cause of reform in England. In many towns reformers began to organize, and did so without any great harassment from the authorities. By 1792 the temper changed dramatically. The Revolution had apparently changed its character, declaring war on its own citizens and on the European powers. Changed international circumstances rapidly made themselves felt in provincial England. The rise and fall of provincial radicalism was captured in cameo by the Leicester 'Revolution Club', which was formed in 1784 to celebrate the English Revolution of 1688 and to press for further constitutional and religious reform. In 1790 and 1791 the club was thriving, and drawing together reformers from the gentry and the local bourgeoisie. The events of 1792 threw the club into crisis, the respectable largely withdrew, and local Painites appear briefly to have seized control before the club collapsed.[7] Throughout the summer of 1792, Quarter Sessions, boroughs, and other incorporated bodies rushed to declare their allegiance to king and constitution, in a striking display of loyalism. By September some 386 loyal addresses had been received.[8] In November an initiative by John Reeves led to the formation of Loyalist Associations throughout the country. Although distinguished more by word than by deed, these short-lived Loyalist Associations played a role in politicizing local communities.[9] By 1794 the government was seeking to translate loyalist sentiment in the localities into concrete action in defence both of the constitution and of the Kingdom. As a result Volunteer Corps were formed, officered by local elites, and drawing on a strong local patriotism. In Devon some £5998 was initially pledged to support

the Devon Volunteers, while in places such as Bury St Edmunds
and Chelmsford volunteering gave a new focus for civic pride.[10] In
Stroud the Stroud Loyal Volunteers mustered a captain (John
Hollings, a retired mercer, banker, and JP), two lieutenants, an
ensign, four sergeants, four corporals, and 84 privates, two drum-
mers, two fifers, and a drum-major, a chaplain, and a surgeon. Its
band consisted of six clarinets, one bassoon, one serpent, two
French horns, one triangle, and one double drum. Here local
ambition invented new civic rituals, achieving a rich cultural
fusion in the context of a national emergency.[11]

Local patriotism was not to be presumed on. English
'Jacobinism' embodied a critique of the unrepresentative nature
of the English polity. While this critique had parliamentary
reform as its central focus, a shift in the social distribution of
power in provincial England was always implicit and often explicit
in its programmes. It would have been difficult to read the
London Corresponding Society's *Address to the Inhabitants of Great
Britain, on the Subject of Parliamentary Reform* of 6 August 1792, with
its vision of 'liberties restored, the press free, judges unbiassed,
juries independent, needless places and pensions retrenched,
immoderate salaries reduced ... and sumptuous feasts, at the
expense of the starving poor, less frequent', without seeing a profound shift in the social distribution of public power as an
intended consequence of parliamentary reform.[12] With a sometimes ruthless efficiency, magistrates closed down the public space
available to radicals. In Birmingham, the 'Church and King' riots
of 1791 saw loyalist crowds attacking known radicals and, with a
dismal symbolism, ransacking the library of the radical scientist
Joseph Priestley, while local magistrates at least silently abetted
the crowds by their inaction.[13] In Manchester, magistrates let it be
known that the licences of publicans who hosted radical meetings
were at risk, and 186 local innkeepers put their signatures to a
resolution calculated to keep their licences, if not perhaps their
consciences, intact: '*we will not suffer* any meeting to be held in
our houses of any CLUB or societies, however *specious* or *plausible*
their titles may be, that have a tendency to put in force what those
INFERNALS so *ardently* and *devoutly wish for*, namely, the
DESTRUCTION OF THIS COUNTRY ... [and] OUR MUCH-
ADMIRED AND MOST EXCELLENT CONSTITUTION'.
'Church and King' riots similar to those in Birmingham followed,

and one local magistrate was reported to have refused to bestir himself to stop 'so trifling a business as breaking a few windows'.[14] Magisterial complicity with loyalist crowds might be effective, but it was crude politics. More imaginative, if more costly, initiatives were taken by corporations such as that of Leicester, which sought positively to reward loyalism. In 1794 it subscribed 100 guineas to the Leicestershire Militia, and in 1801 it responded to the Peace Preliminaries by voting a further 100 guineas to enable the mayor to 'distribute some ale to the populace and treat them with roasted ox'. A further sum was voted for the publication of a Peace Sermon. When hostilities resumed in 1803, the corporation responded by voting 500 guineas to support volunteers and their families, and in 1813 matching grants of 100 guineas were given to the Leicester poor and 'to the fund for the relief of the Russians who have suffered by the invasion of the French'.[15] This kind of municipal patriotism was not uncommon.[16] As a result, provincial public opinion was mobilized and shaped in ways which blunted the reformers' case during the war years, and in the process a provincial reform movement which might have blossomed from the reforming initiatives of the 1780s was snuffed out.[17]

Enclosure and the Challenge to Customary Regulation

Perhaps the most striking transformation in rural England in the eighteenth and early nineteenth centuries followed enclosure. The dimensions of parliamentary enclosure in the century after 1730 are spectacular. Some 3945 Enclosure Acts were passed, enclosing 5.8 million acres. Put another way, around one-third of English parishes were enclosed and 18 per cent of the land of England was the subject of enclosure orders. In the period of the French Wars alone (1793–1815), 8.9 per cent of the land was reallocated in 1969 Acts.[18] The process of enclosing England's parishes combined social and statutory power in revealing and characteristic ways. Petitions for Enclosure Acts were promoted by the principal local landowners. Would-be enclosers' ambitions were grounded in local status and facilitated by their access to professional services and parliamentary time.[19] The effectiveness of opposition to enclosure has almost certainly been under-estimated.[20] Jeanette Neeson's work on Northamptonshire suggests that the most effective moment for opposition was immediately after an enclosure was first mooted. Many enclosure initiatives met brooding local opposition, divided village communities, and foundered before finding formal expression in an enclosure bill.[21] A few enclosure proposals, such as that to enclose the low-lying wetland of Otmoor in Oxfordshire, were violently contested. In the case of Otmoor, enclosure proposals foundered in 1787 and 1800, and when an Act was finally secured in 1815 it took some 14 years for the enclosure commissioners to complete their work. Once work on the enclosure began, anti-enclosure riots exploded and continued for the best part of five years.[22]

The enclosure movement had important consequences for English rural society. Most obviously, it represented a substantial reallocation of property and property rights. Common land was appropriated to private property, and 30 per cent of land included in Enclosure Acts was common or wasteland.[23] Those with rights of access to common land were compensated with other land grants, but the use value of such grants was substantially less than the marginal value of commoning rights.[24] Immediately, landownership was demarcated in new and emphatic ways. Hedges, ditches, and fences were the visible markers of new farms. Behind these hedges new agricultural techniques, new patterns of cultivation, and new social relations of production began to emerge. The enclosure movement was the centrepiece of a new agrarian capitalism which etched individuals' economic status with a stark clarity. The percentage of landless labourers in rural England increased from around 63 per cent in 1688 to 73 per cent by 1831.[25] More importantly, perhaps, a whole world of makeshifts and customary rights – including gleaning, common grazing, access to domestic fuel, and even small substance holdings – came under threat.[26] It is no coincidence that intensive enclosure soon resulted in inflated poor rates, and to some extent the higher levels of poor relief in rural England from the later eighteenth century onwards should be regarded as the price of buying out customary rights.[27]

The veiled consequences of enclosure may, however, be its most profound legacy. Agrarian capitalism not only developed new social relations of production but it also intruded a new social ideology. The fruits of this are clearest in the move towards high farming in the mid-nineteenth century, when English agriculture self-consciously emulated industry with intensive capitalization, the extension of mechanization, and growing market specialization.[28] It is no coincidence that a response came in the form of agricultural trades unionism in the 1870s, the absolute fall in rural population from the same date, and the beginnings of a reconceptualization of the 'rural', in which people played an increasingly less important role and the landscape created by enclosure itself came to constitute a new aesthetic that defined the economic imperatives of an earlier age as both 'natural' and 'beautiful'.[29]

Enclosure also heralded a decisive shift in the social regulation of rural England. As customary patterns of land-holding gave way to a new propertied order, so customary modes of communal regulation gave way to stronger legal definitions of status and entitlement. Enclosure Acts either subordinated custom to statute or, implicitly, translated the language of custom into the currency of a new propertied allocation. The new economic order was to be regulated and policed in novel ways. Magistrates from the late eighteenth century ceased even to attempt to use their power to regulate wages and to determine the price of bread. Here magistrates bowed to a belief in market regulation long before parliament formally abolished their power to regulate wages in 1813 and the assize of bread in 1836.[30] Moreover, when the new propertied order was challenged, as it was for example in the Otmoor riots of 1829–35, magistrates came to recognize, reluctantly perhaps, that new economic relations would entail new police powers to make them work. Oxfordshire magistrates therefore hired a professional police force, of officers trained in the new Metropolitan Police Force, to police Otmoor and to protect the works of the enclosers between 1832 and 1835.[31] In agrarian England, as much as in industrial England, the context for policy-making changed profoundly from the later eighteenth century.

Poverty and Political Transformation

Historians' intermittent preoccupation with 'revolutions in government' has, perhaps, done more to hinder than to help our understanding of the growth of government in provincial England. No-one has yet discovered a 'revolution in government' in eighteenth-century England, but that should not obscure the realities of England's becoming a more intensely governed country. To be sure, this process was subtle and incremental rather than dramatic or sudden, but it was significant nonetheless. As we have seen urban improvement commissions were invested with substantial powers to raise revenue and regulate the urban environment. In an important readjustment of private rights and public advantages, Improvement Acts, such as the Cheltenham Acts of 1806 and 1821, began to invest commissions with limited powers of compulsory purchase as well as more substantial powers to enforce minimum sanitary and building regulations in all new developments.[32] Turnpike and Canal Acts similarly gave their beneficiaries substantial powers of quasi-compulsory purchase. While it would be misleading to suggest that the growth of statutory bodies in Hanoverian England represented a serious erosion of property rights, their emergence did begin to subject property itself, and the exercise of property rights, to greater public regulation. In this respect at least, the Georgian splendour of Bath and Cheltenham represented the marriage of monied leisure, a new urban vision, and a new disposition to public regulation.

While the emergence of improvement commissions with regulatory powers rested on parliament's willingness to grant new permissive powers, the initiative for their formation lay in the localities. Parliament facilitated but did not initiate or direct the process of improvement in the eighteenth century. A similar division of labour underlay the development of a more ambitious, more explicitly interventionist social policy in Hanoverian England. Local authorities pushed their existing powers to the limit, made full use of their discretionary authority, and supplemented their statutory powers through local acts. Poor rate revenue is a fair proxy for total spending by local government. The poor rates were collected as a general rate, and from poor rate receipts parishes paid their county rate subventions. Between 1748 and 1750 the poor rates in England and Wales averaged £730 000 per annum, representing some 6.5 per cent of total spending by central and local government. By 1848–50 this had risen to £7 587 000, or 13 per cent of total spending. Raw figures can, of course, be misleading, but if we look at real per capita spending by local government, this stood at £0.12 in 1750 and £0.38 in 1850.[33] These increases are accounted for principally by changes in poor law and penal policies, and developments in these spheres merit closer investigation.

In important ways, the administration of the old poor law defined social relations and structures of power in provincial England. The old poor law divided provincial society into four broad categories: those habitually dependent on public relief, those intermittently dependent on public relief, those who enjoyed genuine independence, and those who administered the poor law. Those permanently dependent on poor relief included the elderly, the disabled, single mothers, orphans, and soldiers' families. In 1802–3 those permanently dependent on relief in England and Wales amounted to 734 817, or 8.1 per cent of the population. By 1815 this had fallen to 495 002, or 4.5 per cent of the population. The so-called casual poor were a much larger group. In 1802–3, a bad year but by no means as bad as the two preceding years, a further 305 899 occasionally received relief, bringing the total in receipt of relief that year to some 11.4 per cent of the population. In depressed rural areas the figures were much higher, and in Sussex in 1802–3, 22.6 per cent of the population were in receipt of poor relief, with 22.1 per cent receiving relief in Wiltshire.[34] Given the seasonality of much rural employment and the impact of the trade cycle in urban and industrial employment, many saw becoming dependent 'on the parish' at some point as a real or distant prospect. Only those with substantial property, significant and marketable skills, meaningful savings, or genuinely independent means could rest secure in their private and familial independence. This articulation between the genuinely independent and the potentially or actually dependent drove a social and moral fault line through provincial society. Simultaneously, it created a political frontier between the empowered and the disempowered. One correspondent told the Royal Commission on the Poor Laws in 1834 that 'The Persons who hold sway in the vestries would, from what I have observed in many instances, be averse to any measures which would render the labourer independent of parish assistance, which, by keeping him to its confines, retains him always at their command when wanted for urgent work'.[35] In parishes there was a class of office-holders whose administration of the poor law further distanced them from the mass of the labouring poor, leading Mr Stuart to suggest to the Poor Law Commissioners that 'each parish forms a

small and separate society'.[36] The county magistracy enjoyed
status as the appellate jurisdiction for all poor law matters, a judicial authority which mirrored magistrates' social status. In some,
although by no means all, urban areas a partial democratization
of political culture led to the emergence of populist vestries in
which the contest between ratepayers' fiscal liabilities and the
poor's sense of social entitlement was weighted more towards
recipient than provider.[37] Whatever its precise form, the politics
of poverty was a politics of social definition.

How the poor viewed those whom the poor law invested with
power is not easily rediscovered, and doubtless attitudes and experiences varied. We can glimpse something of individuals'
responses from Buckinghamshire evidence. Unusually, one
Buckinghamshire labourer, Joseph Mayett (1783–1839), wrote an
autobiography in the 1830s. Mayett's life, embracing the uncer-
tainties of soldiering and the increasingly fragile world of farm
labour, had seen him drift in and out of poor relief. By 1824,
Mayett was back in Quainton and feeling responsible for his
ageing and infirm parents. His attempts to secure an additional
sixpence per week from the parish were frustrated by his
brother's wife who 'objected to my going to [the overseers]
because she was appointed by the Parish to do for my mother in
her illness for which they gave her three shillings per week and
She was the proper person to go to the vestry'. Family strife
became entwined in the world of local officialdom. Mayett's sister-
in-law appears to have been given increased benefit but then kept
this back from Mayett's parents. Mayett protested to her, and she
threatened 'to take me before the Magistrate for scandleizing
[sic] her Character'. Mayett denounced her and promised to 'go
to the vestry next night and report her abominations to the Parish
Officers'.[38] This sad cameo simultaneously confirms the central
role of poor relief in determining social status and the real
authority of local officialdom. Moreover, Mayett's sense of being
entitled to some form of relief and his anger when this was dispensed in a niggardly or paternalistic spirit may well have been
widely shared. Thomas Fowler, an overseer at Aston Clinton in
Buckinghamshire, told two assistant poor law commissioners in
1833 'that the young men of the parish dress very smart on a
Sunday, and come to the overseer the next day. When they earn
money at harvest time, they spend it on something fine, not

caring about the durability, and will come to the overseer immediately after harvest; if we refuse them they run to the magistrates, who always side with the poor since the [Swing] riots'.[39] Again the poor's sense of entitlement is strongly implied, as is their willingness to play the system and to invoke the superior authority of magistrates. Fowler's comments also hint at the labouring poor's desire for what might be thought short-term respectability, an aspiration which privileged spending over saving, and immediate over deferred gratification.

The poor's inclination to live for the moment represented a perfectly logical response to their economic circumstances. The classes which save generally have a considerable margin on their disposable income and enjoy relative stability of employment. David Davies, rector of Barkham in Berkshire, insisted in his *The Case of Labourers in Husbandry* (1795) that 'the charge of mismanagement made against the labouring people, seems to rest on no solid ground', and indeed suggested that the labouring poor were a palpably 'deserving class of people'.[40] Thus the poor experienced poverty rather than made it; they were its victims, not its architects. Their lifestyle exploited the few moments of gratification that came their way. Yet however logical the poor's disposition to spend for enjoyment and status might have been, it excited hostile responses from many in authority. Two years after Davies's *Case of Labourers in Husbandry* appeared, Sir Frederick Morton Eden published his magisterial survey, *The State of the Poor*, which argued forcefully that much poverty was contingent rather than structural, rooted in cultural and moral roots and habits rather than the iron laws of economics. Eden's celebration of northern dietary habits (soup and potatoes most notably) rather than southerners' preference for refined bread, cheese, and meat led to a series of attempts to alter the diets of the poor.[41] An avalanche of improving pamphlets from bodies such as the evangelical Society for Bettering the Condition and Increasing the Comforts of the Poor, between 1798 and 1817, left the poor largely unmoved and their dietary preferences largely unchanged.[42] Had they been less remorselessly hostile to the power of custom, habit, and social expectation, political economists and their political allies might have come to appreciate that even the most powerful instrument of the market – hunger – changed habits only slowly.

The moral discourse on poverty shaped the broad parameters of policy, and these parameters were changing markedly in the early nineteenth century.[43] The publication of Malthus's *Essay on the Principle of Population* in 1798 offered an account of poverty which attributed the experience of the poor directly to demographic pressure on the means of subsistence, and argued that poverty occurred when the demand for basic foodstuffs outstripped supply, creating food price inflation and acute shortages.[44] If accepted, the Malthusian account would have huge implications both for poor law administration and for social relations in rural society. All poor relief, Malthus suggested, was counterproductive, increasing demand while not acting on supply. Thus transfer payments to the poor simply added to inflationary pressures. Moreover, by fuelling price inflation the poor law added to the number of claimants, undermining the position of the so-called 'independent labourer'. For Malthus the central objective of policy ought to be to 'draw a more marked line between the dependent and independent labourer', and the moral meaning of such a social demarcation would be at least as potent as its economic meaning.[45] This was a moral as well as an economic argument. Malthus was inclined to attribute excessive demographic pressures to 'improvident' marriage and, through the redistributive mechanisms of the poor law, the improvident undermined the provident. Malthus's solution was the phased abolition of public relief. If Malthus's moral argument cut materially at the position of the poor (who would lose entitlement to public relief), it cut politically at provincial elites (who would lose the power that poor relief administration invested in them). Either way, the implications of Malthusianism for provincial society were profound.[46]

Provincial political elites, and magistrates in particular, were inclined to view poverty differently – as a problem to be confronted rather than phased out. Throughout the eighteenth century there had been a disposition to experiment in different ways of administering poor relief. The foundation of policy remained the 1601 Act – the famous 43rd of Elizabeth – which had confirmed that the parish was the basic unit for rating purposes, and that primary responsibility for relief of the poor law lay with churchwardens and with overseers elected by, and accountable to, parish ratepayers. The Elizabethan poor law emphasized the discretionary authority of officials, the right of appeal to magistrates, and the desirability of setting the poor to work. In effect, the 1601 statute established a strong fiscal base and weak, or flexible, mechanisms for delivering relief. In the parish context this generally resulted in responses to poverty which were immediate responses to knowledge of a claimant's circumstances.[47] Certainly parish officers were willing to go to some lengths to acquire information and they were unlikely to spare the reputations of claimants. At Stow-on-the-Wold the vestry resolved in 1822 'That the names of Paupers and the several sums they receive be printed quarterly and put up in the public houses in this town and the names of parents of illegitimate children be also added and a request that any person knowing anything of the conduct or condition of said paupers be requested to communicate it to the Overseers'.[48] Parishes also experimented in mechanisms for delivering relief more effectively, and sought to marry a belief in labour discipline with local labour requirements. A frequently adopted practice was to send the poor 'on the rounds'. Able-bodied claimants would either have to undertake the rounds of local employers in search of work, or assemble in the village for a kind of informal hiring fair.[49] Only when they had thus established a willingness to work would they be entitled to relief. Joseph Mayett recalled how, probably in 1800, he 'went to the overseer for work and he sent me one week to a master in the parish to work and gave me eight pence per day and the next week he sent me to another master at the same price or wages'.[50] Supporters of the 'roundsman system' regarded it as a necessary attempt to impose labour discipline, while critics saw it as little short of an abuse of the system by local employers in search of cheap labour and wage subsidies in the form of poor relief paid to labourers taken on at below subsistence wages. Certainly wage subsidies were paid regularly, and the parish elites who ran vestries were well placed to translate the politics of oligarchy into the economics of parish subsidies.[51] Given the structure of the rural economy, the decline of rural industry from the later eighteenth century, and the cultural and statutory disincentives to labour mobility, wage subsidies are best regarded as central to make-work schemes in depressed local economies. Certainly the ending of wage subsidies after 1834 could cause acute problems, as at Long Crendon in Buckinghamshire, where the Reverend Thomas

Hayton, himself a supporter of the New Poor Law, felt obliged to inform the Poor Law Commissioners that 'The system of paying the wages of labour out of the poor-rates has at length been abolished, a consequence of which is that there is much animosity and considerable difficulty arising from this very temper respecting the best means of employing the surplus labour now entirely at a *standstill.* In fact, we are in a very awkward dilemma, totally at a loss how to employ the labour alluded to'.[52]

Some parishes, especially larger rural parishes and urban parishes, experimented with workhouses. Enthusiasm for incarcerating the poor fluctuated after an Act of 1723 facilitated the construction of workhouses.[53] The framers of the 1723 Act might have regarded the workhouse as a deterrent, and in the 1780s and 1790s parishes such as Bampton in Oxfordshire certainly tried to use their workhouses as a way of reducing expenditure.[54] In the main, though, workhouses tended to become quasi-asylums for the young, single mothers, and the infirm, and thus came to specialize in providing more long-term forms of relief. In towns such as Oxford and Shrewsbury, the evidence suggests that some might even consider entering the workhouse as a necessary expedient when illness, unemployment, or life-cycle changes impacted adversely on them, but that entry to the workhouse carried no particular social stigma and certainly was not marked by any strong institutional deterrence.[55] Thomas Gilbert's Act of 1782, which was important in facilitating unions between parishes for the purpose of constructing and running workhouses, was part of a movement which saw workhouses as efficient providers rather than symbols of deterrence.[56]

This pattern of parochial experimentation in patterns of relief within the broad framework of the Elizabethan legislation was encouraged by magistrates. In 1795 magistrates intervened dramatically by sanctioning the payment of wage subsidies linked to bread prices. The so-called 'Speenhamland System' took its name from the meeting of Berkshire magistrates, in adjourned Sessions, at the *Pelican Inn* in the Speenhamland division of Berkshire in May 1795.[57] The term, and indeed the conventional accounts of its genesis, mislead. Similar decisions had been taken by magistrates in Oxfordshire and Buckinghamshire in January 1795, and the probable architect of the scheme was Sir Christopher Willoughby, Chairman of the Oxfordshire Quarter Sessions.

Moreover, Willoughby was well aware of trends in real wages, grain prices, and food supply from his work with the Board of Agriculture, which had surveyed rural areas in 1794–5.[58] Moreover, he was equally well aware, as were his Berkshire colleagues, that parishes had been experimenting with bread scales and similar systems for determining relief. Thus the decisions of 1795 represented a formalization of practice and an indication that, henceforth, magistrates would employ scales in determining appropriate levels of relief. Once this was done, though, the die was cast and magistrates were in effect establishing minimum entitlements and diminishing the effective authority of parish officers.[59]

In terms of the distribution of power within the British polity, two aspects of the decisions of 1795 merit particular comment. In the first place these decisions taken by magistrates underscored the extent of their discretionary authority. Many – most notably the authors of the *Report from the Royal Commission on the Poor Laws* of 1834 – thought that magistrates came close in 1795 to reinventing the poor law. It was they who regularized the allowance system as a mechanism for settling 'the weekly income of the poor', and it was they who institutionalized the practice by insisting on the publication of tables of allowances, thereby instituting a new 'common law' within the administration of the poor law.[60] This perhaps exaggerated the novelty of the system, but it did confirm the freedom that magistrates had to make policy and to sanction new policy initiatives. Prime Minister Pitt's attempt to pass a poor law bill in the 1796 session collapsed, partly because of opposition from local magistrates, confirming the extent to which central and local government operated as separate spheres of authority.[61] In retrospect, though, it is clear that 1795 represented the high water mark of magistrates' authority. The report from the Select Committee on the Poor Laws of 1817 and the Sturges Bourne reforms of 1818 and 1819 signalled a move towards regarding a reordered parish, coupled with salaried overseers and streamlined bureaucratic procedures, as the building blocks of a reformed poor law administration.[62]

The Sturges Bourne reforms moved with stealth, partly no doubt because of Sturges Bourne's own political temperament and partly because he was himself an active magistrate and sometime Chairman of the Hampshire Quarter Sessions.[63] With the publication of the 1834 *Report from the Royal Commission on the Poor Laws*, stealth gave way to outright opposition. The *Report* had no hesitation in portraying magistrates as part of the problem, and their political emasculation as part of the solution to the crisis of the poor law. In place of the negotiated authority of parish officers and magistrates, the Poor Law Amendment Act established the carefully modulated authority of elected Boards of Guardians with responsibility for policy within newly established Poor Law unions. Simultaneously, the older pattern of relief at the discretion of officers, subject to appeal to magistrates, was replaced by a system of relief that aimed at being self-acting, given shape by the institutional forms of workhouses and a universal workhouse test, and subject to surveillance by a newly established central Poor Law Commission. The parliamentary passage of the Poor Law Amendment Act, which radically redefined both the entitlement of the poor and the structure of authority in provincial England, was remarkably smooth. Opposition was neutered partly by the sheer attrition of the Commissioners' massive 12 volumes of evidence, much of it mendacious but carefully marshalled in defence of reform. The New Poor Law was constructed, in part, from bureaucratic half-truths about the old.[64] Simultaneously, the two front benches united in support of poor law reform. The Royal Commissioners' insistence that a discretionary system of poor relief should be replaced by a mechanistic 'self-acting system' accorded with a certain modernizing vision of the English polity.[65] The Commissioners' proposals appealed to Peelite managerialism as much as they appealed to Whig reformism, still eager to dismantle Tory citadels but carefully casting political reform in the language of efficiency.[66] Lord Althorp, Whig Leader of the House of Commons, went so far as suggesting to the House in 1834 that the old poor law compelled magistrates 'to act on bad and erroneous principles'.[67] One of the Bill's most enthusiastic supporters, Sir James Scarlett (Member for Norwich) trumpeted the evils of localism, proclaiming 'uniformity' of administration 'extremely advantageous'. In the minds of men such as Scarlett, localism equated to parochial prejudice, and officers' discretion to little more than structural incoherence: 'One of the greatest defects of the present administration of the Poor-laws consisted in the local prejudices, and local feelings, and local occasions, which presented themselves everywhere, and caused a different system to be adopted in different parts of the country'.[68]

Only Tory Radicals and Radicals opposed the New Poor Law, and such minority support was doomed by mere deficiency of numbers. Fifty members opposed the bill's third reading. Their opposition inverted Scarlett's critique of localism. Where Scarlett saw efficiency in uniformity, the bill's opponents saw tyranny in centralization. Where the Royal Commissioners and the bill's advocates hailed the new Poor Law Commission as replacing the uncertain discretion of magistrates with an informed and efficient bureaucracy, the bill's opponents saw traditional governing elites being displaced by a new, unaccountable, officialdom. Thus George Robinson (Member for Worcester) thought the bill 'a measure which conferred powers altogether unconstitutional, and hitherto unknown to the history of the country, on a body of irresponsible men, having powers of delegation to others, irresponsible like themselves – powers which want to take away from people, their right of control over their own affairs, of appointing those who should levy taxes upon them'.[69] This latter point, that the 1834 Poor Law decisively undermined the authority of elected parish officers over the levying of local taxation, was not fully appreciated in the debates of 1834. Nevertheless, opinion outdoors soon recognized the radicalism of the Whigs' reforming *coup*. John Walter, Member for Berkshire and editor of *The Times*, denounced the workhouse system to his electors in 1834 and quickly positioned *The Times* in opposition to the Poor Law Commissioners, the 'three tyrants of Somerset House'.[70] Meanwhile, Assistant Commissioners were about their work, constructing new unions and initiating the building of workhouses. The Poor Law Unions were conceived as wholly new administrative units, and the fact that these new unions frequently straddled county boundaries was anything but coincidental. A new administrative idiom was being defined within a new political geography.[71] Anti-poor law riots in the south in 1835 prefigured much more dramatic and sustained popular opposition in the north in 1837. The poor, and more importantly those who thought they *might become* poor, deeply resented the ways in which the state had diminished social entitlement.[72] Those who had traditionally administered the provinces, in parishes and on the bench, came to recognize, and in many cases resent, their loss of influence.

Some historians have argued that the ex officio status of magistrates as Guardians protected the old social distribution of power. Others have pointed to the active role of some members of the gentry within the new Poor Law Unions.[73] Nevertheless, it is important to recognize that the terms on which power was being exercised had changed.[74] Magistrates shared power with elected Guardians, and all Guardians were subject to policy determined, in significant measure, by a central Board. The Poor Law Commission was in no doubt as to the political effect of poor law reform. In February 1835 Thomas Hayton, Perpetual Curate of Long Crendon and soon to be an active Guardian, wrote to the Poor Law Commissioners complaining that parish officers were blocking an emigration scheme that he favoured. The Commissioners' reply offered solace and the prospect of a new political order: '... the powers now exercised by Parish and Elected Vestries ... will in great measure be suppressed when the management of Poor Law affairs is placed in the Hands of Boards of Guardians'.[75] Along with the New Poor Law, a new political order was to be constructed.

The English Penal Revolution; or Magistrates as Modernizers

If poor law policy had been constructed through a sometimes tense contest between parish officers and magistrates, penal policy had fallen more or less wholly within the domain of magistrates and county officials. The late eighteenth and nineteenth centuries were marked by ambitious experiments in penal policy. The most obvious and dramatic consequence of these new directions in penal policy was the development of a national system of penitentiaries, with Millbank being built in London between 1812 and 1817 at a cost of some £450 000, and the remorselessly identical cells of Pentonville Prison opening in 1842.[76] It is tempting to construct the story of the English prison as a story of grand institutional evolution, with the early-modern goals and Houses of Correction giving way to the more ambitious and capacious modern prison. There were indeed continuities in policy and experiments in penal policy were features of seventeenth- and early-eighteenth-century England, notably in the development of bridewells in the counties.[77] Moreover, the prison population comprised four quite distinct categories of inmate: those confined awaiting trial; those confined awaiting non-custodial punishments (transportation, execution, or corporal punishment); those sentenced to a term of imprisonment; and undischarged debtors. Of necessity, the presence of all four categories, and the fluctuation in their numbers, rendered county gaols multi-functional institutions, in which regimes were often improvised rather than prescribed. The character of eighteenth-century prisons was further complicated by venality. Gaolers were entailed to fees: from debtors for services, from the county for prisoners confined, and from inmates for privileges, both authorized and unauthorized. We should guard against uncritically accepting the critique of nineteenth-century reformers who regarded privately managed prisons as necessarily inefficient or corrupt. Nevertheless, neither uniformity of practice nor consistency of penal idiom were features of the early-modern prison.[78]

In a period in which policy dictated that those guilty of serious offences would either be transported or executed, the role of the prison within the penal system was limited. Underlying this were moral and prudential assumptions which privileged punishment over rehabilitation, and tended therefore to rid society of serious offenders rather than seek their reform and reintegration. The dramatic change of policy which led to a massive prison-building programme in the English counties in the 60 or so years after John Howard published his *State of Prisons* in 1777 is usually attributed to pressures of numbers on the English penal system. Rises in reported crime, coupled with the suspension of transportation between the closing of America in 1776 and the opening of Australia in 1787, created huge pressures on a crowded and creaking domestic prison system. Typhus – 'gaol fever' – was an ever-present threat. Howard's *State of Prisons* chronicled the combined effects of this crisis of the English prison system.[79] It is, however, equally important to recognize the impact of broader ideological changes on penal policy. The penal revolution that led to the modern penitentiary had its origins in the powerful combination of optimism and the disposition to social regulation that lay at the heart of the Enlightenment.[80] Central to Enlightenment penal theory was a sensationalist psychology in which sin gave way to socialization as the primary explanation for criminal behaviour. Vicious men were the product of a vicious social environment. By changing the social environment, bad men might be rendered good. This is not to suggest that the Enlightenment abandoned notions of punishment and deterrence; but rather, that it married them to new-found faith in the reformability of delinquents and unequivocal assertions of the state's power to embark on social and personal re-engineering.[81]

The penal experiment of the late eighteenth and nineteenth centuries was, then, far more than a grand expedient in better accommodating a growing prison population. It represented a profound realignment of the relationship with state and society, and offered a new framework through which the boundaries between individual rights and social requirements could be forceably negotiated. What is, perhaps, most striking about this new departure in penal policy is that its principal architects were not Members of Parliament but members of Commissions of the Peace, and as a result a national system of penitentiaries was created through the coordinated actions not of central but of local government. Nor, on this occasion at least, did the English invent through experimental empiricism what the Europeans created through theoretical imagination. Sir George Onesiphorous Paul's personal library contained not only Blackstone's *Principles of Penal Law* and Howard's *State of Prisons*, but Beccaria's *Dei Delitte e Delle Pene*, Vilaine's *Moyen de Corriger les Malfaiteurs*, *Théorie de Peines et de Récompenses*, the *Commentaire Criminelle*, and the *Commentaire Civile* of 1767, and his holdings on penal theory were constantly updated.[82] We have already seen that Paul was part of an extensive network of chairmen of Quarter Sessions and other leading magistrates, embracing men such as Zouch in Yorkshire, Willoughby in Oxfordshire, and Bayley in Lancashire. Paul's own speeches on penal reform were frequently published and widely read, and he, like Willoughby, carried considerable weight in official circles as an advisor on penal policy.[83] These networks were deep as well as wide. George Holford, an MP and leading prison reformer, had no hesitation in suggesting in 1821 that the control of magistrates over prisons and penal policy should be extended still further.[84] The Reverend J. T. Becher, a noted advocate of poor law reform and the workhouse system, shared this Enlightenment vision of the reformatory and corrective role of institutional confinement and was equally committed to prison reform. Becher was closely connected to Paul and George

Holford, who played a key role in shaping the reports from the 1810–11 select committee on penitentiaries.[85] George Frederick Stratton was an Oxfordshire magistrate who served as high sheriff in 1806. Stratton went on to rewrite the *Rules* for Oxfordshire's county gaol in 1809. Stratton probably knew Paul personally; he was certainly familiar with his work and with the penal regime that he had developed in Gloucestershire's county gaols. Stratton was equally familiar with penal experiments in Philadelphia and was an Honorary Member of the Society for Diffusing Information on the Subject of Capital Punishment and Prison Discipline, formed in London in 1808.[86] Stratton's *Rules* carefully grounded policy in theory. There were, Stratton insisted, four objects to punishment: to reform the criminal, to remove from society those who have shown by their temper of crime that they are not fit to live in it, to make reparation for injury done to society or one of its members, and to deter others from committing like offences. Stratton's *Rules* were predicated on an inversion of the traditional economy of deterrence, privileging not deterrence or retribution, but rather reformation and rehabilitation. Similarly, Stratton's emphasis on a carefully calibrated penal regime which eschewed physical punishment, and emphasized the disciplines of labour, education, and religion, was wholly consonant with the penal traditions of Enlightenment thought.[87]

Despite variations in local practice, the central features of magistrates' penal experiments were a careful classification of prisoners into distinctive groups, specific regimes for specific categories of inmate, purpose-built prisons, and a faith in the reformatory capacity of labour discipline, when combined with education and religion. The cost of new county gaols was striking. The estimated cost of the new Bedford prison, constructed between 1798 and 1801, was £6850. This was comparatively modest when set alongside the £25 892 that Gloucestershire had spent on its new gaol by 1792, and the £19 000 that Oxfordshire spent on its gaol between 1784 and 1805. Largely as a result of penal policy, expenditure in Lancashire rose from £4000 in 1787 to £47 000 in 1815, and £75 000 by 1820.[88] Equally striking was magistrates' willingness to increase the fiscal burden on ratepayers, believing that this represented a public investment in a more efficient and more humane penal system. By 1834 county expenditure on gaols had reached £214 424, or one-third of total county expenditure.[89]

The Enlightenment optimism that infused the reforming English magistracy eventually ran its course, but not before magistrates had laid the foundations of the modern prison system. County by county, as new prisons were built, new regimes of inspection were set in place. Committees of visiting magistrates were established in most counties long before they were required by Peel's 1823 Gaols Act. Similarly, this Act effectively codified the classification of prisons that counties such as Gloucestershire, Lancashire, and Oxfordshire had pioneered a generation earlier.[90] Simultaneously, prison governance was being professionalized. The fee-receiving gaoler gave way to the salaried prison governor. Governors' salaries came to reflect both their status and the expectations that they shouldered. In Lancashire the county gaoler was receiving an annual salary of £1000 by the 1830s.[91] Prison chaplains came to lavish far greater time on their penal responsibilities, and prison education was taken more seriously and offered more systematically. Treadwheels were installed at considerable expense in the early nineteenth century by magistrates who welcomed the prospect that they offered of calibrating work-discipline. What was being created were totalizing institutions which aspired to create a controlled environment within which the criminal would be reconstructed.[92]

What local government began, central government would ultimately claim. In the heyday of local prisons, national penitentiaries were constructed at Newgate and Pentonville. Moreover, in the counties themselves ambition often outreached achievement, and ratepayers' faith in the fruits of increased penal expenditure was far from unlimited. Hertfordshire magistrates, for example, found themselves financially stretched after modernizing their prison system in the later 1820s and were reluctant to undertake further significant reforms in the 1830s.[93] Sheer pressure of numbers were also beginning to tell. Criminal committals in England and Wales, which had stood at 4605 in 1805, reached 27 187 by 1840. Even the rate of committals per 100 000 of population rose from 48 in 1805 to 173 by 1840.[94] The very existence of larger prisons, and the claims made in support of reformed prison discipline, almost certainly began to influence not only sentencing policy but also the disposition to commit suspects for trial. As Margaret de Lacy has suggested, the unintended consequences of penal reforms sentenced magistrates to a treadwheel of permanent policy reform. In a sense, therefore, the prison reformers who built larger prisons might have helped to create the problem that they wished to solve.[95] Examples of poor management were not difficult to find, and Parliamentary Committees such as the Lords Select Committee Appointed to Inquire into the Present State of Gaols and Houses of Correction in 1835 shared the fashion for focusing tightly on the deficiencies of local government and local management.[96] Penal theory had moved on, and hopes were coming to be invested in the separate, silent cellular prison. In order to facilitate this further instalment of reform, new grants-in-aid of local rates were offered, a prison inspectorate was established in 1835, and power began to shift towards the centre. An ironic centenary celebration of Howard's *State of Prisons*, that manifesto of a local revolution in prison management, was the 1877 Prisons Act, which nationalized prison administration in the Home Office.[97]

From Local Police to Policeman State

The political economy of policing was significantly different from that of penal policy. It is tempting to think of eighteenth-century England as an underpoliced society, and some have succumbed to this temptation. In 1929 Edwin Chadwick told readers of the *London Review* that 'Our system of police consists of disjointed bodies of men, governed separately, under heterogeneous regulations, and acting, for the most part, under the earliest set of expedients: and then only being called upon, seizing or receiving charge of an offender and handing him over to the judicature for punishment'.[98] But this is to constitute modern notions of order, street culture, and the legitimate scope of state coercion as ideal points of reference. Indeed, Chadwick himself, who was to dominate the 1836–9 Royal Commission on the Best Means of Establishing an Efficient Constabulary Force, was firmly committed to a preventative police, with considerable powers of surveillance, and structurally 'well organized'.[99] Hanoverian society was differently ordered, constructed its liberties in different ways, and was suspicious of the cost, intrusiveness, and connotations of regular police forces. Other states – most notably France and Prussia – had different modes of policing, but opinion in

England, certainly in the English provinces, regarded both the style and political leanings of continental police forces as profoundly alien.[100] England's traditional system of police preferred liberty and local control to rigour and surveillance. Its apparent linchpin was the parish constables, appointed annually by magistrates but in reality nominated by local village elites. Many constables served for years, built on their local knowledge, and developed some skills. Nevertheless, in an important sense, they were figures of their local communities, and the system that they represented was essentially one of communal self-regulation. In the words of one guide to constables' responsibilities, the constable was the village community's 'most ancient, most constitutional and most useful officer'.[101] Some parishes did began to establish small paid watch forces to supplement their constables, and some even tried to fund these from the rates, but there were always uneasy tensions between the desire for greater security and the desire for economy. Less contentious than supplementary watch committees were prosecution associations, which sought to deter crime not by increasing the police presence but by underwriting the costs of prosecution through members' subscriptions. In Essex between 1785 and 1791, at least 42 prosecution associations were active.[102] Village prosecution associations were the most significant components in a programme to deter crime in later Hanoverian England without abandoning traditional forms of communal policing.

The situation in urban areas was significantly different. Here population densities gave crime greater anonymity, demographic mobility both encouraged and abetted criminality, and communal disciplines were probably weaker. Improvement Acts frequently established an enhanced police presence and invested the Commissioners, *de facto*, with new police powers. At Cheltenham a postwar crime wave led to the town's being divided into eight districts in 1816, each with its own paid watchman, under the supervision of a superintendent answerable to the Commissioners. The system was strengthened in 1823, and a struggle for control ensued between magistrates and the Commissioners.[103] Many smaller industrial towns in Lancashire turned to Improvement Acts with police powers in the same period. A Police Commission was established under the 1825 Rochdale Improvement Act, and a force of a dozen watchmen then instituted; while two years later the nearby Oldham Commissioner established a paid force of ten constables.[104] Gradually, a police presence was becoming a more prominent part of the street culture of provincial England.

Thus, while it would be misleading to imply that provincial England viewed its police arrangements with panglossian equanimity, until the close of the Napoleonic Wars at least there was a disposition to work within the established framework of amateur local forces supplemented by limited numbers of paid watchmen. The specific economic of deterrence, punishment, and liberty that Hanoverian policing and penal systems established commanded broad support. The price of the liberty that came from lightly policed streets was a high level of ambient crime and a constant extension of capital punishment, from around 50 capital statutes in 1688 to over 200 by 1820.[105] The forces that conspired to promote a shift to a new, more intensive policing idiom are complex. Perhaps the most obvious was the pressures on the traditional economy of deterrence and punishment posed by rapid social, economic, and demographic change. A larger, more densely settled population of itself challenged customary assumptions concerning appropriate patterns of policing. The village constable was both rooted in and reflected the values of village communities. Town watches were developed, in the main through subscriptions and voluntary endeavour, without statutory powers, and under the control of local propertied elites. Neither the traditional constable, nor supplementary systems of watch, were well adapted to new urban conditions and the defence of new forms of property. Nor was it clear how traditional policing systems could be reinforced to meet new challenges. In a celebrated passage, the 1822 Select Committee on Policing the Metropolis concluded that 'It is difficult to reconcile an effective system of policing with that perfect freedom of action and exemption from interference, which are the great blessings and privileges of this country; and your committee think that the forfeiture or curtailment of such advantages would be too great a sacrifice for improvements in police, or facilities in detection of crime, however, desirable in themselves if abstractly considered'.[106] What is less often remarked is that this was the last time that the English state was to take this view, and every subsequent official report recommended an extension of police powers and a move away from traditional, communal, methods of policing.

Changes in social conditions are a necessary but not a sufficient explanation of changes in policing in England in the first half of the nineteenth century. Ideological transformation was at least as important as political transformation. Even as traditional a figure as William Blackstone in the late 1760s perceived a growing structural deficiency in the established economy of deterrence, policing, and punishment. The tendency to increase the nominal scope of the capital deterrent, in default of elaborate systems of police and detection, was in Blackstone's view beginning to diminish the capacity of the death penalty to deter.[107] This sense of the declining efficiency of the death penalty was reinforced by a powerful fusion of late-Enlightenment humanitarianism and evangelical philanthropy, culminating in sustained pressure for the abatement of capital punishment in the early nineteenth century. Societies such as the Society for Diffusing Information on Punishment by Death, and William Allen's influential journal *The Philanthropist*, might have been organized in Regency London, but they had supporters and a readership in the provinces.[108] The implication of reducing the number of capital statutes, as pressed in parliament by Sir Samuel Romilly and Sir James Mackintosh, was a reconfiguration in the economy of deterrence, in which a more efficient police led to a more certain enforcement of the law, which was seen as constituting a more effective deterrent. No-one insisted more strongly on the association of penal and police reform than Robert Peel who, at the Home Office between 1822 and 1830, carried substantial measures of prison reform and a series of Acts designed to liberalize and partially to codify the criminal law. Peel's modernizing vision culminated in the establishment of the Metropolitan Police in 1829.[109]

Peel clearly intended that the Metropolitan Force would offer the provinces both a model of reformed policing and a reservoir of trained officers from which senior officers for borough and county forces might be drawn. Peel was abetted in his reforming drive by newly available criminal statistics. Annual records of committals to trial had been kept since 1805. By the late 1820s these figures seemed to tell an inexorably and dismal story, with committals rising from 48 per 100 000 of population in 1805 to 137 per 1000 by 1829.[110] As a statistical representation of trends in crime, still less as a revelation of the criminal disposition, such statistics concealed as much as they revealed.[111] Nevertheless, in the new context of policy-making in the later 1820s and against a background of growing anxiety with existing policing methods, statistics could be seized upon as empirically establishing a problem, and legitimating solutions, which had already been theorized.

If there was a crime wave and an associated crisis of policing – and the Royal Commission on Establishing a Constabulary Force, which sat between 1836 and 1939, certainly thought there was – this was not confined to the new industrial cities.[112] Thomas Plint combed the official statistics and established that crime was rising more rapidly in rural counties, such as Bedfordshire, Buckinghamshire, Herefordshire, and Somerset, than it was in urban areas such as Middlesex, Nottinghamshire, and Lancashire.[113] Nor were the governors of provincial England insensitive to the problems that they faced. Paid watches became increasingly common, sometimes funded out of the rates, but more generally through a subscription of the major ratepayers who were well aware that paying police officers a salary from the rate was legally dubious. Thus at Stow-on-the-Wold when a paid watch was established in 1834 following a brutal local murder, the vestry initially voted £10 towards the salary and then rapidly switched to meeting salary costs from a subscription.[114] Cheshire magistrates secured a local act to establish a new County Constabulary in 1829, based on hundreds under the control of stipendiary high constables.[115] A number of counties began experiments with new methods of policing in the 1830s, and as early as January 1831 Shropshire magistrates were considering establishing a paid county constabulary.[116] In February 1839, Shropshire magistrates carried a motion that 'a body of constables appointed by the magistrates, paid out of the county rate, and disposable at any point in the Shire where their services might be required, would be highly desirable'.[117] This resolution was seized upon by Lord John Russell, as Home Secretary, and circulated by him to all chairmen of Quarter Sessions. The effect was to put reform of county constabularies firmly on the political agenda well before the Royal Commission of Constabulary Force reported later in the year. Throughout the 1830s the Whig governments had been seeking ways in which to carry forward the momentum established by Peel's Metropolitan Police Act in 1829. Police reform was clearly integral to the social and political vision that helped to drive the reform of the poor laws, prisons, education, factories, and municipal corporations. An ambitious scheme, which would have established paid police forces under the control of a national system of stipendiary magistrates appointed by the Home Secretary, failed in 1832 when Tories signalled opposition and Lord Melbourne, as Home Secretary, concentrated parliamentary time and political capital on carrying poor law reform.[118] The 1835 Municipal Corporations Act established paid police forces under the control of police committees of the reformed councils.[119] A year later, the government established the Royal Commission on Establishing a Constabulary Force. Under Edwin Chadwick's eager tutelage, the Commission gathered prodigious volumes of evidence and moved inexorably towards recommending the establishment of the kind of national force that Chadwick had been advocating sine 1829.

With magistrates known to be committed to retaining their control over the appointment of constables and patterns of policing in the English counties, the Shropshire Quarter Sessions' motion came as a godsend to Lord John Russell. Faced with known structural problems and, in many areas, the spectre of Chartist disturbances, most Quarter Sessions agreed that police reform was imperative, always provided that it was carried within the framework of local magisterial control.[120] The 1839 Rural Constabulary Act provided for the establishment of paid county forces under the direction of Chief Constables appointed by, and responsible to, magistrates.[121] The Act was permissive, and vigorous debate ensued in Quarter Sessions over adoption. In the event, 22 English counties adopted the Act within two years of its being passed, including all counties with sizeable urban populations. Other counties placed their faith in the 1842 Parish Constables Act, which provided for the appointment of salaried constables under existing jurisdictions.[122] Within little more than a decade, the framework for a new policing infrastructure had been elaborated.

What is striking about police reform, as it emerged in the Municipal Corporations and the Rural Constabulary Acts, was that it acknowledged the legitimacy of control by local authorities. It promulgated centralized ideas of what now constituted good practice, but it did not centralize control. Many in power in provincial England were happy to embrace police reform on these terms.

For others, though, the fear of centralization was sufficiently strong for them to see a centralizing agenda lurking behind the mask of permissive or limited reform. Kent Quarter Sessions had fierce debates over police reform in 1839, and rejected adopting the new Act by the narrow margin of three votes a year later. By 1849 resistance had hardened, and a motion to adopt the Act was lost by 30 votes. One magistrate told his colleagues in 1839 that 'The System would go far to complete that principle of centralization ... [would] interfere with the administration of the law by the unpaid magistracy ... [and] is bound to be followed by a paid magistracy'.[123] On 16 August 1839, the Corporation at Exeter passed a motion protesting that the appointment of commissioners of police paid from local taxation was 'contrary to the spirit of the constitution'.[124] Nevertheless, Exeter's experience after the 1835 Act was not untypical. It moved swiftly to a new style force, experienced acute problems initially in recruiting and retaining suitable officers, but by 1847 had a force led by a superintendent, on the far from niggardly annual salary of £120, supported by five inspectors, three sergeants, and 17 constables.[125] Similarly, at Banbury the Watch Committee that managed the new force after the passage of the Municipal Corporations Act began by trying to modernize its existing watch and inculcate a new discipline. By 1840 it abandoned its policy of putting new wine into old skins, gave notice to the watch, and started afresh.[126] These local experiences underline the acute problems in making the transition from traditional modes of watching to a more activist policing idiom.[127]

Those who perceived a centralizing intention in police reform were vindicated, in part at least, by the prescriptive Terms of the County and Borough Police Act of 1856.[128] The Act obliged those counties which had not adopted the 1839 Act to establish constabulary forces with immediate effect. Central grants-in-aid were now made available to help support the costs of policing in the counties, and three inspectors of constabulary were appointed with powers to designate local forces efficient, or not.[129] The move towards a professional police was decisively consolidated. The civic republicans of Exeter remained trenchantly, if vainly, opposed to developments in policing, protesting against the 1856 Act and claiming that 'the general principle of centralization which characterizes the whole Bill, taking from local Rate payers and Local Authorities all power and justification within their ancient limits

and vesting them in individual members of a Government to
whom the Bill gives absolute powers, is contrary to the constitution of the country and an uncalled for and unnecessary innovation'.[130] In fact, the 1856 Act did not create a centralized system
so much as impose a centralized idea of policing on administra-
tively semi-autonomous county constabularies. What was being
constructed was not a police state but a 'policeman state'.[131] It is
difficult to measure the efficiency of these new forces in any
general sense. What does seem to have been generally true,
though, was that a more professional police was initially very
effective in reducing petty crime. Characteristically poorly organized working class crime, typically petty larceny, did decline in
the later nineteenth century.[132] The decline of theft is clearly
etched in the criminal statistics of later Victorian England, and it
is not difficult to imagine the cultural and ideological changes
that this implied and reflected. Ideas of domesticity, an expansive
private domain, and the security of property were all wholly consonant with a more ostentatiously and rigorously policed society.

Equally significant for contemporaries, and less obviously nar-
rated in the statistical records, was the change in the street culture
of provincial England. Sensible of ratepayers' hostility to what
they might regard as needless inflation in local taxation, police
committees concentrated on policies that might persuade ratepayers of the value of new forces. Campaigns against street violence,
vagrants, disorderly behaviour, and petty street crime were thus
commonplace.[133] A relatively untrained force, as yet imbued with
only a rudimentary policing ethic and bereft of a sophisticated
culture of detection, was well suited to the straightforward policing of public spaces. In rural villages traditional amusements were
often vigorously challenged. Public spaces became more ordered,
decorous, and sanitized. By the later nineteenth century police
were doing above ground what new sewers were doing below
ground, creating an environment which was visibly cleaner,
healthier, and safer. Prisons, workhouses, lunatic asylums, and
hospitals removed ever greater numbers of the sick, the wander-
ing, the delinquent, and those given to molesting the respectable
by begging, vagrancy, and abuse. It is important not to draw this
picture too starkly, but it does sketch something of profound
ideological and cultural importance. Slowly, hesitantly, and in a
very distinctive way, provincial England had passed from the

world of Hogarth and Fielding to the world of Chadwick and Mrs Oliphant. In the process, the relationship between society and state had been renegotiated, and an old order in provincial England was gradually passing away.

NOTES

1. Peter Borsay, '"All the Town's a Stage": Urban Ritual and Ceremony', in Peter Clark (ed.), *The Transformation of English Provincial Towns 1600–1800* (London, 1984), pp. 228–58, here at p. 230.
2. Vernon, *Politics and the People*, pp. 70–1.
3. Cirket (ed.), *Samuel Whitbread's Notebooks*.
4. Alun Howkins, 'The English Farm Labourer in the Nineteenth Century: Farm, Family and Community', in Brian Short (ed.), *The English Rural Community. Image and Analysis* (Cambridge, 1992), pp. 85–104; Jefferies, *Hodge and his Masters*, pp. 15–21, 44–5.
5. See above, pp. 29–30.
6. C. H. E. Zangerl, 'The Social Composition of the County Magistracy in England and Wales 1831–87', *Journal of British Studies*, xi (1971), 113–25.
7. Temple Patterson, *Radical Leicester*, pp. 64–70.
8. Public Records Office, HO 42/21/478, MS 'List of Addresses which have been sent to His Majesty'.
9. Mark Philp, 'Vulgar Conservatism, 1792–3', *English Historical Review*, cx (1995), 42–69; Robert Dozier, *For King, Constitution, and Country. The English Loyalists and the French Revolution* (Lexington KY, 1983), pp. 55–171; Austin Mitchell, 'The Association Movement of 1792–3', *Historical Journal*, iv (1961), 56–77; D. E. Ginter, 'The Loyalist Association Movement of 1792–3', *Historical Journal*, ix (1966), 179–90; Watson, 'Liberty, Loyalty, and Locality'.
10. John Cookson, 'The English Volunteer Movement of the French Wars, 1793–1815: Some Contexts', *Historical Journal*, xxxii (1989), 867–91; Eastwood, 'Patriotism and the English State', 158–60.
11. Fisher, *Notes and Recollections of Stroud*, p. 80.
12. London Corresponding Society, '*Address to the Inhabitants of Great Britain, on the Subject of Parliamentary Reform*' [1792]; reprinted in Cobban (ed.), *The Debate on the French Revolution*, pp. 206–7.
13. R. B. Rose, 'The Priestley Riots of 1791', *Past and Present*, no. 18 (1960), 68–88; Money, *Experience and Identity*, pp. 223–9, 261–3, 276–82.
14. Prentice, *Historical Sketches and Personal Recollections of Manchester*, pp. 8, 10; original emphases.
15. *Records of the Borough of Leicester*, pp. 284, 325–6, 330, 394.
16. M. G. Hobson (ed.), *Oxford Council Acts 1792–1801* (Oxford, 1962), pp. 222, 256, 269; Dozier, *For King, Constitution, and Country*, pp. 55–171.

17.   Although for the resilience of reformism in the later war years, see J. E. Cookson, *The Friends of Peace: Anti-war Liberalism in England, 1793–1815* (Cambridge, 1982).

18.   Michael Turner, *English Parliamentary Enclosure. Its Geography and Economic History* (Folkestone, 1980), 66–82.

19.   W. E. Tate, 'The Cost of Parliamentary Enclosure in England (with Special Reference to the County of Oxford)', *Economic History Review*, 2nd ser., v (1952), 258–65; W. E. Tate, *The Village Community and the Enclosure Movements* (London, 1967).

20.   The standard accounts include W. E. Tate, 'Opposition to Parliamentary Enclosure in Eighteenth-century England', *Agricultural History Review*, xix (1945), 137–42; W. E. Tate, 'Parliamentary Counter-petitions during the Enclosures of the Eighteenth and Nineteenth Centuries', *English Historical Review*, lix (1944), 393–403; J. D. Chambers and G. E. Mingay, *The Agricultural Revolution 1750–1880* (London, 1966), pp. 77–105; G. E. Mingay, *Enclosure and the Small Farmer in the Age of the Industrial Revolution* (London and Basingstoke, 1968). An important reassessment was developed by Keith Snell in *Annals of the Labouring Poor*, pp. 138–227.

21.   J. M. Neeson, *Commoners; Common Right, Enclosure and Social Change in England, 1700–1820* (Cambridge, 1993), esp. pp. 259–93; J. M. Neeson, 'The Opponents of Enclosure in Eighteenth-century Northamptonshire', *Past and Present*, 105 (1984), 114–39.

22.   David Eastwood, 'Communities, Protest and Police in Early-nineteenth-century Oxfordshire: the Enclosure of Otmoor Reconsidered', *Agricultural History Review*, xliv (1996), 35–46; A. V. Brown, 'The Last Phase of the Enclosure of Otmoor', *Oxoniensia*, xxxii (1967), 35–52; B. Reaney, *The Class Struggle in Nineteenth-century Oxfordshire. The Social and Communal Background to the Otmoor Disturbances* (Oxford, 1970).

23.   Turner, *English Parliamentary Enclosure*, p. 71.

24.   Neeson, *Commoners*, pp. 110–84, 221–58; Thompson, *Customs in Common*, pp. 97–184.

25.   J. H. Clapham, 'The Growth of an Agricultural Proletariat 1688–1832, a Statistical Note', *Cambridge Historical Journal*, i (1923), 92–5.

26.   Peter King, 'Gleaners, Farmers and the Failure of Legal Sanctions in England 1750–1850', *Past and Present*, 125 (1989), 116–50; Peter King, 'Customary Rights and Women's Earnings: the Importance of Gleaning to the Rural Labouring Poor, 1750–1850', *Economic History Review*, xliv (1991), 461–76.

27.   As is demonstrated in Snell, *Annals of the Labouring Poor*, pp. 194–207. I am sceptical of George R. Boyer's brief restatement of the counter-case to enclosure's contributing to inflation in real levels of per capita poor relief, in *Economic History of the English Poor Law*, p. 143.

28.   James Caird, *English Agriculture in 1850–51* [1852], new edn, intro. G. E. Mingay (New York, 1967), esp. pp. 473–530; F. M. L. Thompson, 'The Second Agricultural Revolution, 1815–1880', *Economic History Review*, 2nd ser., xxi (1968), 62–77; E. L. Jones, 'The Changing Basis of English Agricultural Prosperity, 1853–73', *Agricultural History*

Review, x (1962), 102–19; Chambers and Mingay, *Agricultural Revolution*, pp. 170–98.

29. For a helpful survey, see Alun Howkins, *Reshaping Rural England A Social History 1850–1925* (London, 1991). For responses, see W. J. Keith, *The Rural Tradition* (Hassocks, 1975), pp. 105–252; E. W. Martin (ed.), *Country Life in England* (London, 1966), pp. 180–232.

30. S. and B. Webb, 'The Assize of Bread', *Economic Journal*, xiv (1904), 196–218; William Smart, *Economic Annals of the Nineteenth Century*, 2 vols (London, 1910/17), i, pp. 368–9, 199–400; Boyd Hilton, *Corn, Cash, Commerce. The Economic Policies of the Tory Governments 1815–1830* (Oxford, 1977), pp. 26–8, 102–6; Eastwood, *Governing Rural England*, pp. 44–6.

31. Eastwood, 'The Enclosure of Otmoor Reconsidered'.

32. Hart, *History of Cheltenham*, pp. 244, 269; cf. Prest, *Liberty and Locality*, pp. 4, 57.

33. Figures are given in 1750 prices and calculated from *Local Taxation Return*, P.P., 1839, xliv (562); B. R. Mitchell, *Abstract of British Historical Statistics* (Cambridge, 1962); and Woods, *The Population of Britain in the Nineteenth Century*. The Schumpeter–Gilboy and Gayer, Rostow, and Schwarz indices were used as deflators, and the figures should be treated with considerable caution.

34. *Abstract of the Poor*, P.P., 1803–4, xiii (175); *Abstract of the Poor [1813–1815]*, P.P., 1818, xix (82); Karel Williams, *From Pauperism to Poverty* (London, 1981), 149.

35. *Poor Law Report of 1834*, p. 193.

36. Ibid., p. 194.

37. *Reports from Select Committee on Select Vestries*, P.P., 1829, iv (25 & 215).

38. Joseph Mayett, *The Autobiography of Joseph Mayett of Quainton 1783–1839*, ed. Ann Kussmaul, Buckinghamshire Record Society, 23 (1986), 77–8; original capitalization and spelling.

39. *Report from the Royal Commissioner on the Poor Laws. Reports of Assistant Commissioners*, P.P., 1834, xxviii (44), 156A.

40. David Davies, *The Case of Labourers in Husbandry Stated and Considered* (London, 1795); quotations at pp. 40 and 4.

41. Eden, *State of the Poor*, esp. pp. i, 85–128.

42. *Reports of the Society for Bettering the Condition and Increasing the Comforts of the Poor*, 7 vols (London, 1798–1817); cf. Wells, *Wretched Faces*, pp. 202–29.

43. Eastwood, 'Rethinking the Debates on the Poor Law in Early Nineteenth-century England'.

44. Malthus's position was set out most starkly and most dramatically in *An Essay on the Principle of Population* [1798], ed. A. Flew (Harmondsworth, 1970), pp. 73–103.

45. T. R. Malthus, 'A Letter to Samuel Whitbread Esq. on the Subject of the Poor Laws' [1807] printed in D. V. Glass (ed.), *Introduction to Malthus* (London, 1959), p. 191. See also Anne Digby, 'Malthus and the Reform of the English Poor Law', in M. Turner (ed.), *Malthus and his Time* (London, 1986), pp. 157–69.

46.   J. R. Poynter, *Society and Pauperism. English Ideas on Poor Relief,
1795–1834* (London, 1969), pp. 144–77; G. Himmelfarb, *The Idea of
Poverty* (London, 1984), pp. 100–44; James Huzel, 'Demographic Impact
of the Old Poor Law', *Economic History Review*, 2nd ser., xxxiii (1980),
367–81; James Huzel, 'Malthus, the Poor Law, and Population', *Economic
History Review*, 2nd ser., xxii (1969) 430–52.
47.   Slack, *The English Poor Law*, pp. 17–34, 49–58; Hampson,
Treatment of Poverty in Cambridgeshire 1597–1834; Webbs, *Old Poor Law*,
pp. 60–95.
48.   Cited in Joan Johnson, *Stow-on-the-Wold* (Gloucester, 1980),
p. 115.
49.   Eastwood, *Governing Rural England*, pp. 156–7, 169–72; Snell,
Annals of the Labouring Poor, pp. 106–8, 128.
50.   Mayett, *Autobiography*, p. 10.
51.   Boyer, *Economic History of the English Poor Law*, pp. 85–145, argues
this case in considerable statistical detail.
52.   Hayton to Poor Law Commissioners, 31 October 1834, printed in
Donald (ed.), *Letters of Thomas Hayton*.
53.   James S. Taylor, 'The Unreformed Workhouse', in E. W. Martin
(ed.), *Comparative Development in Social Welfare* (London, 1972), pp. 57–84.
54.   Hans Meier, 'Welfare and Health of Children and Adolescents in
Early Modern England and Southern Germany. Case Studies of Bampton
(Oxfordshire) and Oettingen (Southern Germany) in the Seventeenth
and Eighteenth Centuries', D.Phil. thesis, University of Oxford (1995);
Eastwood, 'The Republic in the English Village'.
55.   Alannah Tomkins, 'The Experience of Urban Poverty – a
Comparison of Oxford and Shrewsbury 1740 to 1770', D.Phil. thesis,
University of Oxford (1994).
56.   22 Geo. III c. 83; T. Gilbert, *A Scheme for the Better Relief and
Employment of the Poor …* (London, 1764); T. Gilbert, *Plan for the Better
Relief of the Poor* (London, 1781); T. Gilbert, *Heads of a Bill for the Better
Relief and Employment of the Poor* (London, 1787).
57.   Mark Neuman, 'A Suggestion Regarding the Origins of the
Speenhamland Plan', *English Historical Review*, lxxxiv (1969), 317–22;
Neuman, *The Speenhamland County*, pp. 80–1, 85–6.
58.   R. Mitchison, 'The Old Board of Agriculture (1793–1822)',
English Historical Review, lxxiv (1959), 41–69.
59.   Peter Dunkley, *The Crisis of the Old Poor Law in England
1795–1834. An Interpretative Essay* (New York and London, 1982),
pp. 80–91, 142–6; Boyer, *Economic History of the English Poor Law*,
pp. 10–14, 71–83; Eastwood, *Governing Rural England*, pp. 112–17, 136–54.
60.   *Poor Law Report of 1834*, pp. 215–17.
61.   Pitt Papers, P.R.O. 30/8/307, fos 248–312.
62.   *Report from Select Committee on Poor Laws, P.P.*, 1817, vi (462); *Report
of the Lords Select Committee on the Poor Laws, P.P.*, 1818, v (400); Eastwood,
'Rethinking the Debates on the Poor Law'.
63.   Foster, *The Politics of County Power*, p. 44.

64.   M. Blaug, 'The Myth of the Old Poor Law and the Making of the New', reprinted in M. W. Flinn and T. C. Smout (eds), *Essays in Social History* (Oxford, 1974), pp. 123–53; M. Blaug, 'The Poor Law Report Reexamined', *Journal of Economic History*, xxiv (1964), 229–45; Anthony Brundage, *Making of the New Poor Law, 1832–39*, (London, 1978), pp. 15–74.

65.   See William Day, *An Inquiry into the Poor Law and Surplus Labour, and their Mutual Reaction*, 2nd edn (London, 1833).

66.   Peter Dunkley, 'Whigs and Paupers: The Reform of the English Poor Laws, 1830–1834', *Journal of British Studies*, xx (1981), 124–49; Peter Mandler, *Aristocratic Government in the Age of Reform. Whigs and Liberals 1830–1852* (Oxford, 1990), pp. 131–41.

67.   Hansard, 3rd ser., 1834, xxii, 885.

68.   Hansard, 3rd ser., 1834, xxiii, 996.

69.   Hansard, 3rd ser., 1834, xxiii, 963.

70.   John Walter, *A Letter to the Electors of Berkshire* (London, 1834); Nicholas C. Edsall, *The Anti-Poor Law Movement 1834–44* (Manchester, 1971), pp. 15–21; Himmelfarb, *The Idea of Poverty*, pp. 177–80.

71.   Driver, *Power and Pauperism*, pp. 32–57.

72.   John Knott, *Popular Opposition to the 1834 Poor Law* (London, 1986); Edsall, *The Anti-Poor Law Movement*.

73.   Notably Anthony Brundage in *The Making of the New Poor Law*, pp. 105–44; 'Landed Interest and the New Poor Law', *English Historical Review* lxxxvii (1972), 27–48; 'English Poor Law of 1834 and the Cohesion of Agricultural Society', *Agricultural History*, xlix (1974), 405–17.

74.   William Apfel and Peter Dunkley, 'English Rural Society and the New Poor Law: Bedfordshire 1834–1847', *Social History*, x (1985), 37–68; Philip Harling, 'The Power of Pauperism: Central Authority, Local Bureaucracy and the New Poor Law, *English Historical Review*, cvii (1992), 30–53.

75.   Thomas Hayton to Poor Law Commissioners, 12 February 1835, printed in Donald (ed.), *Letters of Thomas Hayton*, p. 20.

76.   Ignatieff, *A Just Measure of Pain*, pp. 3–14; 170–3; S. and B. Webb, *English Prisons Under Local Government*, pp. 45–8.

77.   Joanna Innes, 'Prisons for the Poor: English Bridewells, 1555–1800', in Francis Snyder and Douglas Hay (eds), *Labour, Law, and Crime. An Historical Perspective* (London, 1987), pp. 42–122.

78.   The classic statement of the venality of eighteenth-century prisons in the Webbs, *English Prisons under Local Government*, pp. 1–31. Margaret de Lacy offers a somewhat modified picture in *Prison Reform in Lancashire, 1700–1850*, pp. 15–69. Joanna Innes's work is particularly important: see 'Prisons for the Poor', and 'The King's Bench Prison in the Later Eighteenth Century: Law, Authority, and Order in a London Debtors' Prison', in John Brewer and John Styles (eds), *An Ungovernable People. The English and Their Law in the Seventeenth and Eighteenth Centuries* (London, 1980), pp. 250–98.

79.   Howard, *The State of Prisons*; de Lacy, *Prison Reform in Lancashire*, pp. 18–19.

80.   Ignatieff, *A Just Measure of Pain*, pp. 44–79.

81.   This remaking of the economy of punishment is put in starkest terms in Michel Foucault, *Discipline and Punish. The Birth of the Prison*, Penguin edn (Harmondsworth, 1979).

82.   Moir, 'Sir George Onesiphorous Paul', 199.

83.   G. O. Paul, *A Statement of the Proceedings on the Subject of a Reform of the Prisons Within the County of Gloucester* (Gloucester, 1783); *idem, Address to the Justices of the County of Glocester Assembled at their Michaelmas General Quarter Sessions* (Gloucester, 1789); *idem, An Address to the Magistrates of the County of Glocester* (1978); *idem, Address to His Majesty's Justices of the Peace for the County of Glocester, on the Administration and Practical Effects of the System, of Prison Regulation* ... (Gloucester, 1809).

84.   Holford, *Thoughts on the Criminal Prisons of this Country*, pp. 12–24.

85.   Sean McConville, *History of English Prison Administration*, pp. 112–34; Webbs, *English Prisons under Local Government*, pp. 60–72.

86.   *Address of the Society for Diffusing Information on the Subject of Capital Punishment and Prison Discipline* (London, 1817), p. 9.

87.   G. F. Stratton, *Proposed Rules, Orders and Regulations for the Castle Gaol at Oxford* (Cheltenham, 1809).

88.   J. R. S. Whiting, *Prison Reform in Gloucestershire 1776–1820* (London, 1975), pp. 14–15; Oxfordshire Archives, Clerk of the Peace's Notebook, CPN I, p. 1; Stockdale, *Study of Bedford Prison*, p. 87; de Lacy, *Prison Reform in Lancashire*, pp. 154–7.

89.   *Royal Commission on County Rates*, 'Particulars of County Rate Expenditure', 1834, *P.P.*, 1836, xxvii (58), 284–5.

90.   4 George IV c. 64.

91.   de Lacy, *Prison Reform in Lancashire*, p. 166.

92.   William James Forsythe, *The Reform of Prisoners 1830–1900* (London, 1987), pp. 1–43; Randall McGowen, 'A Powerful Sympathy: Terror, the Prison, and Humanitarian Reform in Early Nineteenth-century Britain', *Journal of British Studies*, xxv (1986), 312–34.

93.   W. J. Hardy, *Hertford County Records*, 10 vols (Hertford, 1905–57), x, 200, 211–15.

94.   *Returns on Committals*, *P.P.*, 1819, xvii (59); 1831/2, xxxiii (282); 1835, xlv (217); 1841, xviii (318).

95.   *Prison Reform in Lancashire*, p. 64.

96.   *Reports from the Lords Select Committee Appointed to Inquire into the Present State of Gaols and Houses of Correction, P. P.*, 1835, vii (438), xi (42).

97.   William James Forsythe, 'Centralization and Local Autonomy: the Experience of English Prisons 1820–1877', *Journal of Historical Sociology*, iv (1991), 317–45; McConville, *History of English Prison Administration*, pp. 468–82.

98.	[Edwin Chadwick], 'Preventative Police', *London Review*, i, (1829), 252; cf. J. J. Tobias, *Crime and Industrial Society in the Nineteenth Century*, Penguin edn (Harmondsworth, 1972), p. 268.

99.	Chadwick, 'Preventative Police', 252–3.

100.	Clive Emsley, *Policing and its Context 1750–1870* (London and Basingstoke, 1983), pp. 8–75.

101.	J. Ritson, *The Office of Constable* (London, 1791), p. iii.

102.	Peter King, 'Prosecution Associations and Their Impact in Eighteenth-century Essex', in Douglas Hay and Francis Synder (eds), *Policing and Prosecution in Britain 1750–1850* (Oxford, 1989), pp. 171–207, here at pp. 185–8.

103.	Hart, *History of Cheltenham*, pp. 273–5.

104.	E. C. Midwinter, *Social Administration in Lancashire 1830–1860* (Manchester, 1969), p. 137.

105.	The real impact of new capital status was attenuated by the highly particularistic nature of the English law: see Joanna Innes and John Styles, 'The Crime Wave: Recent Writing on Crime and Criminal Justice in Eighteenth-century England', *Journal of British Studies*, xxv (1986), 380–435.

106.	*Report from the Select Committee on Policing the Metropolis, P.P.*, 1822, iv (440), 11.

107.	Blackstone, *Commentaries on the Laws of England*, iv. pp. 16–19.

108.	David Eastwood, 'Men, Morals, and the Machinery of Social Legislation, 1790–1840', *Parliamentary History*, xiii (1994), 190–205, here at 192–8.

109.	V. A. C. Gattrell, *The Hanging Tree. Execution and the English People 1770–1868* (Oxford, 1994), pp. 566–85.

110.	*Returns on Committals, P.P.*, 1819, xvii (59), 313; 1831/2, xxxii (282); 1835, xlv (217).

111.	V. A. C. Gatrell and T. B. Hadden, 'Criminal Statistics and their Interpretation', in E. A. Wrigley (ed.), *Nineteenth Century Society* (Cambridge, 1972).

112.	*Report from the Royal Commission on Constabulary Force, P.P.*, 1839, xix (169).

113.	T. Plint, *Crime in England, its Relation, Character and Extent as Developed from 1801 to 1848* (London, 1851), pp. 14–25. Plint did not examine the real incidence of crime, merely trends in recorded statistics.

114.	Johnson, *Stow-on-the-Wold*, p. 183.

115.	Clive Emsley, *Crime and Society in England 1750–1900* (London, 1987), p. 183.

116.	Experiments in policing in the 1830s have been admirably discussed in Robert D. Storch, 'Policing Rural Southern England before the Police: Opinion and Practice, 1830–1856', in Douglas Hay and Francis Synder (eds), *Policing and Prosecution in Britain 1750–1850* (Oxford, 1989), 211–64. For Shropshire, see Douglas J. Elliott, *Policing Shropshire 1836–1967* (Studley, 1984), p. 13.

117.	*Constabulary Force. Circular Letter of Lord John Russell to Chairman of Quarter Sessions, P.P.*, xlvii, 517–22.

118.   David Philips and Robert D. Storch, 'Whigs and Coppers: The Grey Ministry's National Police Scheme, 1832', *Historical Research*, 1xvii (1994), 75–90.
119.   Jennifer Hart, 'The Reform of the Borough Police, 1835–1856', *English Historical Review*, 1xx (1955), 411–27.
120.   *P. P.*, 1839, x1vii, 517–22; F. C. Mather, *Public Order in the Age of the Chartists* (Manchester, 1959), pp. 75–140.
121.   3 & 4 Vic. c. 93; Storch, 'Policing Rural Southern England', 236–42.
122.   *Select Committee on the Parish Constables Bill, P.P.*, 1842, xiv (107–10).
123.   Carolyn Steedman, *Policing the Victorian Community. The Formation of English Provincial Police Forces, 1856–80* (London, 1984), pp. 18–19.
124.   Newton, *Victorian Exeter*, p. 62.
125.   Newton, *Victorian Exeter*, p. 64.
126.   Oxfordshire Archives, Minutes of the Banbury Watch Committee 1836–66, B. B. V/ii/1.
127.   David Philips, *Crime and Authority in Victorian England. The Black Country 1835–1860* (London, 1977), pp. 53–95; B. J. Davey, *Lawless and Immoral. Policing a Country Town, 1838–1857* (Leicester, 1983); Michael Weaver, 'The New Science on Policing: Crime and the Birmingham Police', *Albion*, xxvi (1994), 289–308.
128.   19 & 20 Vic. c. 69.
129.   Steedman, *Policing The Victorian Community*, pp. 27, 38.
130.   Minutes of Corporation, 19 February 1856, printed in Newton, *Victorian Exeter*, p. 62.
131.   The term is Dr Gatrell's: see V. A. C. Gatrell, 'Crime, Authority, and the Policeman State', in F. M. L. Thompson (ed.), *The Cambridge Social History of Britain 1750–1950*, 3 vols (Cambridge, 1990), iii, pp. 243–310.
132.   V. A. C. Gatrell, 'The Decline of Theft and Violence in Victorian England and Wales', in V. A. C. Gatrell, B. Lenman, and G. Parker (eds), *Crime and the Law: the Social History of Crime in Western Europe since 1500* (London, 1980).
133.   Robert D. Storch, '"The Plague of Blue Locusts": Police Reform and Popular Resistance in Northern England, 1840–57', *International Review of Social History*, xx (1975), 61–90; Robert D. Storch, 'The Policeman as Domestic Missionary: Urban Discipline and Popular Culture in Northern England, 1850–1880', *Journal of Social History*, ix (1976), 481–509.

6 Remaking the Public Domain in Provincial England

Describing the Present and Theorizing Change

Viewed from the perspective of the provinces, the English polity of the mid-nineteenth century differed profoundly from that of the mid-eighteenth. The state's institutional superstructure had been dramatically modified. The Old Poor Law had given way to the New; Municipal Corporations had been remodelled, given a representative character, and were being extended to new industrial towns; the challenge of public health was increasingly likely to be confronted not by traditional authorities but by new public health unions; constables were becoming policemen; and inspectors of factories, prisons, and schools, were busily carrying a gospel of efficiency and good practice from the centre into the localities. The changes which were remodelling the English state were often couched in the language of 'reform'. The transition from the eighteenth-century language of improvement to the nineteenth-century language of reform is of itself important, but the language of reform, at least as deployed in the years after 1820, carried increasingly heavy ideological and social baggage. Behind changes in the superstructural apparatus of the English state lay perhaps more important – and certainly more elusive – transitions in the social distribution of power.

Something of this emerges from the strikingly dialectical discourses on the nature and ideological form of the English state in the mid-nineteenth century. At one extreme was Joshua Toulmin Smith and the 'Association of Parochial Representatives', who inveighed against centralization as an abstract idea and sought to expose it as the governing principle of public health legislation in

155

the 1850s.[1] Toulmin Smith's formulation of the centralizing principle was nothing if not polemical: 'The system of Centralization ... is one by which the energies and activity and enterprise of men in their political, social, moral, and intellectual relations are fettered and tied down, and subjected to the caprice and made liable to the arbitrary will of a few irresponsible functionaries'. The disposition of centralizers was, Toulmin Smith concluded, 'in direct and perpetual antagonism' with local self-government.[2] Toulmin Smith himself was deeply involved in the campaign against the 1848 Public Health Act, which he saw as creating the circumstances for 'the widest possible extension of the centralizing principle'. In a stance which flatly opposed that of Edwin Chadwick, Sir John Simon, and Lord Morpeth, Toulmin Smith believed that matters such as public health, being 'so nearly connected with individual well-being and social comfort', were 'necessarily Local in their character' and thus fell 'peculiarly within the range and duty of Local Self-Government'.[3] At another extreme was Edwin Chadwick, who persisted in seeing local authorities as irrational obstacles to urgently necessary reforms, responsible for frustrating the New Poor Law, slowing the pace of police reform, and ensuring that the mountainous reports on the public health problem in the 1840s brought forth a mouse in the form of the 1848 Public Health Act. Chadwick's 1842 *Report on the Sanitary Condition of the Labouring Population of Great Britain*, like the 1834 *Report from the Royal Commissioners on the Poor Law* which he co-authored, embodied a sustained indictment of the competence and motivation of the present governors of provincial England. In calling for the establishment of new Sanitary Districts and new Boards of Health, Chadwick stressed 'the necessity of lifting these important branches of administration out of the influence of petty and sinister interests'.[4] Chadwick never denied the importance of local interests or the need for limited local control: what he did continually insist upon, though, was that local control should be vested in a different class of men, differently accountable, and under the superintendence of a central board with widely ramified powers.

Toulmin Smith and Chadwick indicate something of the starkness of debate over directions in English political formation in the early Victorian period, but representing the debate in these polarized terms is to risk oversimplification. Profound changes notwithstanding, older traditions and political cultures survived, albeit in modified forms. Hippolyte Taine, writing in the early 1860s, described an English polity which was sharply differentiated from that of Bonapartist France. Voluntarism and localism retained their place in English political culture, with English elite social attitudes still informed by a sense of local attachment, and local patriotism. As a result, a member of old or new elites 'gives and gives readily, a part of his time and money towards consolidating and improving the community which harbours him and will harbour his posterity'. Yet even here Taine is careful not to present too static a picture. The English polity was being reformed but, he suggests, in a distinctively English way: 'Here the new generation does not break with its predecessor: reforms are superimposed upon institutions; and the present, resting on the past, continues it'. Taine sees a similar marriage of the Burkean and the Benthamite in 'the antiquity of "self-government", and the wide diffusion of knowledge of political economy'. What is striking here about Taine's account is not so much the perceptiveness of its social observation but its careful calibration of subtle changes in the distribution of political power. When summarizing the persistence of gentry status, note how he carefully modifies his description of their power: 'they have kept in touch with the people ... and they have remained the ruling class, or at least the most influential class, in both parish and State'.[5] It is far from perverse to suggest that processes of social transformation are most powerful when they are most elusive.

Taine's English contemporary, Matthew Arnold, evaluated both patterns of change and ideological imperatives rather differently. In *Culture and Anarchy* Arnold advocated greater state power precisely because he believed that in England the cultural checks on over-centralization were sufficient to attenuate its more illiberal effects. For Arnold an enfeebled state was dangerously co-terminus with cultural impoverishment. Moreover, debates over state formation and state power in England were constrained by a persistent class rivalry that led different social groups to colonize different domains within the polity. Thus, Arnold concluded, the landed classes continued to cherish the decorative inutilities of county government and the middle class to crave local office for reasons of class, sect, and status:

Our leading class is an aristocracy, and no aristocracy likes the notion of a State-authority greater than itself, with a stringent administrative machinery superseding the decorative inutilities of lord-lieutenancy, deputy lieutenancy, and the *posse comitatus*, which are all in its own hands. Our middle class, the great representative of trade and Dissent, with its maxims of every man for himself in business, and every man for himself in religion, dreads a powerful administration which might somehow interfere with it; and besides, it has its own decorative inutilities of vestrymanship and guardianship, which are to his class what lord lieutenancy and the county magistracy are to the aristocratic class.[6]

Arnold, too, saw the transformation of English political culture in gradualist terms. Arnold's own vision – unlike Taine's – was of a strong state and a substantially expanded domain for state action. Nevertheless, where Taine saw the power of the gentry perhaps beginning to recede, Arnold saw the stirrings of a popular, Liberal reformism: 'Through the length and breadth of our nation a sense, – vague and obscure as yet, – of weariness with the old organisations, of a desire for transformation, works and grows'.[7]

The years after 1850 also saw an attempt, or perhaps rather a series of attempts, to understand, theorize, and attribute normative political significance to 'village communities'. It is hardly coincidental that this preoccupation with what the great medieval historian William Stubbs called 'the lower ranges of the [state] fabric' was synchronous with the elaboration of a stronger central state. For Henry Maine part of the attraction of the 'village community' idea lay in the political leverage that it gave against utilitarian ideas of government. The euclidean certainties of utilitarianism opened the way to seeing government as science constructed from abstract principles. Maine's invoking of a quasi-organic 'village community' was part of a wider attempt to suggest that government could only be properly understood by men of historical knowledge and administrative experience. John Burrow has suggested that this historiographical moment was deeply politicized, and that Stubbs, E. A. Freeman, and J. R. Green 'were all imbued with a sense of the importance of local institutions, recognizing local self-government as an important element in

English freedom and stability'.[8] Indeed, this historiographical moment was part of a more pervasive Tory nostalgia which embraced Young England's commitment to maintaining the 'parochial constitution' of England, and a revived gothicism which celebrated – even sentimentalized – the distinctiveness of England's institutional development.[9]

Private Bills, Parliament, and Public Health

Meanwhile, of course, the contours of the English polity were changing. The debate over 'the nineteenth-century revolution in government' was preoccupied principally with agencies, officialdom, and extra-parliamentary developments. Jennifer Hart has suggested that one effect of this approach was to construct an administrative history with the ideas left out.[10] Given the centrality of Benthamism to English historical writing from the work of A. V. Dicey onwards, this criticism is perhaps rather overdrawn.[11] A more serious problem was that we were in danger of developing an administrative history with the politics left out.[12] Nowhere was this more impoverishing than in our understanding of the evolving relationship between centre and locality. As John Prest has recently argued, relations between central and local government in the nineteenth century were worked out in parliament.[13] An important part of the currency of these negotiations between centre and locality were local and private bills; and it is striking that, between 1800 and 1884, local and private acts continued to outnumber Public General Acts, by 18 497 to 9556. John Prest has explained the propensity to favour permissive legislation partly in terms of an evolving political relationship between centre and locality and partly as a search for an appropriate agency to confront the increasingly complex governmental problems within a rapidly industrializing, demographically pressured, and socially more fissiparous society. From the late 1820s to the mid-1840s, both Whigs and Peelites were genuinely unsure about which kinds of agency should enjoy primary executive authority within reformed administrative and political structures. Unpaid county justices, traditional parish officials, and the existing networks of county authorities offered one kind of agency; new administrative unions, paid officials, and enhanced central direction another.

Behind the debate over agency lay another equally important struggle to establish the extent of ratepayers' rights to determine policy and patterns of expenditure in their localities. Faced with burgeoning social problems, central government sought to navigate between civic improving traditions, the energies of which were far from spent, and a more centralized, or at any rate more prescriptive, reformism. Between 1828 and 1833 parliament sought to enhance the likely effectiveness of local reforming initiatives by passing a series of model clauses acts which substantially lessened the costs associated with securing local acts. More importantly, the 1833 Lighting and Watching Act offered parishes the prospect of a paid constabulary force and substantially improved civic amenities wherever two-thirds of ratepayers resolved to adopt the Act.[14] Precisely the same permissive principle was embodied in the 1839 Rural Constabulary Act.[15] Meanwhile, a parallel but quite distinct body of centralizing and prescriptive reforming statutes was being elaborated. The classic example was the 1834 Poor Law Amendment Act, which imposed new agencies at both central and local level, but similar principles were being applied to factory, education, and prison reform.[16] However, it was to be public health legislation which did most to define the relationship between the centre and urban England in the mid-nineteenth century.

Largely unregulated industrial capitalism had brought in its train a largely unregulated urban environment. The public health problem by the 1840s had assumed enormous and complex proportions. Between 1801 and 1851 the urban population of England and Wales had grown by 322 per cent, and despite house-building's having accounted for around 30 per cent of gross domestic fixed capital formation between 1800 and 1830, the housing stock was inadequate both in terms of volume and basic quality.[17] In the early 1840s Liverpool had 8000 inhabited cellars, and one estimate put the number living in these cramped, badly ventilated, and frequently flooded cellars at around 40 000.[18] Typhus, typhoid, and even cholera, in 1831–2, 1848–49, and 1853–4, were sinister spectres on the urban horizon.[19] In Ipswich in 1850 there were 228 gas lamps and ten oil lamps, and 60 of 127 streets and lanes were unlit. The situation below ground was little different, with some 38 streets having no drains and a further 16 only surface drains. Such drains as there were often lacked sufficient water pressure, while as many as 51 streets were unpaved or only partially paved. The contemporary commentator who painted this unhappy urban landscape concluded that, so far as public health was concerned, 'Nature has done much; art but little'.[20] Edwin Chadwick's 1842, *Report on the Sanitary Condition of the Labouring Poor*, the Report of the 1843–5 Royal Commission on the Health of Towns, and myriad local inquiries not only transformed the public health question into a question of national efficiency; they also created an irresistible pressure for serious legislative responses, and, soon after the dust settled on the Corn Law crisis and the 1847 election, the Russell government carried the 1848 Public Health Act.[21]

The 1848 Public Health Act has generally been evaluated – and found wanting – as a straightforward piece of social legislation.[22] Certainly the Act had technical shortcomings, although it probably went as far as any serious legislative initiative could given the current capacity of civil engineering. However, viewed as a *political* measure the 1848 Act was profoundly significant. Chadwick, notoriously, inveighed against the 1848 Act because of its permissive character. As the legislation stood, Chadwick saw 'no probability whatsoever of the introduction of the measure into the most important places'.[23] In fact, the 1848 Act was permissive in a new and highly particular sense. It was, for example, obligatory in areas where the mortality rate exceeded 23 in 1000. Even more strikingly, whereas measures such as the 1833 Lighting and Watching Act had required the approval of a two-thirds majority amongst ratepayers to secure adoption, the 1848 Public Health Act could be triggered by *one-tenth* of ratepayers petitioning the General Board of Health, and the original bill had allowed for the introduction of Public Health Boards on the petition of a mere 2 per cent of ratepayers.[24] As a result, not only could a small minority of ratepayers precipitate the imposition of expensive public health measures on a locality, but they could also inaugurate a partial remodelling of local government. As Prest has noted, 'where there was a body of Improvement Commissioners but no Town Council, the ratepayers were, in effect, being given an open invitation by parliament to substitute a Local Board of Health for the Commission they already had'. In other words, embedded in what Chadwick regarded as the anodyne terms of the 1848 Act was Lord Morpeth's intention further to extend the reform of local government begun by the Whigs in the 1830s. Viewed in this way the 1848 Act was, in part, an attempt by government to 'discover an acceptable degree of central intervention'.[25] As this experiment took place Morpeth himself became a member of the General Board of Health, and public health unions were created independently of the poor law unions, thereby creating another tier of local government. In Lancashire alone some 26 Local Boards of Health were established in the decade after 1848. These new boards embarked on improvement schemes which involved mortgaging local rates for up to 25 years and mobilizing local resources on a quite unprecedented scale.[26]

Towards the Modern State

The campaign to improve public health and tame the urban environment constituted one context within which the relationship between central and local government was renegotiated. Here governance itself was being expanded, and the long litany of public health Acts that followed the 1848 Act was central to the processes through which England became a much more intensely governed country. As a consequence local authorities came to exercise new powers of construction, compulsory purchase, and of planning. The 'municipal socialism' which reshaped urban geographies and generated new urban amenities in the later nineteenth century was the most dramatic and enduring product of this essay in greater government.[27] But in other areas of policy power was moving perceptibly from the provinces to the centre.

   If the 1848 Public Health Act was part of an attempt by the executive to discover an acceptable degree of central intervention, that same experiment had begun in prison administration a generation earlier. Peel's 1823 and 1824 Gaols Acts prescribed quite precise systems of classification, but left inspection in the hands of magistrates. The 1835 Prisons Act established an inspectorate and thereby extended the degree of central influence and the intensity of regulatory control.[28] This new inspectorate sought to develop an official language which would both prescribe policy and control local administration. The inspectors' presentation of good practice was specifically designed to pressure local authorities into adopting specific policies; notably the separate, silent systems of cellular confinement, which were extended massively in the 1840s and 1850s, despite the widespread scepticism of magistrates.[29] After 1846 the word became flesh with the advent of central grants-in-aid of local rates to meet part of the cost of local prison administration. As the financial pressures on local authorities grew in the mid-century, grants-in-aid became an ever more powerful lever over policy. In 1847, grants-in-aid to counties totalled £148 000, while expenditure on prisons and prisoners was running at £349 000. By 1870, grants-in-aid had risen to £526 000, while expenditure on prisons and prisoners was at £494 000.[30] Nevertheless, this tensely negotiated partnership between centre and locality, and between experts and lay administrators, did not survive. The 1877 Prisons Act transferred not only control of prisons to the Home Office but also their ownership.[31] Benjamin Disraeli, whose ministry carried the 1877 Prisons Act, described it as 'a most important measure'.[32] Indeed it was, for it embodied a principle – that what the localities built and owned the centre might appropriate and even dispose of – which contributed to a redefinition of property relationships within the polity, and also tentatively constructed a politics within which local government can be regarded as a mere executive agency, and dispossessed accordingly.

In an earlier incarnation, Disraeli had steadfastly opposed the Whig reforms of the 1830s. In the wake of the passage of the Municipal Corporations Act, Disraeli described the Reform and Municipal Corporations Acts as 'the two most comprehensive' measures which the Whigs have succeeded in carrying. By this he, and other Tory Radicals, meant that they had decisively disturbed the settled territorial constitution of England. New principles and new social groups had been intruded into the polity: Dissenters, new wealth, commerce, experts, officials, policemen, and inspectors. The intentions behind this reforming programme might have been complex, but one of its effects was to diminish the power and public standing of the gentry, the traditional governors of provincial England. For Disraeli the politics of party and the politics of interests were of a piece, and he accused the Whig aristocracy of 'playing town against country to overcome the authority of the gentry'. He went on:

The reform of the municipal corporations of England is a covert attack on the authority of the English gentry ... By this apparently democratic act the county magistrate is driven from the towns where he before exercised a just influence, while an elective magistrate from the towns jostles him on the bench at quarter sessions ... Here is a lever to raise the question of county reform whenever an obstinate shire may venture to elect a representative in Parliament hostile to the liberal oligarchs.[33]

Certainly the Whigs, and Lord John Russell in particular, were forcibly opening up local government to new wealth and naming industrialists to previously exclusively landed Commissions of the Peace.[34] That the social distribution of power within the English state had changed in the eighteenth century and would change still more dramatically in the nineteenth is now surely palpable. While Whigs, and later Peelite Conservatives, abetted by political means a process driven largely by cultural and economic change, Tories resisted or sought to retard the pace of change. Nevertheless, without ever denying their political intentions, Whigs such as Lord John Russell presented the reform of policy and polity in a quite different way from that of their Tory opponents. In the Commons in 1837, Russell insisted that to see the New Poor Law as an attack on local government was 'a gross misrepresentation'. The real objective, Russell claimed, 'was to establish self-government ... The consequence [of the Act] was, that a kind of local government was established, acting certainly under such general rules and general directions as the intelligence and experience of the Poor-law Commissioners had prescribed, but with respect to details, acting according to the judgement of the magistrates, country gentlemen, the farmers, and the ratepayers connected with the district'.[35] It would be perverse to deny the Whigs' commitment to local self-government.[36] The New Poor Law, the Municipal Corporations Act, and the 1848 Public Health Act all brought into being new, representative bodies, elected on a ratepayer franchise, and having definite connections with a defined locality. What is equally clear from Russell's speech, and indeed from Liberal thinkers such as John Stuart Mill, was that the domain of local power was being differently conceived. 'General rules and directions' were increasingly becoming the prerogative of the centre, and 'details' the substance and limit of local discretion.[37]

Again, though, what were emerging were new directions in state formation; processes of change remained hesitant, improvised, and contested. Thus in the 1840s central government continued to deploy both prescriptive and permissive instruments. The New Poor Law was extended to Scotland in 1844–5, despite considerable opposition, and the Mines Act of 1842 and the Factory Acts of 1844 and 1847 confirmed the transfer of responsibility for workplace conditions from magistrates to inspectorates.[38] By contrast, the 1842 Parish Constables Act, like the 1848 Public Health Act, attenuated centralizing solutions in the search for local co-operation and compliance. Nevertheless, what was becoming clearer was that, in the search for appropriate agencies, the elective principle was displacing the power of customary elites; the interests of ratepayers was supplanting the interest of land in political languages which legitimated public power; and the systematic understanding of the expert was devaluing the less self-conscious knowledge of the gentleman administrator.

Changes in the superstructure and in dominant political discourses were felt throughout provincial England. Municipal elections, Poor Law Guardians elections, and elections to Public Health Boards contributed to the development of a reformed political culture in provincial England after 1832. Where before local politics had been given a partisan edge by custom, tradition, and the prerogatives of status, the period after 1832 saw the emergence of a local political culture which was more formally, even structurally, partisan. Embryonic party organizations moved from organizing registration drives and parliamentary elections to local elections and canvassing local issues.[39] In the major industrial centres this marked the heyday of local government by an new industrial plutocracy. But one should beware of reading this as the displacement of one economic elite by another. The factory masters who took power in mid-nineteenth-century Manchester, Salford, Bolton, and Rochdale constructed new rituals and symbols of public power. Religious politics, Dissent, and an emboldened reforming Liberalism were powerful components of this new municipal politics.[40] Moreover, the 'Cotton Masters' who dominated Lancashire cities in the 1840s, 1850s, and 1860s were, by the 1870s, beginning to withdraw from municipal politics.[41] Those who defended both the urban world and municipal politics recognized that their very dynamism was, of itself, unsettling if not destabilizing, but argued that from this self-consciously modernizing political culture different freedoms might be won and an

. expanded public domain constructed: 'The relations ... of lord and vassal, of proprietor and serf, have no place in modern society. Hence, uncertainty, with regard to social relationship, is more or less everywhere. But the evil resulting from this change is in great part counteracted by the good it brings along with it. Men change masters more frequently than in feudal times, but the moral feeling which bound them to one man, or to one household, now binds them to their class or society'.[42]

If urban England acquired new political forms and forged a vibrant political culture after 1830, the rural parish found itself politically enervated. The vestry ceased to be a theatre of real policy formation. Overseers who had previously made policy now did little more than collect the rates. Decisions which before 1834 had been taken at parish level were now taken by Poor Law Guardians at Board meetings. With this, power passed from a parish elite, who had dominated the vestry, to men of greater means and leisure, who could command regional status and thus support as Poor Law Guardians. As they sought to live with the realities of the New Poor Law, the vestry of St George the Martyr and St Andrew, Holborn, carried a motion protesting that 'that infamous Act [the 1834 Poor Law Amendment Act] deprived them, as ratepayers, of the local right of self-government, what was the privilege of their forefathers, and it operated in a most arbitrary and oppressive manner on the helpless yet deserving poor'.[43] Significantly, the limited discretion of the elected overseer was replaced in parish life by a salaried functionary appointed by the Guardians, the relieving officer.[44] Indeed, the intrusion of a new petty officialdom into the life of the parish was perhaps the most visible sign of the decline of its own political institutions and the rise of a new culture of government. The policeman was the most salient symbol of this new order; the school inspector was later to become another less prominent one. Writing of a slightly later period and yet another official, the district nurse Flora Thompson captured something of the cultural friction between the world of custom and the new certainties of officialdom: 'The trained district nurses, when they came a few years later, were a great blessing in the country districts; but the old midwife also had her good points, for which she now receives no credit. She was no superior person coming into the house to strain its resources to the utmost and to shame the patient by forced confessions that she did not possess this or that'. Similarly when 'the Sanitary Inspector appeared for the first time at the hamlet [he] shook his head over the pigsties and privies'.[45]

In some ways what was happening in rural England may have been more significant for the long-run development of the English state than the efflorescence of municipal government. By the mid-nineteenth century many old political communities in England had been, or were now being, dissolved. The parish, the hundred, the Quarter Sessions, and the old improvement commissions had lost their vitality. New political communities were being forged, although in the main these were urban political communities, founded on new wealth, new municipalities, and new patterns of class relations. There were attempts to recreate more traditional rural political communities, but these principally took the form of nostalgic rediscoveries in the works of Toulmin Smith, Henry Maine, Stubbs, Freeman, and Green. The Parish Councils Act of 1894 came too late to transpose the old participatory culture of the vestry into the representative era. Counties, even after the County Councils Act of 1888, had lost deep cultural roots and much of their sense of political identity. The dominant idiom of reformed county government has therefore been administrative rather than political, and it is no coincidence that the twentieth century has witnessed constant remodelling of the spatial and political framework of local government. Parliament venerates itself and its antiquity; since the 1830s it has shown no similar veneration for the other branches of the polity, most notably local government. The quest for administrative efficiency has, in the main, inhibited the development of a genuinely representative, participatory tradition of local government. 'Local government at the King's command' has been only imperfectly translated into local government at parliament's command, and that is one of the tragedies of the modern British state.

NOTES

1. R. A. Lewis, *Edwin Chadwick and the Public Health Movement 1832–1854* (London, 1952), pp. 271, 330; *Chadwick*, p. 403; *Liberty and Locality*, p. 20.
2. J. Toulmin Smith, *Local Self-Government and Centralization* (London, 1851), pp. 67–8.

3.   Ibid., quotations at 336, 344; J. Toulmin Smith, *Local Self-government Un-mystified* (London, 1857).

4.   Edwin Chadwick, *Report on the Sanitary Conditions of the Labouring Population of Great Britain, 1842,* ed. M. W. Flinn (Edinburgh, 1965), pp. 354–410, here at p. 380.

5.   Taine, *Notes on England,* quotations at pp. 173, 126, and 144.

6.   Arnold, *Culture and Anarchy,* pp. 83–4; see also Stefan Collini, *Matthew Arnold. A Critical Portrait* (Oxford, 1994), esp. pp. 88–92.

7.   Arnold, *Culture and Anarchy,* p. 185.

8.   J. W. Burrow, '"The Village Community" and the Uses of History in Late Nineteenth-century England', in N. McKendrick (ed.), *Historical Perspectives. Studies in English Thought and Society* (London, 1974), pp. 255–84; quotation at p. 280. See also Campbell, 'Stubbs and the English State'; Henry Sumner Maine, *Village Communities in East and West'* 3rd edn (London, 1876).

9.   Richard Faber, *Young England* (London, 1987), p. 136; Smith, *Gothic Bequest,* pp. 191–200.

10.   Jennifer Hart, 'Nineteenth-century Social Reform: a Tory Interpretation of History', *Past and Present,* xxi (1965), 39–61.

11.   A. V. Dicey, *Lectures on the Relation Between Law and Opinion in England During the Nineteenth Century* [1905], 2nd edn (London, 1948), pp. 126–210; Elie Halévy, *The Triumph of Reform,* 2nd edn (London, 1950), pp. 60–129; S. E. Finer, 'The Transmission of Benthamite Ideas 1820–50', in Gillian Sutherland (ed.), *Studies in the Growth of Nineteenth-century Government* (London, 1972), pp. 11–32.

12.   Eastwood, 'Rethinking the Debates on the Poor Law', 97–104.

13.   For what follows, I am deeply indebted to Prest, *Liberty and Locality.*

14.   3 & 4 Will. IV c. 46.

15.   Anthony Brundage, 'Ministers, Magistrates and Reformers: the Genesis of the Rural Constabulary Act of 1839', *Parliamentary History,* v (1986), 56–64.

16.   William C. Lubenow, *The Politics of Government Growth. Early Victorian Attitudes Towards State Intervention 1833–1848* (Newton Abbot, 1971), pp. 15–29, 69–188.

17.   Rodger, *Housing in Urban Britain,* pp. 7, 19.

18.   Chadwick, *Sanitary Condition of the Labouring Population,* p. 105.

19.   For a classic contemporary indictment, see Peter Gaskell's study of Manchester in the mid-1830s, *Artisans and Machinery;* R. J. Morris, *Cholera 1832* (London, 1976); Lewis, *Edwin Chadwick and the Public Health Movement,* pp. 34–6, 42–3, 150–1, 181-215; Lees, *Cities Perceived,* pp. 16–39.

20.   Glyde, *Moral, Social and Religious Condition of Ipswich,* pp. 30, 34–5.

21.   Lewis, *Edwin Chadwick and the Public Health Movement,* pp. 29–215; Finer, *Chadwick,* pp. 209–353; Prest, *Liberty and Locality,* pp. 24–47.

22.   Asa Briggs, *The Age of Improvement, 1783–1867* (London, 1959), p. 335; Norman Gash, *Aristocracy and People. Britain 1815–1865* (London, 1979), pp. 341–2.

23.   Quoted in Finer, *Chadwick,* p. 324.

24. Anthony Brundage, *England's "Prussian Minister". Edwin Chadwick and the Politics of Government Growth 1832–1854* (University Park, PA, 1988), p. 128.

25. Prest, *Liberty and Locality*, pp. 24–37; quotations at pp. 33 and 37.

26. Midwinter, *Social Administration in Lancashire*, pp. 79–120; Prest, *Liberty and Locality*, pp. 48–187; Robert Millward and Sally Sheard, 'The Urban Fiscal Problem, 1870–1914: Government Expenditure and Finance in England and Wales', *Economic History Review*, 2nd ser., xlvii (1995), 501–35.

27. E. P. Hennock, *Fit and Proper Persons. Ideal and Reality in Nineteenth-century Urban Government* (London, 1973), esp. pp. 61–176, 247–91; Asa Briggs, *Victorian Cities*, Penguin edn (Harmondsworth, 1968), pp. 184–240.

28. 5 & 6 Will. IV c. 38; *Reports from the Lords Select Committees Appointed to Inquire into The Present State of Gaols and Houses of Correction*; P.P., 1835, vii (547) and ix (42); McConville, *English Prison Administration*, pp. 170–6.

29. U. R. Q. Henriques, 'The Rise and Fall of the Separate System of Prison Discipline', *Past and Present*, 54 (1972), 61–93.

30. Mitchell, *Abstract of British Historical Statistics*, 412–13. Grants-in-aid were not paid simply to cover prison costs but were assumed to contribute to expenditure on prosecutions and policing as well.

31. 40 & 41 Vic. c. 21; Forsythe, 'Centralization and Local Autonomy'; McConville, *English Prisons Administration*, pp. 468–82.

32. W. F. Monypenny and G. E. Buckle, *The Life of Benjamin Disraeli*, rev. 2 vol. edn (London, 1929), ii, p. 836.

33. [Benjamin Disraeli], *The Letters of Runnymede* (London, 1836); quotations at pp. 228, 226, and 231.

34. David Philips, 'The Black County Magistracy 1835–1860', *Midland History*, iii (1976), 161–90; Eastwood, *Governing Rural England*, p. 14.

35. Hansard, 3rd ser., xxvi (1837), 1032–4; cf. Brundage, *Making of the New Poor Law*, pp. 159–60.

36. For an insightful analysis, see Jonathan Parry, *The Rise and Fall of Liberal Government in Victorian Britain* (New Haven and London, 1993), pp. 113–27, 203–7.

37. Eastwood, '"Amplifying the Province of the Legislature"', pp. 291–4.

38. Sir George Nicholls, *A History of the Scotch Poor Law* (London, 1856), pp. 134–84; R. A. Cage, *The Scottish Poor Law 1745–1845* (Edinburgh, 1981), pp. 140–51; R. K. Webb, 'A Whig Inspector', *Journal of Modern History*, xxvii (1955), 352–64; Peter Mandler, 'Cain and Abel: Two Aristocrats and the Early Victorian Factory Acts', *Historical Journal*, xxvii (1984), 83–109; Mandler, *Aristocratic Government in the Age of Reform*, pp. 131–82, 236–67; MacDonagh, *Early Victorian Government*, pp. 42–95.

39. Phillips and Wetherell, 'Parliamentary Parties and Municipal Politics'; Baines, *Life of Baines*, pp. 177–339.

40. John Garrard, *Leadership and Power in Victorian Industrial Towns 1830–88* (Manchester, 1983); Patrick Joyce, *Work, Society and Politics. The Culture of the Factory in later Victorian Britain* (London, 1980), pp. 268–310.

41.   Howe, *Cotton Masters*, pp. 160–1.

42.   Vaughan, *The Age of the Great Cities*, p. 289.

43.   Cited in Andrea Tanner, 'The City of London Poor Law Union 1839–1869', Ph.D. thesis, University of London (1995), 82.

44.   Driver, *Power and Pauperism*, 139–40; [George J. Dew], *Oxfordshire Village Life: The Diaries of George James Dew (1846–1928), Relieving Officer*, ed. Pamela Horn (Abingdon, 1983).

45.   Thompson, *Lark Rise to Candleford*, pp. 136, 246.

Bibliography

Address of the Society for Diffusing Information on the Subject of Capital Punishment and Prison Discipline (London, 1817).

Alexander, Sally, *St Giles's Fair, 1830–1914: Popular Culture and the Industrial Revolution in 19th Century Oxfordshire* (Oxford, 1970).

Allen, W. Gore, *John Heathcoat and His Heritage* (London, 1958).

Anon., *Biographical Memoirs of Thomas Butterworth Bayley* (Manchester, 1802).

Apfel, William and Dunkley, Peter, 'English Rural Society and the New Poor Law: Bedfordshire 1834–1847', *Social History*, x (1985), 37–68.

Arch, Joseph, *From Ploughtail to Parliament. An Autobiography*, new edn, intro. Alun Howkins (The Cresset Library, 1986).

Arnold, Matthew, *Culture and Anarchy and Other Writings,* ed. Stefan Collini (Cambridge, 1993).

Arnold-Baker, Charles, *Parish Administration* (London, 1958).

Ashforth, Adam, 'Reckoning Schemes of Legitimation: on Commissions of Inquiry as Power/Knowledge Forms', *Journal of Historical Sociology*, iii (1990), 1–22.

Aylmer, G. E., *The King's Servants. The Civil Service of Charles I, 1625–1642* (London, 1961).

Aylmer, G. E., *Rebellion or Revolution? England 1640–1660* (Oxford, 1986).

Aylmer, G. E., 'The Peculiarities of the English State', *Journal of Historical Sociology*, iii (1990), 91–108.

Baernreither, J. M., *English Associations of Working Men* (London, 1889).

Bagehot, Walter, *The English Constitution*, ed. R. H. S. Crossman (London, 1963).

Baines, Edward, Jr, *The Social, Educational, and Religious State of the Manufacturing Districts*, 2nd edn (London, 1843).

Baines, Edward, *The Life of Edward Baines* (London and Leeds, 1851).

Baker, Keith Michael, *Inventing the French Revolution* (Cambridge, 1990).

Barber, Brian, 'Municipal Government in Leeds 1835–1914', in Derek Fraser (ed.), *Municipal Reform and the Industrial City* (Leicester, 1982).

Barker, Hannah, 'Press, Politics and Reform: 1779–1785', D.Phil. thesis, University of Oxford (1994).

171

Barker, Hannah, 'Catering for Provincial Tastes: Newspapers, Readership and Profit in Late Eighteenth-century England', *Historical Research*, lix (1996), 42–61.

Barry, Jonathan, 'The Parish in Civic Life: Bristol and its Churches, 1640–1750', in S. J. Walsh (ed.), *Parish, Church, and People: Local Studies in Lay Religion, 1350–1750* (London, 1988).

Barry, Jonathan, 'Provincial Town Culture, 1640–1780: Urbane or Civic', in Joan H. Pittock and Andrew Wear (eds), *Interpretation in Cultural History* (London, 1991).

Barry, Jonathan, 'The Press and the Politics of Culture in Bristol 1660–1775', in Jeremy Black and Jeremy Gregory (eds), *Culture, Politics and Society in Britain 1660–1800* (Manchester, 1991).

Barry, Jonathan, 'Bourgeois Collectivism? Urban Association and the Middling Sort, 1500–1800', in Jonathan Barry and Christopher Brooks (eds), *The Middling Sort of People. Culture, Society and Politics in England 1550–1800* (London, 1994).

Beattie, J. M., *Crime and the Courts in England 1660–1800* (Oxford, 1986), pp. 59–63.

Beckett, J. V., *The Aristocracy in England 1660–1914* (Oxford, 1986).

Belanger, Terry, 'Publishers and Writers in Eighteenth-century England', in Isobel Rivers (ed.), *Books and Their Readers in Eighteenth-century England* (Leicester, 1982).

Bellamy, Christine, *Administering Central–Local Relations. The Local Government Board in its Fiscal and Cultural Context* (Manchester, 1988).

Bennett, James, *The History of Tewksbury* (Tewksbury, 1830).

Bettey, J., 'The Reformation and the Parish Church. Local Responses to National Directives', *The Historian*, xliv (1995), 11–14.

Black, E. C., *The Association. British Extraparliamentary Political Organization 1769–1793* (Cambridge, MA, 1963).

Black, Jeremy, '"Calculated upon a Very Extensive and Useful Plan". The English Provincial Press in the Eighteenth Century', in P. Issac (ed.), *Six Centuries of the Provincial Book Trade in Britain* (Winchester, 1990).

Black, Jeremy, 'The Development of the Provincial Newspaper Press in the Eighteenth Century', *British Journal for Eighteenth-Century Studies*, xv (1991), 159–70.

Black, Jeremy, *Convergence or Divergence? Britain and the Continent* (London, 1994).

Bland, A. E., Brown, P. A., and Tawney, R. H. (eds), *English Economic History. Select Documents* (London, 1914).

Blaug, M., 'The Poor Law Report Reexamined', *Journal of Economic History*, xxiv (1964), 229–45.

Blaug, M., 'The Myth of the Old Poor Law and the Making of the New', reprinted in M. W. Flinn and T. C. Smout (eds), *Essays in Social History* (Oxford, 1974).

Bloomfield, J. C., *History of Finmere* (Buckingham, 1887).

Bohstedt, John, *Riots and Community Politics in England and Wales 1790–1810* (Cambridge, MA, 1983).

Boorman, Julia, 'The Sheriffs of Henry II and the Significance of 1170', in George Garnett and John Hudson (eds), *Law and Government in Medieval England and Normandy* (Cambridge, 1994).

Booth, Alan, 'Food Riots in the North West of England 1790–1800', *Social History*, viii (1983), 295–314.

Borsay, Peter, '"All the Town's a Stage": Urban Ritual and Ceremony', in Peter Clark (ed.), *The Transformation of English Provincial Towns 1600–1800* (London, 1984).

Borsay, Peter, *The English Urban Renaissance. Culture and Society in the Provincial Town, 1660–1770* (Oxford, 1989).

Borsay, Peter, 'The English Urban Renaissance: the Development of Provincial Urban Culture *c.* 1680 – *c.* 1760', in Peter Borsay (ed.), *The Eighteenth Century Town. A Reader in English Urban History 1688–1820* (London, 1990).

Borsay, Peter, 'Image and Counter-image in Georgian Bath', *British Journal for Eighteenth-Century Studies*, xvii (1994), 165–79.

Boyer, George R., *An Economic History of the English Poor Law, 1750–1850* (Cambridge, 1990).

Bradley, James E., *Religion, Revolution and English Radicalism. Nonconformity in Eighteenth-century Politics and Society* (Cambridge, 1990).

Brett, Peter, *The Rise and Fall of the York Whig Club 1818–1830*, University of York, Borthwick Papers no. 76 (1989).

Brewer, John, *The Sinews of Power. War, Money and the English State, 1688–1783* (London, 1989).

Briggs, Asa, 'The Background of the Parliamentary Reform Movement in Three English Cities (1830–1832)', *Cambridge Historical Journal*, x (1952), 293–317.

Briggs, Asa, *The Age of Improvement, 1783–1867* (London, 1959).

Briggs, Asa, 'The Language of "Class" in Early Nineteenth-century England', in A. Briggs and J. Saville (eds), *Essays in Labour History: in Memory of G. D. H. Cole* (London, 1960).

Briggs, Asa, *Victorian Cities*, Penguin edn (Harmondsworth, 1968).

Brock, Michael, *The Great Reform Act* (London, 1973).

Brown, A. L., *The Governance of Late Medieval England 1272–1461* (London, 1989).

Brown, A. V., 'The Last Phase of the Enclosure of Otmoor', *Oxoniensia*, xxxii (1967), 35–52.

Brown, J. B., *The Public and Private Life of John Howard, Philanthropist* (London, 1818).

Brown, J. B., *Memoirs of John Howard* (London, 1823).

Brundage, Anthony, 'Landed Interest and the New Poor Law', *English Historical Review*, lxxxvii (1972), 27–48.

Brundage, Anthony, 'English Poor Law of 1834 and the Cohesion of Agricultural Society', *Agricultural History*, xlix (1974), 405–17.

Brundage, Anthony, *Making of the New Poor Law, 1832–39* (London, 1978).

Brundage, Anthony, 'Ministers, Magistrates and Reformers: the Genesis of the Rural Constabulary Act of 1839', *Parliamentary History*, v (1986), 56–64.

Brundage, Anthony, *England's "Prussian Minister". Edwin Chadwick and the Politics of Government Growth 1832–1854* (University Park, PA, 1988).

Burke, Edmund, *Reflections on the Revolution in France* [1790], ed. C. C. O'Brien (Harmondsworth, 1968).

Burn, R., *Ecclesiastical Law*, 2 vols (London, 1763).

Burn, R., *The Justice of the Peace and the Parish Officer*, 28th edn, 6 vols (London, 1837).

Burroughs, Peter, 'The Northumberland Elections of 1826', *Parliamentary History*, x (1991), 86–97.

Burrow, J. W., '"The Village Community" and the Uses of History in Late Nineteenth-century England', in N. McKendrick (ed.), *Historical Perspectives. Studies in English Thought and Society* (London, 1974).

Butler, Marilyn, *Burke, Paine, Godwin, and the Revolution Controversy* (Cambridge, 1984).

Cage, R. A., *The Scottish Poor Law 1745–1845* (Edinburgh, 1981).

Caird, James, *English Agriculture in 1850–51* [1852], new edn, intro. G. E. Mingay (New York, 1967).

Cairns, David (ed.), *The Memoirs of Hector Berlioz* (London, 1969).

Campbell, James, *Essays in Anglo-Saxon History* (London, 1986).

Campbell, James, *Stubbs and the English State* (Reading, 1989).

Cannan, Edwin, *The History of Local Rates in England*, 2nd edn (London, 1912).

Cannon, John, *Parliamentary Reform 1640–1832* (Cambridge, 1973).

Carpenter, Christine, *Locality and Polity: a Study of Warwickshire Landed Society, 1401–1499* (Cambridge, 1992).

[Chadwick, Edwin], 'Preventative Police', *London Review*, i (1829).

Chadwick, Edwin, *County Government* (London, 1879).

Chadwick, Edwin, *Report on the Sanitary Conditions of the Labouring Population of Great Britain, 1842*, ed. M. W. Flinn (Edinburgh, 1965).

Chadwick, W. O., *Victorian Church*, 2 vols (London, 1966).

Chalkin, C. W., 'Capital Expenditure on Building for Cultural Purposes in Provincial England, 1730–1830', *Business History*, xxii (1980), 51–70.

Chambers, J. D., *Nottinghamshire in the Eighteenth Century. A Study of Life and Labour under the Squirearchy* (London, 1932).

Chambers, J. D. and Mingay, G. E., *The Agricultural Revolution 1750–1880* (London, 1966).

Chandaman, C. D., *The English Public Revenue, 1660–1688* (Oxford, 1975).

Charlton, Barbara, *The Recollections of a Northumbrian Lady 1815–1866*, ed. L. E. O. Charlton (London, 1949).

Checkland, S. G. and Checkland, E. O. A., *The Poor Law Report of 1834* (Harmondsworth, 1974).

Chinnery, G. A. (ed.), *Records of the Borough of Leicester. Hall Books and Papers 1689–1835* (Leicester, 1965).

Chrimes, S. B., Ross, C. D., and Griffiths, R. A., *Fifteenth Century England 1399–1509*, 2nd edn (Stroud, 1995).

Christie, Ian R., *Wilkes, Wyvill and Reform. The Parliamentary Reform Movement in British Politics 1760–1785* (London, 1962).

Church, Roy A., *Economic and Social Change in a Midland Town. Victorian Nottingham 1815–1900* (London, 1966).

Cirket, Alan F. (ed.), *Samuel Whitbread's Notebooks 1810–11, 1813–14*, Bedfordshire Historical Records Society, 1 (1971).

Clark, Peter, *The English Alehouse. A Social History 1200–1830* (London, 1983).

Cobban, Alfred, *The Debate on the French Revolution 1789–1800*, 2nd edn (London, 1960).

Cobbett, William, *Rural Rides* [1830], Penguin edn (Harmondsworth, 1967).

[Cobbett, William], *The Autobiography of William Cobbett*, ed. William Reitzel, new edn (London, 1967).

Cobden, Richard, *Incorporate your Borough* (Manchester, 1837).

Cockburn, J. S., *A History of English Assizes, 1558–1714* (Cambridge, 1972).

Coleby, Andrew M., *Central Government and the Localities: Hampshire 1649–1689* (Cambridge, 1987).

Coleman, Bruce (ed.), *The Idea of the City in Nineteenth-century Britain* (London and Boston, 1973).

Collini, Stefan, *Matthew Arnold. A Critical Portrait* (Oxford, 1994).

Cookson, J. E., *The Friends of Peace: Anti-war Liberalism in England, 1793–1815* (Cambridge, 1982).

Cookson, John, 'The English Volunteer Movement of the French Wars, 1793–1815: some Contexts', *Historical Journal*, xxxii (1989), 867–91.

Cordery, Simon, 'Friendly Societies and the Discourse of Respectability in Britain, 1825–1875', *Journal of British Studies*, xxxiv (1995), 35–58.

Corfield, P. J., *The Impact of English Towns 1700–1800* (Oxford, 1982).

Corfield, Penelope J., 'Class by Name and Number in Eighteenth-century Britain', in Penelope J. Corfield (ed.), *Language, History and Class* (London, 1991).

Corrigan, Philip and Sayer, Derek, *The Great Arch. English State Formation as Cultural Revolution*, new edn (Oxford, 1991).

Costin, W. C. and Watson, J. Steven (eds), *The Law and the Working of the Constitution: Documents 1660–1914*, 2 vols (London, 1952).

[Creevey, Thomas], *The Creevey Papers. A Selection from the Correspondence and Diaries of the Late Thomas Creevey, MP*, ed. Herbert Maxwell, 2 vols (London, 1904).

Cressy, David, *Bonfires and Bells. National Memory and the Protestant Calendar in Elizabethan England* (London, 1989).

Crittal, Elizabeth (ed.), *The Justicing Notebooks of William Hunt 1744–1749*, Wiltshire Record Society, xxxvii (1981).

Cromwell, Valerie, 'Interpretations of Nineteenth-Century Administration: An Analysis', *Victorian Studies*, ix (1966), 245–55.

Daniel, W. B., *Rural Sports*, 4 vols (London, 1812–13).

Darvell, F. O., *Popular Disturbances and Public Order in Regency England*, new edn, intro. Angus Macintyre (Oxford, 1969).

Davenport, J. M., *Oxfordshire Annals* (Oxford, 1869).

Davey, B. J., *Lawless and Immoral. Policing a Country Town, 1838–1857* (Leicester, 1983).

Davies, C. Stella (ed.), *A History of Macclesfield* (Manchester, 1961).

Davies, David, *The Case of Labourers in Husbandry Stated and Considered* (London, 1795).

Davies, Richard W., *Political Change and Continuity 1760–1885. A Buckinghamshire Study* (Newton Abbot, 1972).

Day, William, *An Inquiry into the Poor Law and Surplus Labour, and their Mutual Reaction*, 2nd edn (London, 1833).

Dean, David (ed.), *St Albans Quarter Sessions Rolls 1784–1820*, Hertford Record Society Publications, v (1991).

[Dew, George J.], *Oxfordshire Village Life: the Diaries of George James Dew (1846–1928), Relieving Officer*, ed. Pamela Horn (Abingdon, 1983).

[Dew, George J.], *Oxfordshire Country Life in the 1860s: The Early Diaries of George James Dew (1846–1928) of Lower Heyford*, ed. Pamela Horn (Abingdon, 1986).

Dicey, A. V., *Lectures on the Relation Between Law and Opinion in England During the Nineteenth Century* [1905], 2nd edn (London, 1948).

Dickins, M., *History of Hook Norton* (Banbury, 1928).

Dickinson, H. T., *Liberty and Property. Political Ideology in Eighteenth-century Britain* (London, 1977).

Dickinson, H. T., *The Politics of the People in Eighteenth-century Britain* (London, 1995).

Dickson, P. G. M., *The Financial Revolution in England: a Study in the Development of Public Credit, 1688–1756* (London, 1967).

Digby, Anne, *Pauper Palaces* (London, 1978).

Digby, Anne, 'Malthus and the Reform of the English Poor Law', in M. Turner (ed.), *Malthus and his Time* (London, 1986).

[Disraeli, Benjamin], *The Letters of Runnymede* (London, 1836).

Ditchfield, P. H., *The Parish Clerk* (London, 1907).

Donajgrodzki, A. P., 'The Home Office, 1822–1848', D.Phil. thesis, University of Oxford, (1973).

Dowdell, E. G., *A Hundred Years of Quarter Sessions. The Government of Middlesex from 1660–1760* (Cambridge, 1932).

Doyle, William, *The Ancien Régime* (London, 1986).

Dozier, Robert, *For King, Constitution, and Country. The English Loyalists and the French Revolution* (Lexington, KY, 1983).

Drescher, Seymour, *Tocqueville and England* (Cambridge, MA 1964).

Driver, Felix, *Power and Pauperism. The Workhouse System 1834–1884* (Cambridge, 1993).

Dunbabin, J. P. D., 'The Politics of the Establishment of County Councils', *Historical Journal*, vi (1963), 226–52.

Dunbabin, J. P. D., 'British Local Government Reform in the Nineteenth Century and After', *English Historical Review*, xcii (1977), 777–805.

Dunkley, Peter, 'Whigs and Paupers: the Reform of the English Poor Laws, 1830–1834', *Journal of British Studies*, xx (1981), 124–49.

Dunkley, Peter, *The Crisis of the Old Poor Law in England 1795–1834. An Interpretative Essay* (New York and London, 1982).

Dyck, Ian, *William Cobbett and Rural Popular Culture* (Cambridge, 1992).

Dyer, Christopher, 'The English Medieval Village Community and its Decline', *Journal of British Studies*, 33 (1994), 407–39.

Eastwood, David, 'The Benefits of Brotherhood: the First Century of the Stonesfield Friendly Society, 1765–1865', *Oxfordshire Local History*, ii (1986), 161–8.

Eastwood, David, 'Toryism, Reform and Political Culture in Oxfordshire, 1826–1837', *Parliamentary History*, vii (1988), 98–121.

Eastwood, David, '"Amplifying the Province of the Legislature". The Flow of Information and the English State in the Early Nineteenth Century', *Historical Research*, lxii (1989), 276–94.

Eastwood, David, 'The Triumph of Toryism in Oxfordshire Politics, 1754–1815', *Oxoniensia*, liv (1989), 355–62.

Eastwood, David, 'Patriotism and the English State in the 1790s', in Mark Philp (ed.), *The French Revolution and British Popular Politics* (Cambridge, 1991).

Eastwood, David, 'The Republic in the English Village: Parish and Poor at Bampton, 1780–1834', *Journal of Local and Regional Studies*, xii (1992), 18–28.

Eastwood, David, *Governing Rural England. Tradition and Transformation in Local Government* (Oxford, 1994).

Eastwood, David, 'Rethinking the Debates on the Poor Law in Early Nineteenth-century England', *Utilitas*, vi (1994), 97–116.

Eastwood, David, 'Men, Morals, and the Machinery of Social Legislation, 1790–1840', *Parliamentary History*, xiii (1994), 190–205.

Eastwood, David, 'E. P. Thompson, Britain, and the French Revolution', *History Workshop Journal*, 39 (1995), 79–88.

Eastwood, David, 'Contesting the Politics of Deference', in Miles Taylor and Jon Lawrence (eds), *Party, State and Society: Electoral Behaviour in Modern Britain* (Aldershot, 1996).

Eastwood, David, 'Communities, Protest and Police in Early-nineteenth-century Oxfordshire: the Enclosure of Otmoor Reconsidered', *Agricultural History Review*, xliv (1996) 35–46.

Eden, F. M., *The State of the Poor*, 3 vols (London, 1797).

Eden, F. M., *Observations on Friendly Societies, for the Maintenance of the Industrious Classes, during Sickness, Infirmity, Old Age and other Exigencies* (London, 1801).

Edsall, Nicholas C., *The Anti-Poor Law Movement 1834–44* (Manchester, 1971).

Edsall, Nicholas C., *Richard Cobden. Independent Radical* (Cambridge, MA and London, 1986).

Egerton, John Coker, *Victorian Village. The Diaries of the Reverend John Coker Egerton of Burwash*, ed. Roger Wells (Stroud, 1992).

Elliott, Douglas J., *Policing Shropshire 1836–1967* (Studley, 1984).

Elton, G. R., *The Tudor Revolution in Government: Administrative Changes in the Reign of Henry VIII* (Cambridge, 1953).

Elton, G. R., 'The Tudor Revolution: a Reply', *Past and Present*, 29 (1964), 26–49.

Elton, G. R., *Policy and Police: the Enforcement of the Reformation in the Age of Thomas Cromwell* (London, 1972).

Emsley, Clive, *British Society and the French Wars 1793–1815* (London and Basingstoke, 1979).

Emsley, Clive, 'The Home Office and its Sources of Information and Investigation', *English Historical Review*, xciv (1979), 532–61.

Emsley, Clive, *Policing and its Context 1750–1870* (London and Basingstoke, 1983).

Emsley, Clive, *Crime and Society in England 1750–1900* (London, 1987).

Engels, Friedrich, *The Condition of the Working Class in England*, trans. and ed. W. O. Henderson and W. H. Chaloner (Stanford, CA (1968).

Evans, Eric, 'Some Reasons for the Growth of English Rural Anti-Clericalism *c.* 1750–*c.* 1850', *Past and Present*, no. 66 (1975), 84–109.

Evans, Eric J., *The Contentious Tithe. The Tithe Problem and English Agriculture 1750–1850* (London, 1976).

Evans, R., *The Fabrication of Virtue: English Prison Architecture 1750–1840* (Cambridge, 1982).

Everitt, A. M., *The Community of Kent and the Great Rebellion, 1640–1660* (Leicester, 1966).

Faber, Richard, *Young England* (London, 1987).

Finer, S. E., *Edwin Chadwick* (London, 1952).

Finer, S. E., 'The Transmission of Benthamite Ideas 1820–50', in Gillian Sutherland (ed.), *Studies in the Growth of Nineteenth-century Government* (London, 1972).

Finlayson, G. B. A. M., 'The Politics of Municipal Reform, 1835', *English Historical Review*, lxxxi (1966), 673–92.

Finn, Margot C., *After Chartism. Class and Nation in English Radical Politics, 1848–1874* (Cambridge, 1993).

Fisher, Peter Hawkins, *Notes and Recollections of Stroud [1871]*, new edn, ed. N. M. Herbert (Gloucester, 1986).

Fiske, Jane (ed. and intro.), *The Oakes Diaries. Business, Politics and the Family in Bury St Edmunds 1778–1827*, 2 vols, Suffolk Record Society, xxxii–xxxiii (1990/1991).

Fletcher, Anthony, *Reform in the Provinces; the Government of Stuart England* (New Haven, 1986).

Flick, Carlos, *The Birmingham Political Union and the Movements for Reform in Britain 1830–1839* (Folkestone, 1978).

Foot, Sarah, 'The Making of *Angelcynn*: English Identity Before the Norman Conquest', *Transactions of the Royal Historical Society*, 6th ser., vi (1996).

Forrester, E. G., *Northamptonshire County Elections and Electioneering 1695–1832* (London, 1941).

Fortescue, J. W., *The County Lieutenancies and the Army, 1803–14* (London, 1909).

Forsythe, William James, *The Reform of Prisoners 1830–1900* (London, 1987).

Forsythe, William James, 'Centralization and Local Autonomy: the Experience of English Prisons 1820–1877', *Journal of Historical Sociology*, iv (1991), 317–45.

Foster, Ruscombe, *The Politics of County Power. Wellington and the Hampshire Gentlemen 1820–52* (London, 1990).

Fothergill, Charles, *The Diary of Charles Fothergill 1805*, ed. Paul Romney, Yorkshire Archaeological Society, cxlii (1982).

Foucault, Michel, *Discipline and Punish. The Birth of the Prison*, Penguin edn (Harmondsworth, 1979).

Fraser, Derek, *Urban Politics in Victorian England. The Structure of Politics in Victorian Cities*, new edn (London, 1979).

Galpin, W. F., *The Grain Supply of England during the French Wars* (New York, 1925).

Gammage, R. C., *History of the Chartist Movement 1837–1854* [1854], new edn (London, 1894).

Garrard, John, *Leadership and Power in Victorian Industrial Towns 1830–88* (Manchester, 1983).

Gash, Norman, *Aristocracy and People. Britain 1815–1865* (London, 1979).

Gaskell, Peter, *Artisans and Machinery: the Moral and Physical Condition of the Manufacturing Population* (London, 1836).

Gatrell, V. A. C., 'The Decline of Theft and Violence in Victorian England and Wales', in V. A. C. Gatrell, B. Lenman, and G. Parker (eds), *Crime and the Law: the Social History of Crime in Western Europe since 1500* (London, 1980).

Gatrell, V. A. C., 'Incorporation and the Pursuit of Liberal Hegemony in Manchester 1790–1839', in Derek Fraser (ed.), *Municipal Reform and the Industrial City* (Leicester, 1982).

Gatrell, V. A. C., 'Crime, Authority, and the Policeman State', in F. M. L. Thompson (ed.), *The Cambridge Social History of Britain 1750–1950*, 3 vols (1990), iii, pp. 243–310.

Gattrell, V. A. C., *The Hanging Tree. Execution and the English People 1770–1868* (Oxford, 1994).

Gatrell, V. A. C. and Hadden, T. B., 'Criminal Statistics and their Interpretation', in E. A. Wrigley (ed.), *Nineteenth Century Society* (Cambridge, 1972).

Gilbert, A. D., *Religion and Society in Industrial England. Church, Chapel and Social Change 1740–1914* (London, 1976).

Gilbert, T., *A Scheme for the Better Relief and Employment of the Poor …* (London, 1764).

Gilbert, T., *Plan for the Better Relief of the Poor* (London, 1781).

Gilbert, T., *Heads of a Bill for the Better Relief and Employment of the Poor* (Manchester, 1786).

Gilbert, T., *Considerations on the Bills for the Better Relief and Employment of the Poor* (London, 1787).

Ginter, D. E., 'The Loyalist Association Movement of 1792–3', *Historical Journal*, ix (1966), 179–90.

Gladwin, Irene, *The Sheriff: the Man and his Office* (London, 1974).

Glassey, Lionel K. J., *Politics and the Appointment of Justice of the Peace, 1675–1725* (Oxford, 1979).

Glassey, L. K. J. and Landau, Norma, 'The Commission of the Peace in the Eighteenth Century: a New Source', *Bulletin of the Institute of Historical Research*, xlv (1972), 247–65.

Gleason, J. H., *The Justices of the Peace in England 1558–1640* (Oxford, 1969).

Glover, Richard, *Britain at Bay. Defence against Bounaparte, 1803–14* (London, 1973).

Glyde, John, *The Moral, Social and Religious Condition of Ipswich in the Middle of the Nineteenth Century* (Ipswich, 1850).

Gneist, Rudolph, *The History of the English Constitution,* English edn (London, 1891).

Godber, Joyce, *History of Bedfordshire 1066–1888* (Bedford, 1969).

Godschall, William Man, *General Plan of Provincial and Parochial Police* (London, 1787).

Goodwin, Albert, *The Friends of Liberty. The English Democratic Movement in the Age of the French Revolution* (London, 1979).

Gosden, P. H. J. H., *The Friendly Societies in England 1815–1875* (Manchester, 1961).

Goubert, Pierre, *L'Ancien Régime,* 2 vols (Paris, 1962, 1973).

Gough, Richard, *The History of Myddle,* ed. David Hay (Harmondsworth, 1981).

Griffiths, R. A., *The Reign of King Henry the Sixth* (London, 1981).

Haigh, Christopher, *English Reformations. Religion, Politics, and Society under the Tudors* (Oxford, 1993).

Halévy, Elie, *The Triumph of Reform,* 2nd edn (London, 1950).

Hampson, E., *Poverty in Cambridgeshire, 1597–1834* (Cambridge, 1934).

Harling, Philip, 'The Power of Pauperism: Central Authority, Local Bureaucracy and the New Poor Law, *English Historical Review,* cvii (1992), 30–53.

Hardy, W. J., *Hertford County Records,* 10 vols (Hertford, 1905–57).

Harris, Jose, *Private Lives, Public Spirit: Britain 1870–1914,* Penguin edn (Harmondsworth, 1994).

Hart, Jennifer, 'The Reform of the Borough Police, 1835–1856', *English Historical Review,* lxx (1955), 411–27.

Hart, Jennifer, 'Nineteenth-century Social Reform: a Tory Interpretation of History', *Past and Present,* xxi (1965), 39–61.

Hassell Smith, A., *County and Court. Government and Politics in Norfolk, 1558–1603* (Oxford, 1974).

Hay, Douglas, 'Property, Authority and the Criminal Law', in Douglas Hay *et al., Albion's Fatal Tree. Crime and Society in Eighteenth-century England,* Penguin edn (Harmondsworth, 1977).

Hay, Douglas, 'Poaching and the Game Laws on Cannock Chase', in Hay *et al., Albion's Fatal Tree. Crime and Society in Eighteenth-century England,* Penguin edn (Harmondsworth, 1977).

[Hayton,Thomas], *The Letters of Thomas Hayton. Vicar of Long Crendon Buckinghamshire 1821–1887,* ed. Joyce Donald, Buckinghamshire Record Society, xx (1979).

Heal, Felicity and Holmes, Clive, *The Gentry in England and Wales 1500–1700* (London, 1994).

Hembry, Phyllis, *The English Spa 1560–1815. A Social History* (London, 1990).

Hennock, E. P., *Fit and Proper Persons. Ideal and Reality in Nineteenth-century Urban Government* (London, 1973).

Henriques, U. R. Q., 'The Rise and Fall of the Separate System of Prison Discipline', *Past and Present*, 54 (1972), 61–93.

Hewitt, J., *Guide for Constables and Peace Officers* (London, 1779).

Hill, Christopher, 'The Norman Yoke', in Hill, *Puritanism and Revolution. Studies in Interpretation of the English Revolution of the Seventeenth Century* (London, 1958).

Hill, Christopher, 'Parliament and People in Seventeenth-century England', *Past and Present*, no. 92 (1981), 100–24.

Hill, Francis, *Georgian Lincoln* (Cambridge, 1966).

Hill, Francis, *Victorian Lincoln* (Cambridge, 1974).

Hilton, Boyd, *Corn, Cash, Commerce. The Economic Policies of the Tory Governments 1815–1830* (Oxford, 1977).

Himmelfarb, G., *The Idea of Poverty* (London, 1984).

Hinton, James, *Vindication of the Dissenters of Oxford* (Oxford, 1792).

Hinton, James, *Sermon on the Death of His Late Majesty* (Oxford, 1820).

Hinton, John Howard, *Biographical Portraiture of the late James Hinton* (Oxford, 1824).

Hobsbawm, E. J. and Rudé, George, *Captain Swing*, Penguin edn (Harmondsworth, 1973).

Hobson, M. G. (ed.), *Oxford Council Acts 1792–1801* (Oxford, 1962).

Hogwood, Christopher, *Handel* (London, 1984).

Holford, G., *Thoughts on the Criminal Prisons of this Country* (London, 1821).

Hole, Robert, *Pulpits, Politics and Public Order in England 1760–1832* (Cambridge, 1989).

Holmes, Clive, *Seventeenth-century Lincolnshire* (Lincoln, 1980).

Holt, J. C., *Magna Carta*, 2nd edn (Cambridge, 1992).

Hopkins, Eric, *Working Class Self-help in Nineteenth Century England* (London, 1995).

Horne, Thomas A., *Property Rights and Poverty. Political Argument in Britain, 1605–1834* (Chapel Hill, NC, 1990).

Howard, J., *The State of Prisons in England and Wales* (Warrington, 1777).

Howe, Anthony, *The Cotton Masters 1830–1860* (Oxford, 1984).

Howell, David W., *Patriarchs and Parasites. The Gentry of South-west Wales in the Eighteenth Century* (Cardiff, 1986).

Howkins, Alun, *Witsun in Nineteenth Century Oxfordshire* (Oxford, 1973).

Howkins, Alun, *Reshaping Rural England. A Social History 1850–1925* (London, 1991).

Howkins, Alun, 'The English Farm Labourer in the Nineteenth Century. Farm, Family and Community', in Brian Short (ed.), *The English Rural Community. Image and Analysis* (Cambridge, 1992).

Hueckel, G., 'English Farming Profits during the Napoleonic Wars', *Explorations in Economic History*, 13 (1976), 331–45.

Hughes, Ann, *Politics, Society and Civil War in Warwickshire, 1620–1660* (Cambridge, 1987).

Hughes, Edward, *Studies in Administration and Finance 1558–1825* (Manchester, 1934).

Huzel, James, 'Malthus, the Poor Law, and Population', *Economic History Review*, 2nd ser., xxii (1969) 430–52.

Huzel, James, 'Demographic Impact of the Old Poor Law', *Economic History Review*, 2nd ser., xxxiii (1980), 367–81.

Ignatieff, Michael, *A Just Measure of Pain. The Penitentiary in the Industrial Revolution* (London, 1978).

Innes, Joanna, 'The King's Bench Prison in the Later Eighteenth Century: Law, Authority, and Order in a London Debtors' Prison', in John Brewer and John Styles (eds), *An Ungovernable People. The English and Their Law in the Seventeenth and Eighteenth Centuries* (London, 1980).

Innes, Joanna, 'Prisons for the Poor: English Bridewells, 1555–1800', in Francis Snyder and Douglas Hay (eds), *Labour, Law, and Crime. An Historical Perspective* (London, 1987).

Innes, Joanna, 'Parliament and the Shaping of Eighteenth-century English Social Policy', *Transactions of the Royal Historical Society*, 5th ser., xl (1990), 63–92.

Innes, Joanna, 'Politics and Morals. The Reformation of Manners Movement in Later Eighteenth-century England', in Eckhart Hellmuth (ed.), *The Transformation of Political Culture. England and Germany in the Late Eighteenth Century* (Oxford, 1990).

Innes, Joanna and Styles, John, 'The Crime Wave: Recent Writing on Crime and Criminal Justice in Eighteenth-century England', *Journal of British Studies*, xxv (1986), 380–435.

Jefferies, Richard, *Hodge and his Masters* [1880], new edn, intro. A. M. Richardson (Stroud, 1992).

Jenkins, Philip, *The Making of a Ruling Class. The Glamorgan Gentry 1640–1790* (Cambridge, 1983).

[Jerram, Charles], *Memoirs and a Selection of the Letters of the late Rev. Charles Jerram*, ed. J. Jerram (London, 1855).

Jewell, Helen M., *English Local Administration in the Middle Ages* (Newton Abbot, 1972).

John, A. H., 'Farming in Wartime: 1793–1815', in E. L. Jones and J. D. Chambers (eds), *Land, Labour, and Population in the Industrial Revolution* (London, 1967).

Johnson, Joan, *Stow-on-the-Wold* (Gloucester, 1980).

Jones, E. L., 'The Changing Basis of English Agricultural Prosperity, 1853–73', *Agricultural History Review*, x (1962), 102–19.

Jones, E. L. and Falkus, M. E., 'Urban Improvement and the English Economy in the Seventeenth and Eighteenth Centuries', in Peter Borsay (ed.), *The Eighteenth Century Town. A Reader in English Urban History 1688–1820* (London, 1990).

Jones, Gareth Stedman, 'Rethinking Chartism', in Stedman Jones, *Languages of Class. Studies in English Working Class History 1832–1982* (Cambridge, 1983).

Jones, J. R., *The Revolution of 1688 in England* (London, 1972).

Jordan, J., *History of Enstone* (London, 1857).

Joyce, Patrick, *Work, Society and Politics. The Culture of the Factory in later Victorian Britain* (London, 1980).

Keir, David Lindsey, *The Constitutional History of Modern Britain 1485–1937*, 4th edn (London, 1950).

Keith, W. J., *The Rural Tradition* (Hassocks, 1975).

Keith-Lucas, Bryan, *The Unreformed Local Government System* (London, 1980).

Kent, Joan, 'The Centre and the Localities: State Formation and Parish Government in England, *c.* 1640–1740', *Historical Journal*, xxxviii (1995), 363–404.

King, Peter, 'Prosecution Associations and Their Impact in Eighteenth-century Essex', in Douglas Hay and Francis Snyder (eds), *Policing and Prosecution in Britain 1750–1850* (Oxford, 1989).

King, Peter, 'Gleaners, Farmers and the Failure of Legal Sanctions in England 1750–1850', *Past and Present*, 125 (1989), 116–50.

King, Peter, 'Customary Rights and Women's Earnings: the Importance of Gleaning to the Rural Labouring Poor, 1750–1850', *Economic History Review*, xliv (1991), 461–76.

Knott, John, *Popular Opposition to the 1834 Poor Law* (London, 1986).

Kussmaul, Ann, *Servants in Husbandry in Early Modern England* (Cambridge, 1981).

Lacy, Margaret de, *Prison Reform in Lancashire, 1700–1850. A Study in Local Administration* Chetham Society, xxxiii (Manchester, 1986).

Lacquer, T. W., *Religion and Respectability: Sunday Schools and Working Class Culture 1780–1850* (New Haven, CN, 1976).

Lamonie, Georges (ed.), *Charges to the Grand Jury 1689–1803*, Camden Fourth Ser. , xliii (London, 1992).

Landau, Norma, *The Justices of the Peace, 1689–1760,* (Berkeley, CA, 1984).

Langford, Paul, 'The English Clergy and the American Revolution', in Eckhart Hellmuth (ed.), *The Transformation of Political Culture. England and Germany in the Late Eighteenth Century* (Oxford, 1990), pp. 275–308.

Langford, Paul, *Public Life and the Propertied Englishman 1689–1798* (Oxford, 1991).

Larminie, V. M., *The Godly Magistrate: the Private Philosophy and Public Life of Sir John Newdigate,* Dugdale Society Occasional Papers, 28 (1982).

Lees, Andrew, *Cities Perceived. Urban Society in European and American Thought, 1820–1940* (Manchester, 1985).

Levine, David and Wightson, Keith, *The Making of an Industrial Society: Whickham 1560–1765* (Oxford, 1991).

Lewis, R. A., *Edwin Chadwick and the Public Health Movement 1832–1854* (London, 1952).

Lewis, R. A., 'William Day and the Poor Law Commissioners', *University of Birmingham Historical Journal,* ix (1964), 172–87.

Lipman, V. D., *Local Government Areas 1834–1945* (Oxford, 1949).

Loyn, H. R., *The Governance of Anglo-Saxon England 500–1087* (London, 1984).

Lubenow, William C., *The Politics of Government Growth. Early Victorian Attitudes Towards State Intervention 1833–1848* (Newton Abbot, 1971).

Lucas, Colin (ed.), *The Political Culture of the French Revolution* (Oxford, 1988).

Lucas, Colin (ed.), *Rewriting the French Revolution* (Oxford, 1991).

Lupton, H., *A History of Thame and its Hamlets* (Thame, 1860).

MacDonagh, Oliver, *Early Victorian Government 1830–1870* (London, 1977).

Mackintosh, James, *A Defence of the French Revolution and its English Admirers* in *The Miscellaneous Works of Rt. Hon. Sir James Mackintosh,* 2nd edn (London, 1851).

McClatchey, Diana, *The Oxfordshire Clergy, 1777–1869* (Oxford, 1960).

McConville, Sean, *A History of English Prison Administration. Volume 1 1750–1877* (London, 1981).

McCord, Norman, *The Anti-Corn Law League 1838–1846,* 2nd edn (London, 1968).

McFarlane, K. B., *The Nobility of Later Medieval England* (Oxford, 1978).

McGowen, Randall, 'A Powerful Sympathy: Terror, the Prison, and Humanitarian Reform in Early Nineteenth-century Britain', *Journal of British Studies,* xxv (1986), 312–34.

McLeod, Hugh, *Religion and the Working Class in Nineteenth-century Britain* (Basingstoke, 1984).

McVeigh, Simon, *Concert Life in London in the Age of Haydn and Mozart* (Cambridge, 1993).

Machin, G. I. T., *Politics and the Churches in Great Britain, 1832–68* (Oxford, 1977).

Maddicott, J. R., 'Magna Carta and the Local Community 1215–1259', *Past and Present*, 102 (1984), 25–65.

Maine, Henry Sumner, *Village Communities in East and West*, 3rd edn (London, 1876).

Malcolmson, Robert W., *Popular Recreations in English Society 1700–1850* (Cambridge, 1973).

Malcolmson, Robert W., 'Leisure', in G. E. Mingay (ed.), *The Victorian Countryside*, 2 vols (London, 1981).

Mather, F. C., *Public Order in the Age of the Chartists* (Manchester, 1959).

Malthus, T. R., 'A Letter to Samuel Whitbread Esq. on the Subject of the Poor Laws' [1807], printed. in D. V. Glass (ed.), *Introduction to Malthus* (London, 1959).

Malthus, T. R., *An Essay on the Principle of Population* [1798], ed A. Flew (Harmondsworth, 1970).

Malthus, T. R., *An Essay on the Principle of Population* [1803 edn.], 2 vols, ed. T. H. Hollingsworth (London, 1973).

Mandler, Peter 'Cain and Abel: Two Aristocrats and the Early Victorian Factory Acts', *Historical Journal*, xxvii (1984), 83-109

Mandler, Peter, *Aristocratic Government in the Age of Reform. Whigs and Liberals 1830–1852* (Oxford, 1990).

Marshall, Dorothy, 'The Role of the Justice of the Peace in Social Administration', in *British Government and Administration. Studies Presented to S. B. Chrimes*, ed. H. Hearder and H. R. Loyn (Cardiff, 1974).

Marshall, William, *Review and Abstract of the County Reports of the Board of Agriculture*, 5 vols (York, 1818).

Martin, E. W. (ed.), *Country Life in England* (London, 1966).

Mayett, Joseph, *The Autobiography of Joseph Mayett of Quainton 1783–1839*, ed. Ann Kussmaul, Buckinghamshire Record Society, 23 (1986).

Meier, Hans, 'Welfare and Health of Children and Adolescents in Early Modern England and Southern Germany. Case Studies of Bampton (Oxfordshire) and Oettingen (Southern Germany) in the Seventeenth and Eighteenth Centuries', D.Phil. thesis, University of Oxford (1995).

Midwinter, E. C., *Social Administration in Lancashire 1830–1860* (Manchester, 1969).

Mill, J. S., *On Representative Government*, in *The Collected Works of J. S. Mill*, ed. J. M. Robson *et al.*, 33 vols, (Toronto, 1981–91).

Millward, Robert and Sheard, Sally, 'The Urban Fiscal Problem, 1870–1914: Government Expenditure and Finance in England and Wales, *Economic History Review*, 2nd ser., xlvii (1995), 501–35.

Mingay, G. E., *English Landed Society in the Eighteenth Century* (London, 1964).

Mingay, G. E., *Enclosure and the Small Farmer in the Age of the Industrial Revolution* (London and Basingstoke, 1968).

Mingay, G. E., *The Gentry. The Rise and Fall of a Ruling Class* (London, 1976).

Mitchell, Austin, 'The Association Movement of 1792–3', *Historical Journal*, iv (1961), 56–77.

Mitchell, B. R., *Abstract of British Historical Statistics* (Cambridge, 1962).

Mitchison, R., 'The Old Board of Agriculture (1793–1822)', *English Historical Review*, lxxiv (1959), 41–69.

Moir, E. A. L., 'Sir George Onesiphorous Paul', in H. P. R. Finberg (ed.), *Gloucestershire Studies* (Leicester, 1957).

Moir, Esther, *The Justice of the Peace* (Harmondsworth, 1969).

Money, J., *Experience and Identity. Birmingham and the West Midlands, 1760–1800* (Manchester, 1977).

Monypenny, W. F. and Buckle, G. E., *The Life of Benjamin Disraeli*, revised edn, 2 vols (London, 1929).

Monk, W. J., *History of Witney* (Witney, 1894).

Moore, D. C., 'The Matter of the Missing Contests: Towards a Theory of the Mid-nineteenth Century British Political System', *Albion*, vi (1974), 93–119.

Moore, D. C., *The Politics of Deference. A Study of the Mid-nineteenth Century English Political System* (Hassocks, 1976).

More, Hannah, *Village Politics* (Canterbury, 1793).

Morgan, Richard (ed.), *The Diary of a Bedfordshire Squire (John Thomas Brooks of Flitwick 1794–1858)*, Bedfordshire Historical Records Society, vol. 66 (1987).

[Moritz, Carl Philipp], *Travels of Carl Philipp Moritz in England in 1782*, English trans. 1795 (reprinted London, 1924).

Morley, John *The Life of Richard Cobden*, new edn, (London, 1903).

Morley, John, *Gladstone*, 2 vol. edn (London, 1905/6).

Morrill, J. S., *Cheshire 1630–1660: County Government and Society during the English Revolution* (London, 1974).

Morrill, J. S., *The Revolt of the Provinces. Conservatives and Radicals in the English Civil War 1630–1650* (London, 1976).

Morrill, John, *The Nature of the English Revolution* (London, 1993).

Morris, R. J., *Cholera 1832* (London, 1976).

Morris, R. J., 'Voluntary Societies and British Urban Elites, 1780–1850', *Historical Journal*, xxvi (1983), 95–118.

Morris, R. J., 'Clubs, Societies, and Associations', in F. M. L. Thompson (ed.), *The Cambridge Social History of Britain 1750–1950*, 3 vols (Cambridge, 1990), iii, pp. 395–443.

Morris, R. J., *Class, Sect and Party: the Making of the British Middle Class, Leeds 1820–1850* (Manchester, 1990).

Morris, R. J. and Rodger, Richard (eds), *The Victorian City. A Reader in British Urban History 1820–1914* (London, 1993).

Morris, W. A., *The English Medieval Sheriff to 1300* (Manchester, 1927).

Munch, P. B., *Gentlemen and Poachers* (London, 1981).

Namier, Lewis, *The Structure of Politics at the Accession of George III*, 2nd edn (London, 1957).

Neale, R. S., *Bath: A Social History* (London, 1981).

Neeson, J. M., 'The Opponents of Enclosure in Eighteenth-century Northamptonshire', *Past and Present*, 105 (1984), 114–39.

Neeson, J. M., *Commoners; Common Right, Enclosure and Social Change in England, 1700–1820* (Cambridge, 1993).

Nelson, R. R., *The Home Office, 1782–1801* (Durham, NC, 1969).

Nettel, Reginald, *The Orchestra in England. A Social History* (London, 1946).

Neuman, Mark, 'A Suggestion Regarding the Origins of the Speenhamland Plan', *English Historical Review*, lxxxiv (1969), 317–22.

Neuman, Mark, *The Speenhamland County. Poverty and the Poor Laws in Berkshire 1782–1834* (New York and London, 1982).

Newton, Robert, *Victorian Exeter* (Leicester, 1968).

Newton, Robert, *Eighteenth Century Exeter* (Exeter, 1984).

Nicholls, Sir George, *A History of the Scotch Poor Law* (London, 1856).

Norman, Edward, *Church and Society in England, 1770–1970* (Oxford, 1976).

Nossiter, T. J., *Influence, Opinion and Political Idioms in Reformed England. Case Studies for the North East 1832–1874* (Hassocks, 1975).

Obelkevich, James, *Religion and Rural Society. South Lindsey 1825–1875* (Oxford, 1976).

O'Gorman, Frank, *Voters, Patrons and Parties. The Unreformed Electorate of Hanoverian England, 1734–1832* (Oxford, 1989).

Olney, Richard, *Lincolnshire Politics 1832–1885* (Oxford, 1973).

Olney, Richard, *Rural Society and County Government in Nineteenth Century Lincolnshire* (Lincoln, 1979).

Oxley, Geoffrey W., *Poor Relief in England and Wales 1601–1834* (Newton Abbot, 1974).

Paine, Thomas, *Rights of Man* [1791–2], ed. Eric Foner (Harmondsworth, 1985).

Parry, Jonathan, *The Rise and Fall of Liberal Government in Victorian Britain* (New Haven and London, 1993).

Paul, G. O., *A Statement of the Proceedings on the Subject of a Reform of the Prisons Within the County of Gloucester* (Gloucester, 1783).

Paul, G. O., *Address to the Justices of the County of Glocester Assembled at their Michaelmas General Quarter Sessions* (Gloucester, 1789).

Paul, G.O., *An Address to the Magistrates of the County of Glocester* (1789)

Paul, G. O., *Address to His Majesty's Justices of the Peace for the County of Glocester, on the Administration and Practical Effects of the System, of Prison Regulation …* (Gloucester, 1809).

Patterson, A. Temple, *Radical Leicester. A History of Leicester 1780–1850* (Leicester, 1954).

Philips, David, 'The Black County Magistracy 1835–1860', *Midland History*, iii (1976), 161–90.

Philips, David, *Crime and Authority in Victorian England. The Black Country 1835–1860* (London, 1977).

Philips, David, 'Good Men to Associate and Bad Men to Conspire: Associations for the Prosecution of Felons in England, 1760–1860', in Douglas Hay and Francis Snyder (eds), *Policing and Prosecution in Britain 1750–1850* (Oxford, 1989).

Philips, David and Storch, Robert D., 'Whigs and Coppers: The Grey Ministry's National Police Scheme, 1832', *Historical Research*, lxvii (1994), 75–90.

Phillips, John A., *Electoral Behaviour in Unreformed England, 1761-1802* (Princeton, 1982).

Phillips, John A., 'Municipal Politics in Later Eighteenth-century Maidstone', in Eckhart Hellmuth (ed.), *The Transformation of Political Culture. England and Germany in the Late Eighteenth Century* (Oxford, 1990).

Phillips, John A., *The Great Reform Act in the Boroughs. English Electoral Behaviour 1818–1841* (Oxford, 1992).

Phillips, John A. and Wetherell, Charles, 'Parliamentary Parties and Municipal Politics: 1835 and the Party System', *Parliamentary History*, xiii (1994), 48–85.

Philp, Mark, 'Vulgar Conservatism, 1792–3', *English Historical Review*, cx (1995), 42–69.

Plint, T., *Crime in England, its Relation, Character and Extent as Developed from 1801 to 1848* (London, 1851).

Plomer, William (ed.), *Kilvert's Diary. Selections from the Diary of Rev. Francis Kilvert, 1870–1879*, new edn, 3 vols (London, 1960).

Plumb, J. H., 'The Public, Literature and the Arts in the Eighteenth Century', in Paul Fritz and David Williams (eds), *The Triumph of Culture: Eighteenth Century Perspectives* (Toronto, 1972).

Plumb, J. H., *The Growth of Political Stability in England 1675–1725*, Penguin edn (Harmondsworth, 1973).

Poynter, J. R., *Society and Pauperism. English Ideas on Poor Relief, 1795–1834* (London, 1969).

Prentice, Archibald, *Historical Sketches and Personal Recollections of Manchester. Intended to Illustrate the Progress of Public Opinion from 1792–1832,* 2nd edn (London, 1851).

Pressnell, L. S., *Country Banking in the Industrial Revolution* (Oxford, 1956).

Prest, John, *Politics in the Age of Cobden* (London, 1977).

Prest, John, *Liberty and Locality. Parliament, Permissive Legislation and Ratepayers' Democracies in the Mid-nineteenth Century* (Oxford, 1990).

Price, John, *An Historical Account of the City of Hereford* (Hereford, 1796).

Price, Richard, *A Discourse on the Love of our Country* [1789], printed in D. O. Thomas (ed.), *Richard Price: Political Writings* (Cambridge, 1991).

Pye, H. J., *Summary of the Duties of Justices of the Peace out of Sessions* (London, 1827).

Radcliffe, Philip, *Mendelssohn,* 3rd edn (London, 1990).

Randall, Adrian and Charlesworth, Andrew (eds), *Markets, Market Culture and Popular Protest in Eighteenth-century Britain and Ireland* (Liverpool, 1996).

Ransome, Mary (ed.), *Wiltshire Returns to the Bishop's Visitation Queries 1783,* Wiltshire Records Society, xxvii for 1971.

Read, Donald, *The English Provinces c. 1760–1960. A Study in Influence* (London, 1964).

Read, Donald, *Peel and the Victorians* (Oxford, 1987).

Reaney, B., *The Class Struggle in Nineteenth-century Oxfordshire. The Social and Communal Background to the Otmoor Disturbances* (Oxford, 1970).

Reay, Barry, *The Last Rising of the Agricultural Labourers. Rural Life and Protest in Nineteenth-century England* (Oxford, 1990).

Reports of the Society for Bettering the Condition and Increasing the Comforts of the Poor, 7 vols (London, 1798–1817).

Risley, W. C., *Sermon at the Triennial Visitation of the Bishop of Oxford* (Banbury, n.d., ?1838).

Ritson, J., *The Office of Constable* (London, 1791).

Rivers, Isobel (ed.), *Books and their Readers in Eighteenth-century England* (Leicester, 1982).

Roberts, K., 'English County Members of Parliament 1784–1832', B.Litt. thesis, University of Oxford (1974).

Robertson, John, 'Universal Monarchy and the Liberties of Europe: David Hume's critique of an English Whig Doctrine', in Quentin Skinner and Nicholas Phillipson (eds), *Political Discourse in Early Modern Britain* (Cambridge, 1993).

Redlich, Joseph and Hirst, Francis W., *The History of Local Government in England,* 2nd edn, ed. Bryan Keith-Lucas (London, 1970).

Rochefoucauld, François de la *A Frenchman in England in 1784*, ed. Jean Marchand, trans. S. C. Roberts (Cambridge, 1933).

Rodger, Richard, *Housing in Urban Britain*, new edn (Cambridge, 1995).

Rogers, Nicholas, *Whigs and Cities. Popular Politics in the Age of Walpole and Pitt* (Oxford, 1989).

Rose, R. B., 'The Priestley Riots of 1791', *Past and Present*, no. 18, (1960), 68–88.

Russell, Anthony, *The Clerical Profession* (London, 1980).

Russell, Conrad, *Parliaments and English Politics, 1621–1629* (Oxford, 1979).

Sack, James J., *From Jacobite to Conservative. Reaction and Orthodoxy in Britain c. 1760–1832* (Cambridge, 1993).

Saville, John, *Ernest Jones: Chartist. Selections from the Writings and Speeches of Ernest Jones* (London, 1952).

Saville, John, *1848. The British State and the Chartist Movement* (Cambridge, 1987).

Sellman, Roger G., *Devon Village Schools in the Nineteenth Century* (New York, 1968).

Semper, W. H., 'Local Government and Politics since 1700', in W. B. Stephens (ed.), *History of Congleton* (Manchester, 1970).

Seymour, Charles, *Electoral Reform in England and Wales. The Development and Operation of the Parliamentary Franchise 1832–1885*, new edn (Newton Abbot, 1970).

Seymour, J. H., *Plain Statement of Facts, in a Matter in which the Parishioners of Horley are Interested* (Banbury, 1839).

Siedentop, Larry, *Tocqueville* (Oxford, 1994).

Silver, T., *Memorial to HM Government on the Dangers of Intermeddling with the Church Rates* (Oxford, 1835).

Silver, T., *Letter to the Duke of Marlborough ... on Commutation of Tithes* (Oxford, 1842).

Skinner, John, *Journal of a Somerset Rector 1803–1834*, ed. Howard and Peter Coombs (Oxford, 1984).

Slack, Paul, *Poverty and Policy in Tudor and Stuart England* (London, 1988).

Slack, Paul, *The English Poor Law 1531–1782* (Basingstoke, 1990).

Smart, William, *Economic Annals of the Nineteenth Century*, 2 vols (London, 1910/17).

Smith, E. A., 'The Yorkshire Elections of 1806 and 1807', *Northern History*, xi (1967), 69–90.

[Smith, Mary], *Autobiography of Mary Smith* (London, 1892).

Smith, R. J., *The Gothic Bequest. Medieval Institutions in British Thought, 1688–1863* (Cambridge, 1987).

Snell, K. D. M., *Annals of the Labouring Poor. Social Change and Agrarian England 1660–1900* (Cambridge, 1985).

Snell, K. D. M., *Church and Chapel in the North Midlands: Religious Observance in the Nineteenth Century,* Deptartment of English Local History, Occasional Papers, 4th ser., no. 3 (Leicester, 1991).

Speck, W. A., *Society and Literature in England 1700–60* (Dublin, 1983).

Speck, W. A. *Reluctant Revolutionaries. Englishmen and the Revolution of 1688* (Oxford, 1988).

Stansky, Peter, *The Victorian Revolution. Government and Society in Victoria's Britain* (New York, 1973).

Steedman, Carolyn, *Policing the Victorian Community. The Formation of English Provincial Police Forces, 1856–80* (London, 1984).

Stephens, Edgar, *The Clerks of the Counties, 1360–1960,* Society of Clerks of the Peace (Warwick, 1961).

Stephens, W. B., *Adult Education and Society in an Industrial Town: Warrington 1800–1900* (Exeter, 1980).

Stevenson, John, *Popular Disturbances in England 1700–1870* (London, 1979).

Stevenson, John, 'Sheffield and the French Revolution', in David Williams (ed.), *1789: The Long and the Short of It* (Sheffield, 1991).

Stockdale, Eric, *A Study of Bedford Prison 1660–1877,* Bedfordshire Historical Record Society, vol. 56 for 1977.

Stone, Lawrence (ed.), *An Imperial State at War: Britain from 1689–1815* (London & New York, 1994).

Storch, Robert D., '"The Plague of Blue Locusts": Police Reform and Popular Resistance in Northern England, 1840–57', *International Review of Social History,* xx (1975), 61–90.

Storch, Robert D., 'The Policeman as Domestic Missionary: Urban Discipline and Popular Culture in Northern England, 1850–1880', *Journal of Social History,* ix (1976), 481–509.

Storch, Robert D., 'Policing Rural Southern England before the Police: Opinion and Practice, 1830–1856', in Douglas Hay and Francis Snyder (eds), *Policing and Prosecution in Britain 1750–1850* (Oxford, 1989).

Stratton, G. F., *Proposed Rules, Orders and Regulations for the Castle Gaol at Oxford* (Cheltenham, 1809).

Stubbs, William, *Constitutional History of England,* 3rd edn, 3 vols (London, 1880).

Sturt, George, *William Smith, Potter and Farmer, 1790–1858,* new edn (Firle, Sussex, 1978).

Supple, B. E., 'Legislation and Virtue: An Essay in Working Class Self-Help in the Early-nineteenth Century, in N. McKendrick (ed.), *Historical Perspectives: Studies in English Thought and Society* (London, 1974).

Sutherland, Gillian, 'Education', in F. M. L. Thompson (ed.), *The Cambridge Social History of Britain 1750–1950,* 3 vols (Cambridge, 1990), iii, pp. 119–69.

Sweet, Rosemary, 'The Writing of Urban Histories in Eighteenth-century England', D.Phil thesis, University of Oxford (1993).

Taine, Hippolyte, *Notes on England,* trans. Edward Hyams (London, 1957).

Tanner, Andrea, 'The City of London Poor Law Union 1839–1869', Ph.D. thesis, University of London (1995).

Tate, W. E., 'Opposition to Parliamentary Enclosure in Eighteenth-century England', *Agricultural History Review,* xix (1945), 137–42.

Tate, W. E., 'Parliamentary Counter-petitions during the Enclosures of the Eighteenth and Nineteenth Centuries', *English Historical Review,* lix (1944), 393–403.

Tate, W. E., *The Parish Chest,* 3rd edn (Cambridge, 1969).

Taylor, Audrey M., *Gilletts. Bankers at Banbury and Oxford* (Oxford, 1964).

Taylor, James S., 'The Unreformed Workhouse', in E. W. Martin (ed.), *Comparative Development in Social Welfare* (London, 1972).

Thomis, Malcolm I., *Politics and Society in Nottingham 1785–1835* (Oxford, 1969).

Thompson, Dorothy, *The Chartists. Popular Politics in the Industrial Revolution* (London, 1984).

Thompson, E. P., *Making of the English Working Class,* Penguin edn (Harmondsworth, 1968).

Thompson, E. P., 'The Peculiarities of the English', in E. P. Thompson, *The Poverty of Theory and Other Essays* (London, 1978).

Thompson, E. P., *Customs in Common* (London, 1991).

Thompson, Flora, *Lark Rise to Candleford,* Penguin edn (Harmondsworth, 1973).

Thompson, F. M. L., *English Landed Society in the Nineteenth Century* (London, 1963).

Thompson, F. M. L., 'The Second Agricultural Revolution, 1815–1880', *Economic History Review,* 2nd ser., xxi (1968), 62–77.

Thomson, Gladys Scott, *Lords Lieutenant in the Sixteenth Century. A Study in Tudor Local Administration* (London, 1923).

Tiller, Kate (ed.), *Church and Chapel in Oxfordshire 1851. The Return of the Census of Religious Worship,* Oxfordshire Records Society, vol. 55 (1987).

Tobias, J. J., *Crime and Industrial Society in the Nineteenth Century,* Penguin edn (Harmondsworth, 1972).

Tocqueville, Alexis de, *The Ancien Regime,* English trans, intro. Norman Hampson (London, 1988).

Tocqueville, Alexis de, *Recollections,* intro. J. P. Mayer (London, 1971).

Tomkins, Alannah, 'The Experience of Urban Poverty – A Comparison of Oxford and Shrewsbury 1740 to 1770', D.Phil. thesis, University of Oxford (1994).

Toulmin Smith, J., *Local Self-government and Centralization* (London, 1851).

Toulmin Smith, J., *Local Self-government Un-mystified* (London, 1857).

Townsend, George Flyer, *The Town and Borough of Leominster* (Leominster, [1863]).

Trinder, Barrie, *Victorian Banbury* (Chichester, 1982).

Turner, Michael, *English Parliamentary Enclosure. Its Geography and Economic History* (Folkestone, 1980).

Turner, M. J., 'Gas, Police and the Struggle for Mastery in Manchester in the Eighteen-twenties', *Historical Research*, lxvii (1994), 301–17.

Underdown, David, 'Settlement in the Counties 1653–1658', in G. E. Alymer (ed.), *The Interregnum. The Last Quest for Settlement 1646–1660* (London and Basingstoke, 1972).

Underdown, David, *Somerset in the Civil War and Interregnum* (Newton Abbot, 1973).

Underdown, David, *Revel, Riot, and Rebellion. Popular Politics and Culture in England 1603–1660* (Oxford, 1985).

Underdown, David, *Fire From Heaven. Life in an English Town in the Seventeenth Century* (London, 1992).

Urdank, Albion M., *Religion and Society in a Cotswold Vale. Nailsworth, Gloucestershire, 1780–1865* (Berkeley, CA, 1990).

Vaughan, Robert, *The Age of the Great Cities: or, Modern Society Viewed in its relation to Intelligence, Morals, and Religion* (London, 1843).

Vernon, James, *Politics and the People. A Study in English Political Culture c. 1815–1867* (Cambridge, 1993).

Walsh, John, 'Methodism and the Mob in the Eighteenth Century', *Studies in Church History*, viii (1972), 213–27.

Walsh, John, 'Methodism and the Local Community in the Eighteenth Century', in *Vie Ecclésiale. Communauté et Communautés* (Paris, 1989), pp. 141–51.

Wahrman, Dror, *Imagining the Middle Class. The Political Representation of Class in Britain, c. 1780–1840* (Cambridge, 1995).

Waller, P. J., *Town, City, and Nation. England 1850–1914* (Oxford, 1983).

Walter, John, *A Letter to the Electors of Berkshire* (London, 1834).

Ward, W. R., 'County Government, 1660–1835', *Victoria County History, Wiltshire*, v (1957), 170–94.

Warne, Arthur, *Church and Society in Eighteenth-century Devon* (Newton Abbot, 1969).

Warren, W. L., *Henry II* (London, 1973).

Watson, Kate, 'Liberty, Loyalty, and Locality: The Discourse on Loyalism in Britain, 1790–1815', Ph.D, thesis, Open University (November 1995).

Watson, W. H., *Practical Treatise on the Office of Sheriff*, 2nd edn (London, 1848).

Weaver, Michael, 'The New Science of Policing: Crime and the Birmingham Police Force', *Albion*, xxvi (1994), 289–308.

Webb, R. K., 'A Whig Inspector', *Journal of Modern History*, xxvii (1955), 352–64.

Webb, S. and Webb, B., 'The Assize of Bread', *Economic Journal*, xiv (1904), 196–218.

Webb, S. and Webb, B., *The Parish and the County* (London, 1906).

Webb, S. and Webb, B., *The Manor and the Borough* (London, 1908).

Webb, S. and Webb, B., *English Prisons Under Local Government* (London, 1922).

Webb, S. and Webb, B., *English Poor Law History: Part 1. The Old Poor Law* (London, 1927).

Webber, William, *The Rise of Musical Classics in Eighteenth-century England: a Study in Cannon, Ritual, and Ideology* (Oxford, 1992).

[Weeton, Ellen], *Miss Weeton's Journal of a Governess 1807–1825*, ed. J. J. Bagley, 2 vols (New York, 1969).

Wells, Roger, *Dearth and Distress in Yorkshire, 1793–1802*, Borthwick Paper, no. 52 (1977).

Wells, Roger, 'The Revolt of the South West: a Study in English Popular Protest', *Social History*, vi (1977), 713–44.

Wells, Roger, *Wretched Faces. Famine in Wartime England* (Gloucester, 1988).

Whiting, J. R. S., *Prison Reform in Gloucestershire 1776–1820* (London, 1975).

Wilberforce, R. I. and Wilberforce, S. (eds), *The Life of William Wilberforce*, 5 vols (London, 1838).

Wiles, R. M., 'Provincial Culture in Early Georgian England', in Paul Fritz and David Williams (eds), *The Triumph of Culture: Eighteenth Century Perspectives* (Toronto, 1972).

Williams, Karel, *From Pauperism to Poverty* (London, 1981).

Williams, Penry, *The Tudor Regime* (Oxford, 1979).

Williams, Penry, 'The Crown and the Counties', in C. Haigh (ed.), *The Reign of Elizabeth* (London, 1984).

Williams, Penry and Harriss, G. H., 'A Revolution in Tudor History?', *Past and Present*, 25 (1963), 3–58.

Wilson, Kathleen, *The Sense of the People. Politics, Culture and Imperialism in England, 1715–1785* (Cambridge, 1995).

Wing, William, *Changes in Farming and the Rural Economy during the Fifty-five Years, 1826–1880* (Oxford, 1880).

Wood, Florence and Wood, Kenneth, *A Lancashire Gentleman. The Letters and Journals of Richard Hodgkinson 1763–1847* (Stroud, 1992).

Woodforde, James, *Diary of a Country Parson 1758–1802*, ed. John Beresford (Oxford, 1978).

196 Bibliography

Woods, Robert, *The Population of Britain in the Nineteenth Century*, new edn (Cambridge, 1995).

Woolrych, Austin, 'Last Quests for a Settlement 1657–1660', in G. E. Alymer (ed.), *The Interregnum. The Last Quest for Settlement 1646–1660* (London and Basingstoke, 1972).

Wormald, Patrick, '*Engla lond*: the Making of an Allegiance', *Journal of Historical Sociology*, vii (1994), 1–24.

Wrigley, E. A. and Schofield, R. S., *The Population History of England, 1541–1871. A Reconstruction*, new edn (Cambridge, 1989).

Wrightson, Keith, 'Two Concepts of Law', in John Brewer and John Styles (eds), *An Ungovernable People: the English and their Law in the 17th and 18th Centuries* (London, 1980).

Wrightson, Keith, *English Society 1580–1680* (London, 1982).

Wrightson, Keith and Levine, David, *Poverty and Piety in an English Village: Terling, 1525–1700*, new edn (Oxford, 1995).

Young, Arthur, *General View of the Agriculture of Oxfordshire* (London, 1813).

Youngs, Frederic A., *Guide to the Local Administrative Units of England*, 2 vols (London, 1979/91).

Zangerl, C. H. E., 'The Social Composition of the County Magistracy in England and Wales 1831–87', *Journal of British Studies*, xi (1971), 113–25.

Index